365 DAYS TO

BIOHACK YOUR LIFE

Daily Reflection For Health, Wisdom, And personal Growth

365 Days to biohack your life

Azpeer Academy

2000 PCH

Huntington Beach, CA

92648

AZpeer Academy Publishing

Copyright@ Azpeer Academy 2024

ISBN: 979-8-9917375-1-7

Mauro dos Santos

Mauro dos Santos Public Disclaimer

The information provided in this book results from a wide range of opinions and research on various ideals accumulated over 35 years of experience in the health field, combined with insights gained from working with numerous clients. What's presented here consists of personal experiments by the author and is not intended as medical advice, diagnosis, treatment, or a substitute for the services of a trained health professional. Biohacking focuses on optimizing health through natural methods and resources, without the use of drugs.

Consult with your health professional before making any changes to your nutrition, diet, fasting practices, physical activity, or supplement intake. If you have any medical conditions, limitations, or are currently undergoing treatment, it is essential to approach the guidance provided here cautiously and always discuss it with your doctor beforehand. Always consult your physician before engaging in any physical activities or body-related challenges to prevent potential harm.

Biohacking involves self-experimentation and health improvement. The practices shared in this book are based on what I have successfully implemented for myself and my clients over the years. While I have not encountered harm or negative side effects resulting from my guidance, it is still advisable to proceed with care and responsibility.

The publsher and author disclaim any responsibility for adverse effects or actions taken based on the ideas or opinions presented in this book or in the resources provided.

365 Days to biohack your life

Mauro dos Santos

Index

Introduction

A Journey to Daily Transformation and Lifelong Growth.
What if, every day, you get 1% better?

Helping people transform their lives is what drives me every single day. It's the passion that inspired me to write this book. After more than 35 years of guiding individuals toward better health, personal growth, and a deeper sense of purpose, I've come to understand one crucial truth: transformation is not something that happens overnight. It's a daily practice. Every experience, whether from my work as a personal trainer, my studies in biohacking, or my spiritual and philosophical journey, has shown me the importance of consistent, intentional growth.

This book is designed to be a practical guide for you, pulling together wisdom from so many areas—Stoic philosophy, biblical teachings, health, neuroscience, biohacking, and the lessons I've learned through my own life's work in health, fitness, and healing. Each entry you'll find here is built to give you something valuable to apply in your own life, whether it's a new piece of knowledge, a perspective shift, or a simple action step. The goal is to help you become the best version of yourself—physically, mentally, emotionally, and spiritually.

My own journey began with health and fitness. I helped people build physical strength, push their limits, and discover their potential. But as a Christian who studied to become a minister, I also learned the power of the Bible—not just as a spiritual text but as a powerful manual for life itself. The Bible offers timeless wisdom on overcoming adversity, aligning with a higher purpose, and living with integrity. Its teachings continue to shape how I approach life's challenges, offering clarity, strength, and purpose.

As I continued to evolve, I became a student of Stoic philosophy. The wisdom of the Stoics—people like Marcus Aurelius, Seneca, and Epictetus—gave me a framework for dealing with life's inevitable challenges. They taught me to focus on what I can control, accept what I can't, and view every adversity as an opportunity to grow. These lessons on resilience, virtue, and personal responsibility have become core to my journey and have helped me build a life of balance and emotional strength and even improve my health and physical wellbeing.

Then there's my work in health and fitness, which eventually led me to another revelation—the healing power of touch. Over years of giving massages, I noticed how touch could balance energy, heal emotional wounds, and restore emotional pain and traumas. This discovery opened me up to the world of energy healing. I learned how energy flows within us, how our chakras and energy fields influence our physical and emotional health, and how healing the body is also about healing the mind and spirit. This deeper understanding of energy healing has since become a key part of what I teach today.

But let me be clear—I'm still a student. Every day, I continue to learn, grow, and apply the wisdom I've gained from the Bible, Stoicism, biohacking, and modern science to my own life. Transformation is a process, and it's a lifelong one. This book reflects that journey. It's a collection of lessons, insights, and practices that have shaped my life and the lives of those I've been fortunate enough to help.

Every lesson in these pages serves a meaningful purpose. I've personally used these lessons to overcome obstacles, grow as a person, and achieve more balance in life. They have also helped countless others grow, heal, and break through barriers they didn't even realize were holding them back. Some of these lessons might challenge you, and some might seem simple, but I can assure you that they have led to powerful transformations.

Mauro dos Santos

If there's one thing, I wish I had 40 years ago, or even 10 years ago, it would be a book like this. It would have saved me time, helped me break through challenges more quickly, and given me the tools I needed to navigate life's ups and downs with more wisdom and grace. Now, you have that book in your hands.

This isn't just a book meant for passive reading; it's meant to be **your manual for a better you**, a guide that walks with you through your own journey. As you read, think about how the concepts apply to your life. Every day's entry is designed to help you make small but meaningful changes, one step at a time. And remember, this isn't a race. Take your time. You can read it all at once or day by day—the magic happens when you engage with the teachings and apply them in ways that resonate with you; some will not, that's ok, this is biohacking, self-experimentation and learning.

And here's something I suggest—don't go on this journey alone. One of the most meaningful ways to grow is to share the process with someone else. Growth isn't something we need to do in isolation and will always happen when you have a partner, a mentor or a buddy running with you. Share these teachings with a friend, a partner, or even a coworker. Someone who could also benefit from this wisdom. When we learn and grow together, we reinforce what we've learned, and we create a ripple effect that spreads far beyond ourselves.

Imagine the impact if you found someone to grow alongside you— someone to share in this journey. Not only would you strengthen your own commitment, but you'd also help create an environment of collective growth. That's the beauty of personal development—it doesn't just lift us up, it lifts everyone around us. In the end, this is more than just a book. It's a tool for transformation—not only for you but for those around you. So, as you read, think about who in your life might benefit from these teachings. Share the book, share the knowledge, and together, let's grow into the best versions of ourselves.

Why I wrote this book

Too many people are suffering unnecessarily, holding onto feelings and pain that don't serve them, instead harming their health and well-being in various ways. Emotions are energy, and this energy directly impacts the cells in our bodies, influencing our overall health.

We are not educated on how to let go of our emotions and take care of our health. Instead, most of us are conditioned to hold onto them, maybe pretend they don't exist, or suppress them. Without the proper mechanisms, we can't avoid the negative impact these emotions have on us. Negative emotions contribute to the development of several diseases, from cancer to diabetes. Even our immune system can become weaker or stronger based on our emotions. Yet, we are often conditioned to visit a doctor to treat the specific symptoms rather than addressing the root cause.

Treating a disease with medication without addressing its root cause is like treating a fever without targeting the underlying infection. To effectively treat the infection, we must first identify and address its root cause.

My objective with this book is to give you daily tools to improve your overall health. Each month, we will start by focusing on your physical health, emotional health, spiritual health, social health, and intellectual health.

I don't expect you to follow and do every daily recommendation—it's almost impossible, especially if you are learning some of these concepts for the first time. But my goal is that you take something from here—implement it in your life, reflect on it, become aware of it, or even teach it to someone else. By blessing someone else, you will also be blessing yourself. I always believe in paying it forward and how you can contribute to a better world around you by sharing positive things and spreading good news.

Some lessons from this book will also be available with deeper insights or more detailed instruction at *www.365DaysofWisdom.com*. These resources are designed to help you explore the concepts further and apply them more practically in your life.

Prelude

It wasn't warm outside on this autumn day in the Netherlands when we walked out to the cold bath. I was surprised to see the tank, where we were supposed to bathe for at least two minutes, filled with cold water and then topped up with ice cubes to fill at least half of its capacity. Just placing my hand on the tank made it freeze and become painful.

We went in two at a time while the others watched, waiting their turn. I was almost the last one; I was trying to avoid it until the last moment, but I knew that I would have to go in at a certain point.

I stepped up to the edge and felt my hands freezing as I stepped inside. I tried not to think because, in situations like that, the more you think, the more difficult it becomes. It was painful when I sat down and let the water and ice rise to cover my shoulders. I felt horrible pain in my back, neck, feet, and hands, and I immediately tried to control the pain to see how long I could last. I was getting desperate when the mentor touched my shoulder and, with some magical words, told me, "Dude, calm down and focus on my breath." I can't explain exactly how it happened, but I experienced a complete shift from pain and desperation to total calmness, controlled breathing, and a Zen-like mental state. From somewhere far away, I heard him saying, "Ladies and gentlemen, look at this guy; we have a new ice guru here." I was unsure if I'd listened to those words until later when I asked him, but I was sure of what I felt. I was still in pain, but the pain was not bothering me because, at that moment, I felt heat coming from inside me that put me in total comfort and control of the situation. Two and a half minutes passed, and I was even more comfortable and joyful in that highly uncomfortable situation. Still, I decided to get out to allow others to have their moment of joy.

But why would someone willingly subject themselves to such punishment? Why would a guy from the north of Brazil, where 65°F is already considered too cold, immerse himself in a 35°F bath? This is one of the ways to biohack your body for optimal health and longevity.

Me First

Welcome to my journey of transformation and self-discovery. This book is a culmination of my experiences, teaching, studies, scientific research, and the practical application of biohacking, neuroscience, social science, business principles that have profoundly impacted my life and the lives of those I coach.

At its core, this book is about taking control of your own life, from your emotions to your biology. It's a collection of insights, methods, and notes that I have meticulously gathered and applied to myself over the years. From diving into the latest scientific research to conducting self-experimentation, I've explored various aspects of health and wellness to understand what truly works.

Each chapter unfolds a part of my journey, detailing the experiments I've undertaken and the remarkable outcomes they've yielded. I've delved deep into the realms of nutrition, fitness, mental health, emotional health, social health and longevity, always seeking ways to optimize and enhance human potential.

What sets this book apart is its foundation in real-life application and observable results. My approach has always been hands-on, grounded in the principle of self-experimentation. This means not just relying on existing studies and theories but putting them to the test, understanding their effects firsthand, and refining them for practical, everyday use.

The discoveries and techniques shared here are not just theoretical concepts but have been applied over and over with exceptional results - both in my life and in the lives of hundreds or people that I have mentored or encountered on my way of studies and discoveries. From enhancing physical performance to achieving mental clarity, from managing stress to unlocking the secrets of longevity, this book is a guide to making profound changes in your life.

But more than just a guide, this book is an invitation to question, explore, and experiment. It's an encouragement to step beyond the conventional boundaries of health and wellness and to discover what your body and mind are truly capable of achieving when given the right tools and knowledge.

Whether you're new to the world of biohacking, neuroscience, quantum science or a seasoned explorer in those fields, this book is designed to provide you with a comprehensive understanding of how to take your health and performance to the next level. So, embark on this journey with me, and let's unlock the full potential of our bodies and minds together.

From Struggles to Self-Optimization: A Personal Journey into Biohacking

Life throws us unexpected challenges that force us to reevaluate our priorities and seek new solutions. My journey into the world of biohacking began with a profound realization of the limitations I faced despite living an active and seemingly healthy lifestyle.

From a young age, I was active, immersing myself in various physical pursuits, from practicing karate to competing in track and field. Later, I became a personal trainer, helping others achieve their fitness goals and maintaining a reputation for delivering results. However, as the years passed, I couldn't ignore the signs of my own declining health, diminishing strength, confusing mindset and a body that seemed to be losing its youthful shape.

Then came the day when everything changed. I found myself confined to my bed, unable to walk, and experiencing excruciating pain that surpassed anything I had ever endured. It was a wake-up call, a pivotal moment that compelled me to take charge of my health and seek out new knowledge and strategies to restore my well-being.

Driven by a deep desire to understand the root causes of my deteriorating health, I immersed myself in research, learning everything I could about nutrition, meditation, yoga, pilates and exercise in general, and the human body on the most biological details I could learn. It was during this period of self-discovery that I stumbled, without knowing, upon the world of quantum science, neuroscience and biohacking – a realm where science, technology, and self-experimentation merged to optimize the human body and mind.

Finding my health became my guiding light, searching everywhere for a framework through which I could regain control and transform my health. I realized that despite my dedication to "good nutrition" and rigorous workouts, there were underlying factors that I had overlooked. When I discovered Biohacking, it introduced me to a new way of thinking, challenging traditional notions of health and urging me to explore innovative approaches.

With an open mind and a hunger for knowledge, I embarked on a journey of self-optimization. I embraced the fundamental principles of biohacking – self-experimentation, the quantified self, and the resilience to face setbacks head-on. I developed a growth mindset, knowing that my path to recovery would require adaptability, patience, and unwavering determination.

Through biohacking, I discovered the importance of personalized experimentation, recognizing that what worked for others might not necessarily work for me. Armed with wearable devices, I meticulously tracked my biomarkers, sleep patterns, and nutrition to gather data that would guide my interventions. This data-driven approach empowered me to make informed decisions, tailor interventions to my specific needs, and optimize my lifestyle choices for improved performance.

Ethics and responsible experimentation became vital considerations on my biohacking journey. I understood the need to prioritize safety, privacy, and informed consent. I upheld the values of integrity and credibility within the biohacking community, ensuring that my interventions were grounded in evidence and guided by ethical principles.

My personal experience taught me that biohacking is not a one-size-fits-all solution. It is a deeply personal journey of exploration and self-discovery. It requires the courage to question conventional wisdom, the resilience to face setbacks, and the dedication to uncover the extraordinary potential within.

In the chapters to come, we will explore the realms of cognitive enhancement, physical fitness optimization, neuroscience, quantum science, sleep quality, nutrition, and much more. Drawing from my own experiences and the wealth of knowledge gained along the way, we will navigate the fascinating world of biohacking together.

Get ready to embark on a transformative journey of self-optimization, where the boundaries of what is possible are redefined, and the extraordinary becomes attainable. Stay tuned as we dive into the history of biohacking in the next chapter, tracing its origins from ancient practices to the modern innovations that shape our understanding today.

Stay committed to your own path of self-discovery and let the principles of biohacking guide you toward a healthier, stronger, and more vibrant you.

Understanding Biohacking: A Quest for Optimization

Imagine yourself standing at the threshold of a hidden, vibrant world. Inside, the human body, once a mysterious fortress, reveals itself as a landscape ripe for exploration. This is the realm of biohacking, a burgeoning field where curiosity and science collide to empower you to become the architect of your own well-being.

But before you embark on this thrilling journey, a fundamental question arises: ***what exactly is biohacking?***

At its core, biohacking is the art and science of optimizing the human body and mind, a quest to unlock your latent potential. It's not just about quick fixes or trendy fads; it's a multidisciplinary dance that draws inspiration from diverse fields like biology, medicine, nutrition, psychology, and even technology. Think of it as a personal laboratory where you gather data, experiment with safe and effective tools, and witness the fascinating interplay between your choices and your biology.

Biohacking isn't a one-size-fits-all endeavor. It's about empowering individuals to take control of their own unique biological landscapes. We each have our strengths, weaknesses, and quirks, and the beauty of biohacking lies in its personalized approach. Whether you seek to boost your energy, sharpen your focus, or build resilience against stress, biohacking provides a toolkit to tailor your journey toward optimal living.

My fascination with biohacking stemmed from a deep desire for an optimal life. I yearned to understand the forces that govern my physical and mental performance, to break free from limitations, and to cultivate a vibrant mind and body. Biohacking resonated with this yearning, offering a path to explore my own biology, optimize its functions, and ultimately, become the healthiest, happiest version of myself.

In the coming chapters, we'll dive deeper into the diverse realms of biohacking, exploring the tools and techniques at your disposal. We'll delve into the fascinating science behind sleep, nutrition, exercise, and mental wellbeing, empowering you to make informed choices and witness the transformative power of biohacking within your own being.

So, dear reader, prepare to embark on this thrilling journey of self-discovery. Open your mind to the possibilities, gather your curiosity, and join me as we unlock the secrets of biohacking, one fascinating step at a time. Remember, within you lies a universe of potential, waiting to be optimized. Let's get started!

Self-Experimentation: My Personal Laboratory

Forget passive spectating and embrace the stage! In the realm of biohacking, self-experimentation is my starring role, allowing me to gather data, test hypotheses, and write the narrative of my own optimized life. This isn't reckless recklessness, mind you; it's a carefully orchestrated dance, where curiosity drives the steps and scientific rigor ensures my safety.

Unlike passive recipients of information, biohackers are active co-creators of their own well-being. We design personalized experiments, gather data through wearables, apps, or simple self-tracking techniques, and observe how different interventions affect our unique internal landscapes. This empirical approach, like a personal laboratory tucked within our bodies, unlocks the secrets of individual optimization.

For me, this proactive stance sparked a conversation with my doctor. My request for specific blood tests twice a year, despite a decade of robust health and even conquering COVID-19 without medical intervention, raised an eyebrow. But it also opened a dialogue about preventative care, personalized data-driven health monitoring, and the power of proactive biohacking.

Imagine a world where you aren't simply told what to do, but empowered to explore, question, and actively participate in your own health story. Self-experimentation, guided by proper research and caution, unlocks this potential. By experimenting with sleep hacks, dietary tweaks, or even gentle biohacking supplements, you gather invaluable data about your own unique biology.

Mauro dos Santos

Think of it like a detective story, where you are both the investigator and the subject. The clues are scattered in your sleep patterns, energy levels, stress markers, and even your gut microbiome. By conducting controlled experiments, you observe how certain variables affect these clues, revealing your remarkable machine's hidden connections and patterns.

But remember, caution is our middle name. Always consult your doctor before embarking on any significant changes, especially if you have pre-existing health conditions. Start small, track your results meticulously, and celebrate even the tiniest victories. After all, every biohacking journey is unique, paved with discoveries and insights gleaned from self-experimentation.

How to read this book.

This book is the culmination of over 35 years of experience, countless hours of study, and a deep commitment to personal growth and transformation. It distills wisdom from hundreds of books, teachings, and real-life lessons. What you're holding is more than just a collection of ideas—it's a guide to profound, life-changing insights. Over the years, I've gathered thousands of notes for my personal growth, and from this vast reservoir, I've handpicked the teachings that have had the greatest impact on my life. These lessons have guided me through the heavy challenges life has put in my path, whether they involved my health, discouragement, depression, or unwanted circumstances. These notes became my personal master, my guru, and my fortress.

As you read, some topics may feel familiar—maybe ideas you've encountered but haven't fully embraced. Others might be entirely new, challenging how you currently think. Both reactions are perfectly normal. The power of this book lies in its ability to meet you exactly where you are on your journey—whether that's today, tomorrow, or even years from now. These are insights that resonate and tools you can start using immediately.

This isn't a book for passive reading. It's a companion, designed to be part of your journey toward growth. You can read it straight through, or day by day, applying each insight as suggested. Or use it as a personal manual for facing life's situations. Either way works, if you keep your heart and mind open to absorb and learn from what you read and from your own experiences. As you explore these lessons, think deeply about how they apply to your life, and take notes for future reference. Each lesson has a purpose, but the words here aren't the final truth. My goal is to guide you and help you find your own truth.

A quick story—many people who meet me, especially at the gym, often comment, "You look good for your age." Now, this could be a compliment or an assumption. But remember, when you say, "You look good," especially to a lady, avoid adding "for your age." No one wants their age assumed. Let your compliment stand on its own, honoring the person without assumptions. It's a small gesture, but it means a lot.

The teachings in this book have helped me overcome my own obstacles and become a better person, and they've also guided countless others to heal, grow, and break through barriers they didn't even realize existed. While some lessons may challenge you, they have led to powerful transformations for many, me included.

I wish I'd had this book 40 years ago—or even 20. It would have saved me time and a lot of pain, helping me overcome challenges and equipping me with the wisdom and tools to navigate life more gracefully. But now, it's here for you. This is your chance to experience your own transformation and growth.

As you move through these pages, remember—this isn't a race. Take your time, reflect, and make a commitment to read at least one lesson a day. Start your morning with a new insight or end your day with reflection. This daily practice will help these teachings sink in and become part of your everyday life. The magic happens when you engage with the teachings, reflect on how they fit into your life, and make small, consistent changes. Think of this book as a compass—it points you toward growth, but you're the one steering the journey.

Here's a tip: Don't go on this journey alone. Share these teachings with someone close to you—someone you believe can grow alongside you. Growth is even more powerful when shared. It not only strengthens your commitment but also amplifies the impact of these lessons. Think of the ripple effect these insights can have when shared with someone who matters to you. Reflect together, hold each other accountable, and experience personal growth as a team.

This book isn't just about self-transformation—it's about collective growth. When you share these lessons with others, you're creating a bond that deepens both of your experiences. Whether it's a partner, close friend, or colleague, sharing these insights can lead to mutual transformation. You're offering them the chance to change their life, just as you're changing yours.

Growth doesn't happen in isolation. Imagine how much more fulfilling this journey can be with someone by your side. Share these teachings, find a growth partner, and build a community of people dedicated to becoming the best versions of themselves. Every lesson in these pages was written with intention. They've already helped countless people, and now they're here to help you. These teachings have the power to create real breakthroughs—if you let them.

In the end, this book is more than just a guide—it's a tool for transformation, both for you and those around you. Whether it's your partner, a friend, or a colleague, this is your chance to spread these teachings, create meaningful connections, and help others step into their own evolution. Let's embark on this journey together, and let's make every moment count.

Welcome to your journey of daily transformation.

Let's start from the beginning.

P.S: For further resources related to the insights in this book, visit www.365DaysofWisdom.com/resources. There, you'll find additional tools and materials to support your journey of transformation.

Mauro dos Santos

January

Introduction to January:

January is the month where you plant the seeds for everything that's to come. It's not about making quick changes or setting resolutions that won't last—it's about building a foundation that will carry you throughout the year. Discipline is where it starts. This is your chance to create habits that will make you stronger, more focused, and more energized.

Capricorn's energy helps you stay grounded and focused. It's about staying consistent, day by day, showing up for yourself, and putting in the work. Whether you're managing your time better, setting clear goals, or optimizing your physical health, you're setting yourself up for success.

And then, with Aquarius, comes the innovation. January is also about seeing things differently. How can you improve? Where can you grow? It's the perfect time to reflect and plan, to make sure you're aligned with your purpose. Biohacking techniques—like improving your sleep, energy, and mental clarity—will support you as you move forward.

Remember, this month is about laying the groundwork, finding your rhythm, and building a life that reflects who you are and where you're going. The habits you start now will pay off in the months to come.

January 1: Ice Bath Challenge - Let's Start With a Big Challenge

"Pain is a defense mechanism; suffering is a choice we make."
– Sadhguru

Getting into an ice bath will be painful, no doubt about it. But as the Stoics would say, pain is not inherently bad—it's how we respond to it that matters. This discomfort offers a unique opportunity to practice resilience and self-control. Instead of seeing it as torture, you can choose to embrace it. Your body may scream for you to get out, and your mind might insist that you've reached your limit. But remember, as Epictetus taught, it's not the event itself that causes suffering but your judgment of it. After the first 45 seconds, something remarkable happens: you begin to feel a shift, and you'll be grateful that you didn't give up.

In that moment, you've exercised your power over your own mind, something the Stoics believed was within your control. To endure the cold, keep your hands out of the water, breathe calmly, in meditation, and focus on what is within your grasp: your breath, your thoughts, and your attitude. As Marcus Aurelius once wrote, "You have power over your mind—not outside events. Realize this, and you will find strength.

Trust me, by the end; you'll feel a profound sense of accomplishment—not just because you endured the ice bath, but because you exercised your inner strength, the very thing the Stoics saw as the essence of a good life. Along with this sense of achievement, your body will flood with dopamine and endorphins, rewarding your discipline and resolve.

Today, raise your standards, both in life and health. Take the plunge—just do it. This practice isn't just about physical endurance; it's about training your mind to accept challenges, knowing they make you stronger.

<u>What you will get from doing this:</u>

1. **Pain as perception:** The idea that pain is not inherently bad, but a signal you can choose how to interpret.

2. **Power over your mind:** Your ability to control your response, regardless of external circumstances.

3. **Resilience in discomfort:** Emphasizing that enduring the cold water is a way of exercising your inner strength.

4. **Embracing challenge:** Viewing the ice bath not as torture, but as an opportunity for self-mastery, a key Stoic value.

I encourage you to reflect on some of your painful or difficult situations and consider how you can approach them with greater wisdom and resilience this year. Remember, it's not the situation itself that matters, but how you choose to respond to it.

January 2 - The Power Of Discipline

"Success is nothing more than a few simple disciplines practiced every day." – Jim Rohn

Start your year by identifying small, consistent habits to build discipline. As the Stoics teach, true mastery comes from controlling your own actions and not being swayed by external circumstances. Consider biohacks like the Pomodoro technique to improve your focus—an example of applying deliberate effort to what you can control.

On this journey, many people will be inspired by your actions and tell you they want to change—they want better health, more energy, and to feel younger. But what separates you from the crowd is your dedication to discipline and the Stoic commitment to self-mastery. As **Epictetus** said: *"First say to yourself what you would be; and then do what you have to do."*

Remember, it is not enough to simply want change; it is through consistent action and resilience that transformation occurs.

Hacking Tip: Today, January 2nd, make a promise to yourself: regardless of external challenges or distractions, you will remain disciplined and committed to building your exceptional life. As Marcus Aurelius once said, "You have power over your mind—not outside events. Realize this, and you will find strength."

Tip: Create an actionable to-do list for this month. A clear structure will help you maintain momentum and avoid overwhelm. As the Stoics remind us, it's not enough to talk about goals and plans—true transformation comes from taking deliberate action. **Seneca** said: "While we wait for life, life passes."

Today is about turning your ideas into tangible steps, no matter how big or small is. Every action, however minor, contributes to the larger picture of your success.

Approach these 365 days by breaking them down into manageable steps. This strategy not only keeps you focused but also brings a sense of fulfillment as you progress steadily. Remember, as Epictetus taught, "Small but deliberate actions lead to great outcomes." Progress is made one step at a time, and each small action moves you closer to your ultimate goals.

January 3: Celebrating Achievements And Setting Future Goals

Taking the time to celebrate your achievements is crucial for personal growth and motivation. Acknowledging what you've accomplished not only boosts your confidence but also reinforces your belief in your ability to succeed. The Stoics understood the value of recognizing milestones along the way, as it provides a moment to reflect on your journey and fuels your ambition for the future.

Celebrating your wins—whether big or small—reminds you of the hard work and dedication that got you there. It's a chance to pause and appreciate your efforts, which can inspire you to tackle new challenges. When you take the time to celebrate, you create a positive cycle: the more you recognize your successes, the more motivated you become to pursue further goals. But celebrating achievements is just one side of the coin. Setting future goals is equally important. Goals give you direction and purpose, acting as a roadmap for your ongoing growth. By defining what you want to achieve next, you create a sense of focus and accountability, pushing yourself to dream bigger and strive for excellence.

Hacking **Tip:**
At the end of each month, set aside time to reflect on your accomplishments. Write down everything you've achieved, no matter how small, and give yourself a pat on the back. Then, think about your goals for the coming month. What do you want to learn? What challenges do you want to take on?

By celebrating your achievements and setting new goals, you create a cycle of continuous growth. This practice not only enhances your sense of accomplishment but also keeps your motivation alive as you look ahead. Embrace this journey of reflection and ambition and watch how it transforms your path to success.

January 4th: Resistance Training

Pain and pleasure are close companions. Your workout starts with a decision to go to the gym; you overcome excuses, distractions that cross your way, or even some other pleasurable activity that invites you. Make your fitness a non-negotiable activity until you develop the natural habit, consistency, and discipline.

Stoic Insight: Strength is not just physical but mental. Enduring challenges with grace and persistence builds resilience. The decision to go to the gym, resist distractions, and make fitness non-negotiable reflects the core Stoic principle of **virtue through action**. Marcus Aurelius said, *"The impediment to action advances action. What stands in the way becomes the way."*

Biohacking Tips: Focus on progressive overload during training. This will enhance muscle strength and mental toughness, preparing you to face whatever life has for you. Additionally, pushing your muscles stimulates neuroplasticity, reverses brain age, and builds BDNF, regardless of your sex or age.

P.S.: I always make sure that I drink enough water, have my shake with protein powder, creatine, avocado, and banana before my workout. The protein powder and creatine give my muscles the strength and energy they need and help me recover faster, while the avocado provides healthy fats for sustained energy, and the banana adds a boost of potassium to help prevent cramps during or after. This combination, besides several other benefits, fuels me up, helps me power through my training, and ensures my body is ready for recovery afterward.

Mauro dos Santos

January 5: The Power Of Stillness

"Be still, and know that I am God." — Psalm 46:10

Regardless of your religion or belief, prayer and meditation should be essential practices in your daily life. Are you a tough man? Then pray and meditate every day. Want to grow mentally and spiritually? Make prayer and meditation a habit. Struggling to handle difficult situations? Daily meditation can help you find calm and clarity. The strongest among us practice prayer and meditation because they promote physical, emotional, and mental well-being.

Over 1,400 studies have shown the wide range of benefits of meditation, from reducing stress to enhancing mental clarity and even strengthening the immune system.

Stoic Insight: Stillness brings clarity. As Seneca reminds us, *"We suffer more often in imagination than in reality."* When you control your reactions and find peace in quiet moments, you gain perspective, reducing unnecessary suffering and enhancing your ability to act with purpose.

Biohacking Tip: Meditation reduces stress, sharpens focus, and promotes healing. Start with just five minutes of mindfulness each day to create a space of calm and build mental resilience.

January 6: Run, Not Like Forrest

Cardio is essential for anyone aiming for good health. It increases the growth hormone (BDNF) Brain-Derived Neurotrophic Factor, enhances neuroplasticity, reduces the risk of neurodegenerative diseases, lowers stress, and provides mental clarity. The Stoics believed the body was made for movement, and this vitality is key to a strong life. As Marcus Aurelius said, *"If you seek tranquility, do less,"* but ensure what you do is essential—and physical activity is crucial for vitality.

Biohacking Tips: Engage in high-intensity cardio to improve heart health and mitochondrial function. Cardio boosts dopamine and energy levels but avoid overdoing it—excessive cardio can harm your immune system, drain energy, and affect longevity. In the movie Forrest Gump ran for 3 years, 2 months, 14 days and 16 hours, but trust me, you don't need to! Whether it's running, swimming, biking, or walking, choose the cardio that works for you—and just do like that!

Also, It's important to recognize that balance is key—excessive training can work against you. I didn't realize until later that my intense training for marathons and triathlons was lowering my testosterone levels and weakening my immune system and allowing me to be sick all the time. The training for extreme endurance sports, are not advisable if your goal is to live a long and healthy life.

January 7: Plan Your Day

"Let all your efforts be directed to something, let it keep that end in view." — Seneca, *Letters to Lucilius*

Seneca emphasizes the importance of intentional living. Planning your day ensures your actions are aligned with a higher purpose, bringing order and meaning to each task. For the Stoics, purpose and direction are central to a life well-lived. By organizing your day, you focus on what's in your control and move closer to the life you wish to create.

Biohacking Tip: "Let all your efforts be directed to something, let it keep that end in view." — **Seneca, *Letters to Lucilius***

Just as Seneca teaches purposeful action, time-blocking your day helps you focus on high-impact tasks with intention. By creating a clear plan, you reduce decision fatigue, as you no longer waste energy deciding what to do next. With time-blocking, each task has a designated time, allowing you to focus fully on one thing at a time, boosting productivity and maintaining mental clarity. This method ensures your efforts not only serve your immediate needs but also contribute to the larger vision of the life you wish to create.

January 8: Plan Your Goals, See Where You Want To Go

"Where there is no vision, the people perish." — Proverbs 29:18

The Stoics believed that having clear goals provides purpose and focus. Without direction, effort is scattered and wasted. Setting goals gives you a target and a reason for every action, turning your energy into meaningful progress. It's not just about doing more but doing what matters. Studies show that individuals who set specific goals are over 10 times more likely to achieve them compared to those without clear objectives. Planning your goals ensures that your actions are deliberate, helping you move steadily toward your desired future.

Compelling Reason:
Research by Dr. Gail Matthews, a psychology professor, found that people who write down their goals are 42% more likely to achieve them. Clear, written goals give you a roadmap, allowing you to measure progress and stay accountable. Without goals, life becomes reactive and aimless, but with goals, you direct your path and ensure that every step brings you closer to success.

"When a man does not know what harbor, he is making for, no wind is the right wind." — *Seneca*
Seneca's wisdom reminds us that without a clear goal (the harbor), no amount of effort will get you where you need to go. Planning your goals gives your life direction and purpose, making every action meaningful.

This quote underscores the importance of setting goals. Without a clear direction (the harbor), efforts become ineffective, no matter how hard you try. For the Stoics, a well-defined goal gives meaning to every action and prevents wasted effort.

January 9: Yoga, Also For Discipline

Flexibility is strength. Discipline is built not by rigidity but by adaptability and resilience. The Stoics emphasized that true strength lies in our ability to remain steadfast yet flexible in our approach to challenges. Yoga teaches us this balance—learning to bend without breaking. Discipline doesn't mean harshness or strictness but rather the ability to adapt gracefully, adjust when necessary, and maintain inner control despite external circumstances.

Through practices like yoga, we learn to control our reactions, adapt, and stay disciplined, building inner strength and mental flexibility.

Biohacking Tip: Yoga improves both physical and mental flexibility. It strengthens muscles while increasing mental resilience and clarity. Regular practice of yoga not only enhances physical flexibility but also teaches mindfulness and adaptability, both of which are crucial for staying disciplined and focused on everyday life.

Seneca's quote reminds us that much of the resistance to discipline comes from our own mind. By incorporating yoga, you build resilience in both body and mind, aligning perfectly with the Stoic philosophy of adaptability and control.

January 10: Detachment From Distractions

*"If you are pained by any external thing, it is not this thing that disturbs you, but your own judgment about it. * — Marcus Aurelius*

This quote from Marcus Aurelius underscores the Stoic teaching that external distractions only hold as much power as we give them. By focusing inward and detaching from the external, you can master your mind and direct your attention to what truly matters.

True freedom lies in mastering your attention. Detachment from life's noise allows you to focus on what truly matters. The Stoics taught that distractions—whether material possessions, external opinions, or fleeting desires—hinder personal growth. By detaching from these distractions, you reclaim control over your mind, enabling you to focus on higher purposes and long-term goals. Mastering your attention aligns your actions with your inner values, bringing clarity and intention to your life.

This quote from Marcus Aurelius underscores the Stoic teaching that external distractions only hold as much power as we give them. By focusing inward and detaching from the external, you can master your mind and direct your attention to what truly matters.

Biohacking Tip: Try a digital detox by reducing screen time and interruptions. Practice mindfulness to boost concentration and energy. Digital distractions drain mental energy and fragment attention, so taking regular breaks and focusing on mindfulness keeps you present, productive, and mentally sharp

January 11: Just keep swimming, Just Keep

Swimming, Just Keep Swimming, *(Dory in the movie Finding Nemo)*

"How long are you going to wait before you demand the best for yourself?" — Epictetus

Like Dory, in the cartoon movie, *"Finding Nemo"*, persistence is key—just keep swimming. Success isn't built on occasional bursts of effort, but through steady, consistent action. The Stoics taught that greatness comes from perseverance. Every small step, every small effort, builds the foundation for future success. Even when you feel discouraged, remember that persistence is your greatest ally.

Biohacking Tip:

Focus on consistency, not intensity. Regular, mindful habits—whether in fitness, nutrition, or mental well-being—compound over time, creating lasting results. A steady routine is more effective than intense bursts of effort.

Epictetus' wisdom encourages you to aim for excellence by staying constant in your efforts, knowing that small, consistent actions lead to long-term success.

IF you keep swimming, as long as you are swimming in the right direction, eventually you will get there!

January 12: Inner Power Through Perseverance

"Difficulties strengthen the mind, as labor does the body." —
Seneca

Seneca's wisdom captures the Stoic belief that challenges are essential for growth. Perseverance in the face of difficulty builds true inner power and resilience, preparing you for future adversity. The Stoics emphasized that real strength comes from the mind— mental resilience is the foundation of true power. Each challenge, when faced with courage and persistence, becomes an opportunity for growth. By enduring hardships, you develop self-mastery and an unshakable will.

Biohacking Tip: Challenge your limits to build resilience. Practices like cold showers and intermittent fasting push both your body and mind, cultivating mental toughness and endurance. These biohacks teach you to remain calm under pressure, enhancing your ability to handle stress. Regular exposure to discomfort strengthens both physical and mental fortitude.

Seneca's quote perfectly aligns with the message of perseverance, showing that mental strength, like physical strength, is developed through consistent effort and challenges. This complements the biohacking tip, illustrating how perseverance in biohacks like cold showers and fasting strengthens both body and mind.

teach you to remain calm under pressure, enhancing your ability to handle stress. Regular exposure to discomfort strengthens both physical and mental fortitude.

January 13: Focus And Concentration

Focus is the foundation of achievement. The Stoics taught that directing your energy and attention toward what truly matters is essential for success. By concentrating on what's within your control and blocking out distractions, you harness your power for meaningful progress. Clarity of purpose leads to deeper concentration and effective action, enabling you to achieve your goals without being sidetracked by external noise.

*"You must be single-minded. Drive for the one thing on which you have decided." — **Epictetus**.* Epictetus emphasizes the importance of focus and single-minded determination. By concentrating on a single goal, you eliminate distractions and channel your energy toward what truly matters, ensuring steady progress.

Hacking Tips: Enhance focus with nootropic supplements and mindfulness exercises. These tools improve cognitive function and mental clarity. Create an environment that supports concentration—limit distractions, organize your workspace, and prioritize tasks. Mindfulness helps sharpen attention, allowing you to maintain focus throughout the day.

Focus is when you direct your attention to the immediate task at hand and you are being fully present and engaged in the moment.

Concentration, on the other hand, is about sustaining that focus over time and maintaining attention on a task or goal for an extended period, ensuring you don't lose track of it even with distractions. In another word; be 100% present. Lack of **omega-3** may affect your focus, as it plays a crucial role in brain health and cognitive function. **Ginkgo biloba** has long been reported to help increase blood flow to the brain, while Lion's Mane is a natural nootropic that stimulates brain cell growth and may promote better focus, concentration, and memory by enhancing neuroplasticity. I recommend that you do your own tests and see what makes you feel better. I also enjoy my coffee in the morning.

January 14: Functional Exercises For Strength

Most people focus on one or two areas of fitness, such as cardio, weight training, or flexibility, and forget that fitness is meant to make us functional. Many overlook critical aspects like mobility, explosiveness, movement, speed, posture, balance, agility, coordination, or even the power of recovery. Enhancing your fitness in these areas makes it more efficient, improves your health, and can positively affect your biological aging. Remember, fitness isn't about appearance, but when done properly, you will naturally develop the best version of your body.

True strength lies in function. Train your body for utility and resilience, not merely for aesthetics. In doing so, you prepare yourself to meet the demands of life with both mental and physical strength.

"We should not, like sheep, follow the herd in front of us, making our way where others go, not where we ought to go." — **Seneca**

This quote aligns with the idea that training should be purposeful and tailored to real-world function, not based on external standards or appearances. It emphasizes independence in choosing what is best for long-term strength and endurance.

Biohacking Tip: Incorporate functional exercises like squats and deadlifts to build practical, real-world strength. These compound movements not only increase coordination and balance but also help prevent injuries. Functional exercises mimic the natural movements of daily life, ensuring your body is prepared for any physical challenge it encounters. By focusing on functional strength, you improve overall health and longevity.

January 15: Breathing Techniques For Energy

Breathwork reduces stress by calming the nervous system and lowering cortisol levels. It increases oxygen flow, improving energy and mental clarity. Practicing breathwork helps regulate emotions, enhancing emotional resilience. It also boosts lung capacity, supporting better physical performance and endurance. Breathwork promotes mindfulness, helping you stay present and focused. The Soma breathwork technique helps balance the autonomic nervous system, increasing energy and promoting relaxation. It also boosts oxygen flow to the brain and body.

Control over your breath is control over your mind. In Stoic philosophy, mastery of the self begins with mastery over one's reactions, and breath is the gateway to this control. Deep breathing centers the spirit, enhances mental clarity, and allows you to respond to challenges with calmness and resilience.

"He who lives in harmony with himself lives in harmony with the universe." — *Marcus Aurelius*

This quote aligns with the idea that breathwork connects the mind, body, and spirit. By mastering your breath, you bring yourself into alignment and cultivate inner calm, which enhances your ability to face life's challenges.

Biohacking Tip: Practice breathwork techniques like Wim Hof or Soma breathing to boost energy and mental focus. Controlled breathing reduces stress and oxygenates the body, promoting mental clarity and increased physical endurance. These methods help you stay centered and focused, even in stressful situations.

January 16: Managing Your Energy (Qi or Prana)

Stoic Insight: Energy is the essence of life. In Stoic philosophy, mastery over one's energy is crucial to living a balanced and purposeful life. By becoming aware of your energy (or vital force, often referred to as *Qi* in Chinese tradition or *Prana* in Indian tradition), you gain control over how you engage with the world. Discipline is the key to maintaining this energy, using it wisely in all areas of life without allowing external distractions or emotions to drain it. The Stoics believed that living in harmony with nature requires awareness of your internal resources and the way you spend your mental and physical energy.

"The mind that is anxious about future events is miserable." — *Seneca*

This quote reminds us that wasting energy on things outside of our control, such as anxieties about the future, depletes our vital force. By managing your energy wisely and focusing on the present moment, you conserve your internal strength and maintain resilience.

Biohacking Tip: To manage your energy efficiently, incorporate practices like Tai Chi or Qi Gong into your routine. These ancient energy-balancing exercises help align your mind and body, promoting the flow of Qi (or Prana) through gentle movements and mindfulness. Practicing these methods improves focus, reduces stress, and optimizes energy flow, feeds your cells with more oxygen, enhancing your ability to stay centered and calm throughout the day. By managing your life force with intention, you create balance in both your mental and physical well-being, leading to greater overall vitality.

Here is some breathwork that you can do without the help of a coach or master:
There are several methods of breathwork, each with unique benefits and techniques:

1. Pranayama: An ancient yogic practice focusing on controlled breathing for balancing mind and body energy.

2. Wim Hof Method: Combines breathing exercises with cold exposure to improve endurance, resilience, and mental clarity.

3. Holotropic Breathwork: Uses rapid, deep breathing to access altered states of consciousness for emotional healing.

4. Box Breathing: Involves inhaling, holding, exhaling, and holding again in equal counts to reduce stress.

5. Buteyko Method: Focuses on shallow nasal breathing to improve oxygen efficiency and reduce anxiety.

Each method has distinct effects, catering to physical, emotional, and mental health.

January 17: Remove Your Shoes, You're On Earth!

Getting in touch with the earth is essential for both your physical and mental well-being. The Stoics believed that living in harmony with nature brings balance and clarity. By physically connecting with the ground or simply being mindful in nature, you can find peace and reduce the distractions of daily life. This connection helps you feel calmer, more focused, and emotionally steady. When you align with the natural world, you cultivate inner peace and build resilience.

"Man must consider, not only his own self but everything else in relation to the whole." — Marcus Aurelius

This quote reminds us that we are part of a larger whole. Grounding yourself in nature allows you to acknowledge your place in the world, fostering balance and clarity.

Biohacking Tip:
Grounding, or "earthing," helps reduce inflammation, boosts mood, and balances your body's energy. Whether you're spending time barefoot outdoors or using grounding mats, reconnecting with the earth's natural energy improves your physical and mental health. Regular grounding can lower stress, improve sleep, and speed up recovery from daily challenges—making it an easy yet effective way to support overall well-being.

January 18: Sunlight Exposure For Energy

The sun is an essential source of energy and vitality. For the Stoics, nature provided everything necessary for strength and well-being, including sunlight. By embracing sunlight, we align ourselves with nature's rhythms, restoring energy and sharpening our minds. The Stoics believed in harnessing the elements to promote mental clarity, resilience, and overall health. Just as sunlight illuminates the earth, it can bring clarity and renewal to our minds and bodies.

"Nature does not hurry, yet everything is accomplished." — Lao Tzu While I don't know a specific Stoic quote, it echoes Stoic principles. Life has a natural rhythm, like the steady rise and fall of the sun. When we sync ourselves with these natural cycles, we can find balance, enhance energy, and focus without rushing or forcing outcomes.

Biohacking Tip:
Daily sunlight exposure is key to boosting vitamin D, regulating your circadian rhythm, and improving mood. Aim for 15-20 minutes of morning sunlight to optimize these benefits. This simple practice enhances immune function, strengthens bones, improves sleep, and lifts mental well-being. Making sunlight a daily habit helps energize both your body and mind, keeping you in tune with the natural world's cycles.

While sunlight provides several benefits, it's may not be enough; that's why it's highly recommended that you supplement your daily nutrition with Vitamin D-rich foods like eggs and fatty fish and consider taking a Vitamin D3 (Cholecalciferol) supplement daily.

January 19: Faith And Belie

"Now faith is confidence in what we hope for and assurance about what we do not see." — Hebrews 11:1

This Bible verse reminds us that faith is crucial for shaping the life we want. It fuels our vision and keeps us moving forward, even when the way ahead is uncertain. Faith is also the foundation of inner strength. The Stoics believed that trusting in oneself and the natural flow of life offers hope and endurance, especially during tough times. While they valued reason, the Stoics also understood that having faith—whether in a principle or a higher power—brings calm and resilience when faced with adversity. Faith, in this sense, is about trusting the process, even when we can't see the outcome.

"To bear trials with a calm mind robs misfortune of its strength and burden." — **Seneca**

This quote reminds us that faith and inner strength help us handle difficulties. It encourages us to stay calm, hopeful, and resilient, even when life feels overwhelming.

Biohacking Tip: You can "hack" your faith by practicing gratitude journaling and visualization. Gratitude journaling shifts your brain to focus on the positive, while visualization helps you mentally rehearse success, boosting your confidence. By using these practices, you can build resilience, optimism, and a stronger belief in your abilities and path.

Mauro dos Santos

January 20: If It's Red, It Will Work. Biohacking
Cellular Health With Red Light Therapy

If you want your skin to feel and look younger, here's the magic trick: Red Light Therapy. But it's not just about rejuvenating the skin—it goes far beyond that. Red light therapy can transform not only your appearance but also your brain and overall well-being.

Red light therapy penetrates deep into your cells, boosting mitochondrial function. This enhances energy production, speeds up recovery, and reduces inflammation. Regular exposure to red light can promote skin health, support muscle repair, and boost overall vitality, making it a powerful tool for biohacking your cellular health.

Now, for some scientific facts: red light therapy boosts your body's energy production by stimulating the mitochondria. This doesn't just benefit your skin; it powers up your brain cells, enhancing focus and mental clarity. More energy means sharper thinking, improved memory, and better decision-making as your brain becomes more adaptable and efficient.

Inflammation, particularly in the brain, is a hidden enemy that contributes to cognitive decline and mental fatigue. Red light therapy reduces this inflammation, helping protect your brain from long-term damage. It also enhances the brain's ability to repair itself by promoting neuron regeneration, which protects against neurodegeneration.

Red light therapy offers impressive benefits:
Skin Health: It stimulates collagen production, which improves skin elasticity and reduces wrinkles, fine lines, and acne. It even promotes wound healing.
Muscle Recovery: Red light therapy speeds up muscle repair and reduces soreness by increasing blood flow and lowering inflammation.

Pain Relief: It's often used to reduce chronic pain like arthritis and joint discomfort by promoting cellular repair and reducing inflammation.

Improved Sleep: Red light exposure helps regulate melatonin, leading to better sleep quality.

Rest and recovery are vital for progress. True strength comes from knowing when to pause and let the body heal. The Stoics emphasized balance, and recovery is just as crucial as effort in maintaining long-term health and strength.

Biohacking Tip:

Incorporate red light therapy into your routine to promote cellular repair, reduce inflammation, and enhance recovery. It supports muscle recovery, relieves pain, and improves skin health, while also helping you achieve better sleep. This non-invasive treatment boosts overall well-being and speeds up your body's healing process.

January 21: Inversion Therapy for Relaxation

Relaxation isn't just a luxury—it's a must for growth and sustained effort. The Stoics knew the importance of balancing action with rest. Just as the mind needs clarity, the body needs rejuvenation to stay resilient. Taking time for recovery is key to staying on track with your goals and maintaining well-being.

"The mind that is free from passions is a fortress; people have no stronger place of retreat, and one into which they cannot be received unless they have such a mind." — Marcus Aurelius

A calm, rested mind is just as powerful as a strong body. True relaxation helps you recharge, regain clarity, and keep moving forward.

Biohacking Tip: Inversion therapy is a simple way to decompress your spine, reduce stress, and boost circulation. Just a few minutes in an inverted position each day can relieve tension, ease back pain, and get more blood flowing to your brain. Adding this to your routine can enhance relaxation, support recovery, and improve your overall well-being.

January 22: Emotional Balance

Cheerful Heart as Medicine:

A positive mindset, joy, and laughter truly act like medicine. Keeping a lighthearted attitude boosts your energy, promotes physical health, and helps your body function more efficiently. Emotional well-being is essential to overall vitality.

Crushed Spirit Dries Bones:

On the other hand, a heavy or broken spirit—whether from depression or deep discouragement—can drain your energy and take a physical toll. Emotional distress weakens the body and affects your long-term health.

Stoic Insight:

True strength comes from emotional balance. The Stoics knew that controlling emotions leads to inner peace and resilience. When you calm your mind and manage your emotional responses, you gain a sense of peace that helps you navigate life's challenges without being overwhelmed.

"You have power over your mind—not outside events. Realize this, and you will find strength." — *Marcus Aurelius* This quote perfectly captures the Stoic idea that regulating your emotions and maintaining inner calm is where true strength comes from.

Biohacking Tip: Boost emotional balance by incorporating mindfulness, journaling, and deep breathing into your routine. These practices help you process emotions healthily, reduce stress, and keep your mental well-being in check. Staying centered and emotionally resilient will help you handle whatever comes your way.

You can also support your emotional balance by taking **Omega-3**, especially EPA and DHA, which are essential for brain health and

Mauro dos Santos

can help regulate mood. **Magnesium** plays a key role in the regulation of neurotransmitters that control mood. **B-complex vitamins**, particularly B6, B9 (folate), and B12, support the production of neurotransmitters like serotonin and dopamine. Additionally, I take **Vit D** which receptors are found in many parts of the brain, including areas associated with mood regulation.

January 23: The Role Of Love In Discipline

And now these three remain: faith, hope, and love. But the greatest of these is love. — **1 Corinthians 13:13**

The Power of Love for Health: Love plays a crucial role in reducing stress and promoting a sense of safety and comfort. Emotional connections release hormones like oxytocin, which help lower stress and improve emotional resilience. This has a direct impact on heart health by keeping blood pressure down and reducing the risk of heart disease. Love also boosts overall cardiovascular function and strengthens the immune system, making your body more resilient against illness. The positive emotions tied to love help your immune system respond better, giving your body an extra edge in fighting off disease.

Research shows that people in loving relationships tend to live longer and healthier lives. Emotional stability, reduced stress, and the physical benefits of love all contribute to a longer lifespan and a higher quality of life.

For the Stoics, love was a powerful force that brought meaning to discipline. When discipline is driven by love, it transforms from a rigid routine into a path for growth and connection. Without love, discipline can feel cold, but when it's fueled by love, it leads to fulfillment, not just for yourself but for others as well.

A person's worth is measured by the worth of what he loves. — **Marcus Aurelius**

This quote reminds us that love gives purpose to discipline, turning it into a meaningful act rather than just an exercise in self-control.

Hacking Tip:

Fostering loving relationships is a natural way to boost oxytocin, the "love hormone," which reduces stress. Strong emotional connections not only improve mental well-being but also boost physical health. Love lowers stress, improves heart function, and strengthens the immune system, making it essential for overall wellness. Building and nurturing meaningful relationships is a powerful biohack for both the body and mind, helping promote longevity and resilience.

January 24: Spirituality Isn't Religion, It's For Structure

Spirituality offers a foundation for structure and purpose in life. It provides clarity and helps us align our goals with something deeper. For the Stoics, living a disciplined and focused life meant anchoring oneself in spiritual or philosophical principles. When we root ourselves in spiritual practices, we create a guide that helps us navigate life's challenges with greater peace and intention. *"The happiness of your life depends upon the quality of your thoughts."* — *Marcus Aurelius* This quote reminds us that the thoughts inspired by spiritual practices bring structure and clarity, keeping us aligned with our higher purpose.

Hacking Tip: Add mindfulness or prayer to your daily routine to foster purpose and structure. Spiritual practices like meditation, prayer, or quiet reflection enhance emotional well-being, reduce stress, and keep you grounded. By making spirituality a part of your day, you cultivate peace and direction, which benefit both your mental and physical health.

January 25: Just Do It! The Power Of Determination

Determination is what allows us to overcome obstacles and move forward. The Stoics believed that steady, focused effort is what leads to success, no matter the challenges along the way. With a determined mindset, you stay committed to your purpose and push through whatever life throws at you.

"First say to yourself what you would be; and then do what you have to do." — Epictetus

This quote captures the essence of **self-discipline, determination, and intentional action**. It starts with **clarity of purpose**—knowing what you want to achieve and who you want to become. Before taking any steps, you must first define what success means to you. Whether it's personal growth, hitting a fitness goal, or mastering a new skill, the first step is having a clear vision.

The second part—"and then do what you have to do"—is about taking action. Once your goal is clear, there's no room for hesitation. Epictetus reminds us to pursue our goals with **relentless determination**, focusing on the process and executing with discipline, no matter the challenges that arise. This aligns perfectly with a core Stoic idea: **focus on what you can control**. While you can't always control the outcomes, you can control your actions. By consistently doing what's within your power, you live with **purpose, discipline, and perseverance**.

In practical terms:

1. **Define your goal**—whether it's fitness, career growth, or personal development.
2. **Map out the steps** you need to take to reach that goal.
3. **Take action** with determination, even when obstacles come up. The path won't always be smooth, but staying focused and disciplined will keep you moving forward.

In summary, this quote serves as a powerful reminder that self-discipline begins with knowing what you want and taking consistent, deliberate steps to make it happen.

Hacking Tip: Break larger goals into smaller, manageable tasks. This keeps you from feeling overwhelmed and makes progress more tangible. Consider using a journal to track your progress and maintain motivation. Regularly reviewing what you've achieved and setting clear, actionable steps will help keep your determination strong and your goals within reach.

January 26: Thinking Outside The Box For Self-Growth

Growth happens when we step beyond conventional thinking. The Stoics knew that true self-growth comes from **challenging societal norms and expectations**. To evolve, we need to break out of our comfort zones and embrace new, creative ways of thinking. When we dare to see things differently, we open ourselves to personal transformation, gaining deeper wisdom and insight along the way.

"He who follows reason in all things is both tranquil and active at the same time." — *Marcus Aurelius* Marcus reminds us that by thinking independently and following reason, we can find balance. It's about pushing boundaries but staying grounded, growing and finding peace in the process.

Hacking Tip: Incorporate activities that spark creativity—like journaling, learning something new, or trying your hand at drawing. These novel experiences promote **neuroplasticity**, helping your brain form new connections and pathways. When you challenge yourself with fresh experiences, you not only enhance your creativity but also promote self-growth and build mental resilience. It's a powerful way to think outside the box and expand your potential.

January 27: Creativity And Innovation In Your Routine

Routine doesn't have to be monotonous. The Stoics valued discipline but also recognized that weaving creativity into your daily habits keeps both the mind sharp and the spirit alive. By bringing innovation into your routine—whether it's approaching familiar tasks in a new way or trying something completely different—you prevent stagnation. Creativity can elevate even the simplest parts of life and keep you aligned with your higher purpose.

"Waste no more time arguing about what a good man should be. Be one." — *Marcus Aurelius* This quote emphasizes the importance of taking action. Rather than overthinking, take initiative and improve your routine with meaningful, creative practices.

Hacking Tip: Shake up your routine regularly to prevent stagnation and keep your brain engaged. Try new exercises, pick up a hobby, or learn something unfamiliar. These fresh activities stimulate **neuroplasticity**, enhancing cognitive function and keeping your mind sharp. When you introduce variety, you build mental resilience, making it easier to adapt to new challenges. Novelty fuels growth.

January 28: Sitting In Silence For Mental Clarity

Silence is a powerful tool. Taking just 30 minutes to sit in silence can clear your mind, calm your spirit, and reconnect you with yourself. It promotes inner peace and allows for deeper reflection, helping you find clarity in your thoughts and emotions. In silence, we create the mental stillness needed for understanding and harmony.In *The Seven Spiritual Laws of Success* by Deepak Chopra, the **Law of Pure Potentiality** emphasizes the power of silence, meditation, and connecting with your inner self. By cultivating inner stillness, we tap into our true potential and align with the universe's creative energy. In this space of silence, possibilities are endless, and we access our deepest wisdom and strength.

Chopra explains that practicing silence allows us to disconnect from the constant mental chatter and distractions of life. This not only brings clarity and creativity but also fosters peace and self-awareness. Through silence, we align with our true nature, where all possibilities reside, leading to effortless success and a balanced, fulfilling life.

Stoic Insight: *"Silence is a refuge; in it we find ourselves."* — *Seneca*

For the Stoics, silence was a tool for reconnection and growth. In those moments of stillness, we can reflect deeply, find clarity, and strengthen our sense of purpose. Silence becomes essential for building mental resilience and fortitude.

January 29: Chakra Balancing For Stability

It tool me a long time to recognize and accept that chakras are energy centers in the body and that influence your physical, emotional, and spiritual health, according to ancient Eastern traditions. There are seven main chakras, each linked to different organs and aspects of your psychological well-being. When your chakras are balanced, you feel more grounded and vital. But imbalances can lead to physical, emotional, or spiritual challenges.

- **Root Chakra (Muladhara):** Located at the base of the spine, it controls survival, stability, and grounding. Imbalances may cause fatigue, anxiety, or digestive issues, with physical symptoms like lower back pain or leg problems.
- **Sacral Chakra (Svadhisthana):** Below the navel, it governs creativity, emotions, and sexuality. Imbalances may result in emotional instability, lack of creativity, or sexual dysfunction, with physical issues like reproductive or urinary problems.
- **Solar Plexus Chakra (Manipura):** In the stomach area, this chakra influences personal power, confidence, and control. Blockages can cause digestive problems and low self-esteem, with physical symptoms like ulcers or liver issues.
- **Heart Chakra (Anahata):** Centered in the chest, it governs love and emotional balance. Blockages may lead to loneliness or bitterness, alongside heart or lung problems.
- **Throat Chakra (Vishuddha):** Located in the throat, it affects communication. Imbalances may lead to sore throats, thyroid issues, or difficulty expressing yourself.
- **Third Eye Chakra (Ajna):** Between the eyebrows, it governs intuition and clarity. Imbalances can cause headaches, vision problems, or confusion.
- **Crown Chakra (Sahasrara):** At the top of the head, this chakra connects you to higher spiritual energy. Blockages

may lead to feelings of disconnection, depression, or migraines.

Balancing your chakras through meditation, yoga, or energy healing practices like Reiki helps maintain physical, emotional, and spiritual health.

Stoic Insight: True strength comes from inner alignment. The Stoics, like those who practice chakra balancing, believed in the importance of harmony between mind, body, and spirit. When our internal energies are in balance, we gain clarity, resilience, and a deeper ability to face life's challenges with strength.

*"Be like the cliff against which the waves continually break; but it stands firm and tames the fury of the water around it." — **Marcus Aurelius***

This quote from Marcus Aurelius reminds us that stability comes from within. Just like the cliff standing firm against crashing waves, inner balance helps us remain grounded and unshaken by external challenges.

Hacking Tip: Incorporate chakra-balancing practices like yoga, breathwork, or meditation into your routine. These techniques help align your energy centers, promoting physical, emotional, and spiritual stability. Regular practice enhances overall well-being and builds resilience, giving you a stronger foundation to navigate life's ups and downs.

January 30: Wash Your Hands

Discipline is reflected in our daily habits. The Stoics believed that caring for both the body and mind is essential for living a virtuous life. Self-care and hygiene are more than just routines; they are acts of discipline and respect for oneself. Maintaining cleanliness and caring for your body is a foundation for mental clarity and inner strength.

"Take care of your body as if you were going to live forever; and take care of your soul as if you were going to die tomorrow." — **Marcus Aurelius**

This quote perfectly captures the balance between physical care and mental well-being. By treating your body with the same dedication you would offer to long-term goals, you create a strong foundation for mental and emotional health. At the same time, nurturing your soul through reflection and discipline ensures a life lived with purpose and virtue.

Tip: Do I really need to remind you to wash your hands and take a shower daily? These small acts of self-care are simple but powerful ways to maintain both physical cleanliness and mental well-being.

January 31: Wake Up Early for Productivity

Waking up early is a powerful symbol of discipline and readiness to face the day's challenges. The Stoics believed that the way we begin each day sets the tone for everything that follows. By rising early, you cultivate a mindset of productivity and preparedness, positioning yourself to tackle important tasks without distraction. Early mornings offer a quiet space for reflection, planning, and focused work, laying the foundation for success.

"When you arise in the morning, think of what a precious privilege it is to be alive—to breathe, to think, to enjoy, to love." — Marcus Aurelius

This quote emphasizes the Stoic approach to beginning the day with gratitude and purpose, which enhances both focus and productivity.

Hacking Tip: Waking up early has numerous benefits for both physical and mental health:

- **Better Mental Health:** Early risers often experience reduced stress and anxiety due to the calm start of the day. Studies suggest they are also less likely to suffer from depression, as morning sunlight exposure helps regulate circadian rhythms and boosts serotonin levels, improving mood.
- **Improved Sleep Quality:** Maintaining a consistent early waking schedule aligns with the body's natural circadian rhythm, improving overall sleep quality. Early risers tend to fall asleep more easily and enjoy deeper rest, promoting better recovery.
- **Increased Productivity:** Waking up early offers undisturbed time to focus on important tasks. Cognitive functions, such as memory, problem-solving, and decision-making, are often at their peak during the morning, making it the ideal time for work and creativity.

- **Enhanced Physical Health:** Early risers are more likely to engage in regular exercise during the quiet morning hours, promoting cardiovascular health, stronger muscles, and improved mental clarity. Morning routines also encourage healthier food choices and better digestion throughout the day.
- **Better Time Management and Reduced Procrastination:** Waking up early provides extra time to plan the day, set priorities, and stay organized. This improves time management and reduces procrastination, allowing for more efficient handling of daily responsibilities.

February:

Introduction

Introduction:

February is a month of transformation, where innovation meets emotional depth. With the energy of Aquarius and Pisces guiding you, it's the perfect time to focus on the areas that truly matter— your emotional well-being, your relationships, and your inner creativity. It's about building resilience, not just in how you manage stress, but in how you connect with others and how you express yourself.Emotional resilience is the foundation for everything else. When you know how to stay calm and focused, no matter what's happening around you, you gain clarity and strength. This is the month to explore that, using tools like journaling, meditation, or whatever helps you stay grounded and aware.

At the same time, February invites you to nurture your relationships. Our connections with family, friends, and community shape our lives. How can you show up better for those around you? How can you improve your communication and create more meaningful interactions? Take time this month to deepen these bonds, because they are the support system that fuels your growth.Lastly, don't forget about your creative and spiritual side. This is a great time to reconnect with what inspires you—whether it's art, nature, or simply sitting in silence. Let that inspiration guide you toward a more fulfilling life, and you'll find that everything else falls into place. When you're in touch with your inner world, it naturally reflects in everything you do.

February 1: If You Don't Feel Like Doing It, Just Do It Until You're Done

Resilience is not a means to avoid hardship; instead, it's about resilience—it's all about enduring and overcoming it. The Stoics believed emotional strength is built through the unstoppable challenges of life. It is not in the absence of difficulty that defines resilience, but rather the ability to face adversity with graciousness and inner strength. Each fight is an opportunity for more growth.

"You have power over your mind—not outside events. Realize this, and you will find strength." — **Marcus Aurelius**

This quote captures the very essence of Stoicism: even though the world might be outside of our control, our responses are not. It is within the control of your own mind, in focusing on what's within your control and releasing what is not, that emotional resilience really derives. When you learn true strength is a product of controlling one's thoughts or reactions, you will be resilient no matter what comes your way.

Hacking Tip: Practice gratitude and reframe bad experiences in lighter ways to help your emotional resilience. Gratitude helps shift your thinking to the positive side, while reframing helps to view difficulties as opportunities for growth. Daily, one can weave in mindfulness and journaling—one can even process emotions with this—to build inner strength and long-lasting emotional resilience.

February 2: Developing Mental Clarity

Mental clarity comes when we release the distractions and begin to pay attention to what we can control. The quiet mind will eventually emerge, the Stoics believed, by detaching ourselves from the noise outside and anchoring in on what's in our control. And in shutting out things we don't need to worry or think about, we make room for keener thinking, sounder decision-making, and effective action.

"The happiness of your life depends upon the quality of your thoughts." — **Marcus Aurelius**

This quote clearly underlines that our mental clarity and well-being are deeply connected with the way we handle what lies behind the mind. Paying attention only to that which is most important and cutting distractions enhance clarity while empowering the mind.

Hacking Tip: You can improve your mental clarity with cognitive enhancers such as Lion's Mane or L-theanine. These are supplements that take care of your brain so that it will be clear all day. Add to this meditation or breathwork, and watch how clearing the mind can improve concentration and build mental clarity in both short-term focus and long-term resiliency.

Studies show that Omega-3, B-complex vitamins and Vitamin D are also associated with mental sharpness.

February 3: Smoothing Out Relationships Within *The Family*

Family is all about respect, patience, and understanding. The Stoics regarded family harmony as being able to be kept through listening attentively and with much love in every word or act concerning another. Besides emotional balance, strengthening family ties with acts of kindness fosters a sense of belonging and peace in the mind. *"Whenever there is human life, there is the opportunity for kindness."* — **Seneca**

As this quote says, it is all about kindness, really—the basis of every relationship. Patience can make life much easier in a family, showing and practicing it binds the bonds and keeps your emotions intact.

The Science Behind Family Relationships and Health: Good family bonding assures sound mental and physical health. Research has proved that close family ties bring about emotional support, low levels of stress, and good health in general. Individuals who relate very strongly with their family members have more infrequent levels of anxiety and depression, lower cortisol—the stress hormone—and they live longer. These bonds assure good cardiovascular health, a stronger immune system, and a quicker recovery after sickness. It is also important to recognize that it helps to decrease chronic stress and all the bad influences on the body because of a feeling of membership in your family, which improves the quality of life and longevity.

Hacking Suggestion: The ways to improve family relationships and overall health include active listening and empathy. Give quality time to your loved ones, being present in every interaction or activity undertaken with them. Allow regular times for quality—such as over meals, during activities, or in deep conversations—to improve bonding.

February 4: Friendship Enhancement

One of the biggest strengths in our lives is friendship, especially in really hard times. Friendship for Stoicism was not only support, but a mirror with which to reflect our actions and values. A good friend reminds you of where you come from and keeps your feet on the ground; he or she encourages you and points it out to you when you are wrong. Trust and respect toward each other help us face whatever life throws our way. *"We are born for cooperation, as are feet, hands, and eyes, as the two rows of teeth, upper and lower."* — **Marcus Aurelius**. This quote develops the Stoic view of humans as basically social animals, where cooperation and support are necessary for our well-being and growth.

The Science of Friendship and Health:

Studies have shown that good friendships bolster mental and physical health. The presence of close friends lowers the chance of depression, blood pressure, and even prolongs one's life. Social contacts trigger the release of oxytocin, also commonly known as the "cuddle hormone," which helps lower stress and promotes feelings of pleasure and affiliation. Strong friendships provide emotional support, which has been linked to better immune function and a lower risk of chronic diseases. Friendships also act as a buffer to stress, allowing individuals to bear adversity better. Studies have recorded that people with good supportive friends are more likely to recover faster from illness and will show fewer signs of psychiatric disorders.

Hacking Tip: Nourish your friendships with your presence and gratitude. Let regular check-ins with friends involve meaningful conversations and activities. Small, consistent acts of appreciation and prioritizing time with friends create an emotional connection and add depth to relationships. Friendships are an important part of emotional and overall health; it is vital to use your time to nurture and grow friendships.

February 5: Social Well-Being

The Stoics believed that our well-being is deeply connected to the well-being of those around us. True social health arises from empathy, mutual respect, and recognizing that we are part of a larger community. By investing in the happiness and success of others, we not only help them thrive but also contribute to our own sense of fulfillment and purpose. Social harmony is achieved when we extend kindness and support, fostering bonds that make us stronger collectively. **"What injures the hive, injures the bee."** — *Marcus Aurelius*. This quote emphasizes the Stoic understanding that we are all interconnected, and the health of the community directly affects our individual well-being. When we help others, we help ourselves.

The Science of Social Well-Being:

Strong social connections are essential for mental and physical health. Engaging with others and maintaining positive relationships boosts the release of **oxytocin**, the "bonding hormone," which reduces stress and promotes feelings of well-being. Studies have shown that people with strong social networks have a lower risk of **anxiety**, **depression**, and **chronic illness**, and they tend to live longer, healthier lives.Participating in social activities, such as volunteering or joining community groups, enhances a sense of belonging and purpose. These connections foster resilience, help reduce loneliness, and promote overall life satisfaction. Social well-being also improves **cognitive health**, as maintaining strong relationships has been linked to reduced risk of cognitive decline in older adults.

Hacking Tip: Foster social well-being by investing in your community. Engage in group activities or volunteer work that allow you to connect with others meaningfully. These interactions promote the release of **oxytocin**, improving mood and creating strong emotional bonds. Regularly participating in social activities not only enhances your sense of belonging but also contributes to a happier, healthier life.

February 6th: Spiritual And Creative Thinking

Creativity represents the spirit of human beings and an avenue that can help foster the inner self in connection to the world. To the Stoics, the key that unlocks creative and innovative minds is accessed when we tap into our core values and purpose in life. Spirituality and creativity walk hand in hand since both explore new avenues of thought, creation, and contribution to the world. True creativity flows when we are in alignment with our higher purpose and allow our imagination to be ignited.

"The happiness of your life depends upon the quality of your thoughts." — **Marcus Aurelius**

This reminds us that creativity is a product of the quality of the inner world; through thoughtful, imaginative, and purposed thinking, we make space for innovation and inspiration.

Hacking Tip: Trigger creativity through the act of exposing oneself to new environments and activities. Performing arts, music, or creative writing can unleash creativity in you and boost your mental flexibility. Moreover, there is an effective tool one can use these days: binaural beats to enhance focus and cognition in creative tasks. These fasten the process of creating a state of flow where ideas mount easily. Keep your mind and spirit enthralling with innovative activities that keep challenging your thinking outside the box for soaring creativity.

February 7: Communication Hack

Building and sustaining relationships involves communication. It is important, as the Stoics remind us, to speak with purpose and intention, allowing our words to be thoughtful, measured, and meaningful. True communication involves not speaking, but rather deep listening to understand others and responding with clarity and kindness. This invites stronger, more meaningful connections.

"Better to trip with the feet than with the tongue." — Zeno of Citium

This quote highlights the importance of careful and intentional speech. Just as it's better to stumble physically than to harm with words, thoughtful communication requires mindfulness and purpose in what we say.

Hacking Tip: Improve your interaction with others through the use of active listening. Techniques such as NVC build empathetic understanding and connection with others. NVC invites one into speaking with her heart, speaking with self-awareness while being present to one's interactions. Mindfulness practices will further increase your positive communication by helping you be grounded and present in your moment, bringing a greater depth in your conversations with more productive outcomes.

February 8: Working With Emotions Using Mindfulness

Emotions are temporary; mindfulness is how one gets through them with clarity. The Stoics taught to look to observe the emotions calmly rather than impulsively, allowing them to pass without judgment. And by achieving such a dimension of awareness, one will get hold of the key to one's emotional response and remain unflustered in a storm.

"We suffer more in imagination than in reality." — **Seneca** This quote brings out the very central view of the Stoics, namely, that much of our emotional turmoil emanates from within our own minds, not from the events themselves. Mindfulness enables us to step back from our thoughts and their emotional concomitants; thus, more rational and proportionate responses are thereby enabled.

Hacking Tip: The moment strong emotions arise, practice mindfulness techniques such as body scanning or focused breathing. Body scanning helps to eliminate tension in the body, while focused breathing cogently helps to calm the mind and normalize your emotional responses. The ease with which these basic practices allow improvement in emotional awareness makes the management of difficult emotions considerably easier, thus contributing to better mental-emotional well-being.

February 9: Visualization For Mental Clarity

"For as he thinks in his heart, so is he." — Proverbs 23:7

I don't believe you could find a better verse in the Bible to define the power of your thoughts and how they shape who you are.

The fact is that what we focus on in our minds, we manifest in our reality. The Stoics had a similar understanding—**clear and intentional thoughts, define our belief about ourselves,** drive our actions and ultimately define our outcomes. When we consistently visualize what we want to achieve, with precision and clarity, our thoughts naturally guide us toward purposeful action. Visualization is not just a technique; it's a powerful tool for achieving mental clarity and staying on track with our goals and define us.

The mind shapes your reality, and this is supported by science. What we focus on grows, and by directing our thoughts, we can influence the course of our lives. What you consistently hold in your mind, you naturally begin to attract or create in your reality. By shaping your thoughts and intentions, you are already laying the foundation for how you are living your life and for your future.

"You become what you give your attention to." — *Epictetus* This quote from Epictetus perfectly aligns with the idea that **what we focus on grows**. By directing your attention to specific thoughts and actions, you begin to shape your reality and move closer to your goals. Visualization is key to this process.

Hacking Tip: Incorporate **visualization techniques** like guided imagery into your daily routine to increase focus and help you achieve your goals. When you consistently visualize success, your brain begins to act as if that success is already happening, enhancing your motivation and performance. Whether your goals are personal, professional, or physical, visualization helps sharpen mental clarity and primes you for success.

February 10: Forgiveness As Emotional Healing

Forgiveness is one of the most powerful tools and skill that we have, not just as an act of kindness toward others, but as a way to free ourselves from emotional burdens. It's difficult to understand that when we hold onto grudges, we carry the weight of resentment, which slowly chips away at our well-being adn eat us from iside out. Letting go of this weight creates space for inner peace and healing.

The Stoics understood that **forgiveness** is crucial for emotional well-being. Harboring anger or resentment does more damage to us than the original offense. Letting go of negative emotions allows us to reclaim our mental clarity and emotional balance. True strength lies in our ability to forgive—both others and ourselves.

"Anger, if not restrained, is frequently more hurtful to us than the injury that provokes it." — *Seneca* This quote from Seneca perfectly captures the idea that holding onto anger is more damaging than the initial wrongdoing. Forgiveness frees us from this self-inflicted pain and leads to emotional relief.

Hacking Tip: If you have difficult forgiving engage in **journaling** or **guided meditation** to work through these feelings. Writing down your thoughts or practicing forgiveness meditation helps you process and release lingering emotional weight, allowing you to move forward with greater emotional balance and mental clarity. Sometimes, putting yourself in the other person situation helps.

Buda said that *holding onto anger is like grasping a hot coal with expectation that the other person get burned.* Don't be this person. Free yourself.

February 11: Less Can Be Better

Several studies show that reducing caloric intake by 25% to 40% triggers various longevity factors in our bodies, including reduced oxidative stress, enhanced insulin sensitivity, and increased expression of genes associated with longevity, such as SIRT1 and FOXO. These changes improve cellular repair mechanisms and reduce inflammation, and believe it or not, they give us more energy.

Additionally, research on blue zones, such as Okinawa in Japan, reveals that dietary patterns in these areas emphasize lower calorie intake, which is associated with lower rates of chronic diseases and improved metabolic health—factors that contribute to longevity. On top of that, caloric restriction promotes the production of brain-derived neurotrophic factor (BDNF), a protein essential for the growth, maintenance, and survival of neurons. Higher BDNF levels are associated with improved cognitive function and resilience against neurodegenerative diseases.

Biohacking Tip: Try reducing your portions by 40% or adjusting your eating frequency and notice how you feel. Your body may signal hunger, but your mind will likely appreciate the extra energy, focus, and clarity you'll gain, as well as developing the best natural medicine against Alzheimer's and other cognitive diseases.

February 12: Emotional Control

"But the fruit of the Spirit is love, joy, peace, forbearance, kindness, goodness, faithfulness, gentleness, and self-control." — Galatians 5:22-23

The fruit of the Spirit emphasizes that these qualities are not simply human virtues but rather divine characteristics that manifest in the lives of those who cultivate their relationship with God. These attributes become evident as self-control, wisdom, and peace of mind. Emotional control is not about suppression; it's about mastery. As we cultivate self-control, we allow our emotions to serve us rather than control us.

"You have power over your mind—not outside events. Realize this, and you will find strength." — **Marcus Aurelius**

This quote from Marcus Aurelius encapsulates a core tenet of Stoic philosophy. The Stoics believed in practicing apatheia, a state of being where one is not disturbed by emotions. They taught that through reason and self-reflection, individuals could cultivate a sense of inner peace and make conscious choices rather than reacting impulsively.

Hacking Tip: You have total control over your emotions, but you also have a choice to give it to someone else. If you are triggered, or better said, when you are triggered, try deep breathing, focus on your inner thoughts and feelings, and NEVER respond when you are in a high emotional state. By practicing this, you will eventually find a way of peace over the storm, and nothing will take you out of balance.

February 13: Facing Challenges With Resilience

In the movie *The Pursuit of Happyness,* Chris Gardner, played by Will Smith, faces severe challenges as he becomes homeless while trying to provide for his young son after his wife decides to leave. Despite losing his job and struggling to make ends meet, Chris demonstrates remarkable resilience. He persists through overwhelming obstacles, including a demanding unpaid internship at a brokerage firm, all while caring for his son. Chris's journey embodies extraordinary determination and resilience, showcasing the strength of hope in the pursuit of a better life.

The Stoics believed that every challenge we face is a chance to cultivate resilience and character. Instead of viewing hardships as setbacks, they saw them as essential experiences that strengthen our resolve and teach valuable lessons.

"The impediment to action advances action. What stands in the way becomes the way." — **Marcus Aurelius**

This quote reflects a core Stoic principle: challenges and obstacles are not just barriers but can serve as tools for growth and progress. Things happen in our lives for a reason, and instead of avoiding difficulties, we should confront them, as they often provide opportunities to develop resilience, strength, and wisdom. By shifting our perspective, we can see that what hinders us can also guide us, transforming obstacles into pathways for action and improvement.

Hacking Tip: Build your resilience by regularly stepping out of your comfort zone. Engaging in discomfort—whether through cold showers, fasting, or challenging physical activities—can strengthen your mental fortitude and prepare you to face life's inevitable trials. When confronted with challenges, try to view them from an outside perspective.

February 14: Speaking Clearly And With Intention

As far as I know, every religious book discusses, in one way or another, the power of controlling your words and speaking wisely. *As **Epictetus** said, "We have two ears and one mouth so that we can listen twice as much as we speak."* This quote reminds us that effective communication involves not only expressing our thoughts but also listening attentively. By choosing our words thoughtfully and being open to others, we create an atmosphere of respect and trust. As a matter of fact, the beginning of efficient communication starts with active listening.

To cultivate this practice, reflect on how you express your thoughts. Are your words consistent with your beliefs? Engaging in self-reflection about your communication style can lead to more meaningful conversations.

Hacking Tip: Next time you engage in a conversation, pay attention to how you are paying attention. Are you fully present? Are you listening to understand or thinking about how you are going to respond instead? Try to maintain eye contact while speaking to foster connection and show that you value the conversation. Develop the habit of speaking with intention, and build confidence while creating an environment where others feel heard and respected, reinforcing positive interactions.

In this way, speaking clearly and with intention becomes a powerful tool for personal growth and meaningful engagement with the world around you.

February 15: Self-Superation: Overcoming Limits

"I can do all this through Him who gives me strength." — **Philippians 4:13**This verse reminds us that we are capable of far more than we often believe, especially when we draw strength from faith or a higher purpose. In moments of doubt or difficulty, we can rise above our perceived limits by tapping into inner and outer sources of strength. Sometimes we need a life push to start developing our potential, but it's a lot better and more fun when you do it consciously and by decision. The Stoics believed that the limits we face are often self-imposed; we choose our own limits and keep them rooted in fear, doubt, or a lack of self-belief. When we recognize these internal barriers and learn to transcend them, we master our power. *"You have power over your mind—not outside events. Realize this, and you will find strength."* — **Marcus Aurelius** This Stoic teaching is very clear in telling us that we have the capacity to change our perspective, which, in turn, changes our reality. By pushing ourselves beyond our mental, physical, and emotional limits, we experience growth and self-superation.

Overcoming personal barriers requires courage, resilience, and determination. The Stoics taught that the key to rising above these limitations lies in understanding that obstacles are not enemies but opportunities for growth. When we confront our perceived limits—whether physical, emotional, or intellectual—we tap into a wellspring of untapped potential. I call this "breaking your mental wall."

Hacking Tip: Pushing your limits to break your wall is essential to building resilience. Some ways to try this are by doing an extra push in your exercise routine, incorporating intermittent fasting to challenge your body and mind, or engaging in strength training to push your physical boundaries. Or even practice sitting in silence to challenge your control over your mind. Overcoming discomfort, whether through physical exertion or mental challenges, builds both mental and physical toughness. Engage in that dream you have but think is impossible, and you may realize that everything is impossible until it's done.

Embrace discomfort on a daily basis, and you will find that growth happens when we leave our comfort zones. Start training yourself to become more resilient. The feeling of overcoming these obstacles, both big and small, becomes the foundation for pushing past our limits in all areas of life, and trust me, you will experience a lot of joy in the process.

February 16: Doing Something New Each Day

"You must not think that it is only the living beings that change according to a definite plan, for this change affects all things, even those that seem motionless. How slight the difference is between a person who rests and a person who is weary! Or between someone who is awake and someone who is drowsy! How slight the difference between someone who is sound and someone who is sick! Hence, we must not seek to avoid changes, for these are the conditions that offer opportunities to sharpen our minds and hone our resilience." — **Seneca, *Letter to Lucilius*.**

Seneca reminds us that change is constant, even in things that appear still. Small shifts—like moving from rest to weariness or from health to sickness—can have a big impact on our lives. Instead of avoiding change, look at it as an opportunity for growth. By doing something new each day, you can align yourself with life's natural flow, which sharpens your mind and builds resilience. Even small daily changes will keep you adaptable, fostering continuous growth and mental clarity. True strength comes from engaging with the unknown, not avoiding it.

Doing something new every day may seem simple, but it is a powerful way to shift our perspective and prevent stagnation and mental atrophy. It breaks the monotony of everyday life, keeping our spirit refreshed and fostering continuous personal development. When we approach life with curiosity, adventure, and a willingness to learn, we cultivate innovation in our thinking and actions.

Hacking Tip: One of the most effective ways to boost **neuroplasticity**—the brain's ability to form new neural connections—is by introducing new activities into your routine. This can be something as small as trying a new workout, cooking a different meal, or learning a new skill, and it will increase your neural connections. These seemingly minor changes stimulate the brain and keep it agile, reducing mental rigidity and enhancing cognitive function.

February 17: Avoid Eating Late At Night

Science is increasingly proving how important it is to avoid late-night meals, especially because during deep sleep, the body has the capacity to clean the brain of toxins and waste products. The glymphatic system is most active during deep sleep, and anything that disrupts or reduces deep sleep can impair its ability to effectively cleanse the brain.

To understand a few points about how your meal can affect your brain health:

If digestion is active late into the night—such as after a large meal right before bed—it interferes with sleep quality, particularly the deep stages of sleep. This can indirectly impact the effectiveness of the glymphatic system, as it relies on deep sleep for optimal function.

Also, the body may prioritize digestion over other restorative processes during wakefulness or when eating close to bedtime. Since the glymphatic system primarily works during sleep, if digestion is ongoing when you fall asleep, it could interfere with your ability to achieve the deep sleep necessary for effective brain waste clearance.

Furthermore, the body's circadian rhythm naturally shifts energy toward different systems at different times of the day. The glymphatic system is most active during sleep, while the digestive system is typically active after eating. Eating late at night can disrupt these rhythms and negatively affect the glymphatic process by delaying sleep onset or reducing sleep quality.

Biohacking Tip: To optimize your body's natural rhythms, aim to finish a light meal at least four hours before bed, giving your body time to fully digest before sleep. This helps you sleep better, improves your metabolism, supports overall health and brain function, and helps prevent metabolic diseases.

February 18: Pursuit Of Perfection In Actions

For the Stoics, perfection is not the absence of mistakes (I don't think that would be possible) but the relentless pursuit of excellence in all aspects of life. Stoicism teaches that while external circumstances may be beyond our control, the effort we put into perfecting our actions, thoughts, and character is fully within our grasp. In other words, perfection isn't about achieving flawlessness but about persistently doing our best, day in and day out, regardless of the challenges we may face.

As Epictetus said: *"No man is free who is not master of himself."* This mastery over ourselves comes from continually refining our actions and responses, striving to improve our judgment, and living in accordance with reason and virtue. The Stoic pursuit of perfection is about focusing on progress, acknowledging our shortcomings, and using them as opportunities to grow in wisdom, patience, and resilience.

Hacking Tip: To apply this in daily life, aim to optimize your routines through continuous self-reflection and mindful improvements. Strive to become 1% better than yesterday, whether in your nutrition, exercise, reading, learning something new, meditating, or tracking your habits. Assess your performance and make small adjustments that contribute to your growth. You can also try something new—experiment with intermittent fasting or cold exposure to strengthen your body's resilience, spend time in sunlight, or practice mindfulness. Your actions won't be "perfect," but you can cultivate a mindset of steady progress.

February 19: Learn Calisthenics For Health And Longevity

Imagine having a full gym that you can bring with you wherever you go. And by using this gym, you'll also be developing great fitness for your brain. That's the simplicity and benefit of calisthenics. Calisthenics is a simple and effective form of exercise that uses your own bodyweight and creativity to build strength, flexibility, and endurance. You don't need any equipment—just focus on your natural movements. It's a workout accessible to everyone, anywhere.

Some of the **physical benefits** include building functional strength by engaging multiple muscle groups at once, improving not just muscle size but also how your body moves in daily life. Engaging in calisthenic exercises enhances your core stability, balance, and coordination. Additionally, the full range of motion in these movements promotes mobility and flexibility, which are essential for long-term joint health.

There are also **mental and emotional benefits** that calisthenics develops, such as mental toughness as you gradually progress to harder movements, and creativity as you improvise or adapt to your situation. The discipline required to improve over time strengthens both your mind and body. Every small gain—whether mastering a new exercise or adding reps—helps you build resilience and confidence.

Biohacking Tip: Start with basic exercises and maximize your calisthenics routine by focusing on progressive overload: begin with simple movements and gradually increase difficulty with more challenging variations. The goal is not to get stuck in repetition but to keep incorporating new exercises, improving mobility, and boosting cardiovascular health.

Mauro dos Santos

February 20: Maintaining Your Physical Fitness

Developing and maintaining the best version of your body is about more than just appearance; it's about honoring the body we've been given and ensuring it serves us well throughout life. Caring for our physical health is a form of respect for ourselves and a recognition of the body's potential to carry us through life's challenges.

For the Stoics, physical fitness was a reflection of self-discipline and self-love. Additionally, a strong body fosters a strong mind, and neglecting either creates imbalance. By dedicating time to maintain physical fitness, we sharpen both the body and the mind. Discipline in keeping your body in shape will also help develop discipline in other areas of life.

A healthy, fit body is the most elegant way to present yourself, making it easier to dress stylishly and carry yourself with confidence. It reflects discipline and resilience and prepares you to handle both the mental and emotional stresses that come your way.

Biohacking Tip: Don't focus on quantity on a daily basis, but on consistency and quality. Some days may be tough to work out, but even doing 15 minutes of light exercise will keep you on track. I guarantee you'll see continuous results because that's how I've maintained my fitness for decades.

February 21: A Strong Body Leads To A Strong Mind

Your physical and mental health, as well as your longevity, are a result of the balance between the fat stored in your body and the amount of muscle you have naturally developed. Developing muscle mass naturally is as important to your health as losing weight. High testosterone, for example, is one of the many benefits you gain by maintaining a well-shaped, healthy body.

Biohacking Tip: Don't focus on the scale but on the natural shape of your body. Never use drugs or steroids to gain muscle, especially for men, as it can work against your long-term health.

February 22: Losing Fat For Health

"It is not food or drink that causes human beings to be overweight or unhealthy, but the misuse of them. Eating beyond what is necessary and at improper times, driven by gluttony rather than need, leads to disorder both in body and soul. The one who seeks to master himself must first conquer his desires for food and drink, for excess in these things will always lead to excess in others... Late-night feasting, in particular, is harmful, for it disturbs the natural rhythms of the body. It burdens the stomach when it should be at rest, and it interrupts the tranquility of the night, when the mind and body must prepare for the day ahead. By practicing moderation, eating only at appropriate times, and with restraint, one promotes health, clarity, and peace within." ~ **Musonius Rufus – On Food and Moderation (Lecture 18)**

I don't think Rufus could be clearer about the importance of self-control and moderation when it comes to food, as well as the need to be mindful while eating, avoid bad habits, and develop discipline to achieve physical fitness. We need to be aware that fat stored in your body is a burden, and losing it requires discipline and perseverance. This applies to the body just as much as it does to the mind. Having worked in the fitness industry for decades, I know that shedding excess fat isn't easy—it takes a lot of commitment and discipline, especially when you feel like your efforts aren't bringing results. But the rewards are worth the effort.

Biohacking Tip: Don't push yourself too hard, and forget the scale. Focus on how you feel on a daily basis. Don't get stressed about the results; instead, enjoy the journey of physical activity and eating healthy food.

February 23: The Courage To Be Yourself

"The life we receive is not short, but we make it so; nor do we lack time, but we waste it. Life is long if you know how to use it. Some men are preoccupied with the pursuits of others, chasing approval and losing themselves in the process. Do not let this be you."

The path to happiness lies in self-sufficiency—knowing that you act with integrity and in accordance with your reason. It is not the concern of a wise person to be well-liked by the crowd but to be liked by oneself, to have one's own approval of one's life and actions. In this way, true courage is the ability to live for oneself, free from the need to conform, and free from the anxieties that come with seeking validation from others. — *Seneca, On the Happy Life (Chapter 2)*

Authenticity is courage in action. Being yourself in certain situations can be challenging. It takes true bravery to stand firmly in your truth and live according to your values, especially in a world that often pressures us to fit in by creating expectations. The Stoics believed that living authentically—aligned with reason and virtue—is the path to inner peace and happiness. It's about having the courage to be yourself, regardless of circumstances, external judgments, or expectations.

Hacking Tip: Practice self-reflection through journaling to uncover your true self. This allows you to process your thoughts and explore your values more deeply. Combine this with mindfulness and visualization techniques to reinforce confidence in your authenticity. Before going to bed, reflect on a human interaction, especially in a situation where you felt the need or pressure to please someone. Think about how true you were to yourself.

February 24: Honesty In Your Interactions

"If you ever wish to please anyone, you must expect to be false to yourself and betray your trust. But do you want to be truthful, honest, and consistent? Then never regard anything as more important than truth, for every time you seek to flatter or deceive, you are bartering away your integrity.

Why do you seek approval through dishonesty? You cannot deceive the nature within you, and every falsehood is an injury to your soul. If you hold honesty in the highest esteem, you will not allow anyone or anything to pressure you into being false. The wise man knows that integrity is its own reward, and that to live honestly, even in a world of deceit, is to live in accordance with nature.

Be honest with yourself and others, and you will find that truth is freedom. To lie is to enslave oneself, for you will always be trapped by the fear of being discovered. But truth makes the soul invincible, for nothing can harm one who is aligned with reality." — Epictetus, Discourses (Book 4, Chapter 8)

Honesty is a cornerstone of virtue. For the Stoics, truthfulness is essential in living a life of integrity. It isn't always easy to be honest, especially when you know what the other person expects to hear from you or when you fear your words might hurt them. However, when we are honest, we not only build trust with others but also create clarity and peace within ourselves. Honesty strengthens our relationships, allowing them to be built on a foundation of trust and openness.

Hacking Tip: First, be honest with yourself, then reflect on how you can be 100% honest with others. When you lie, you become a slave to your story, making it difficult to control the damage it may cause. Remember, spoken words never come back, and fixing a lie is much harder than telling the truth in the first place. A wise man once said: "If you don't have something good to say, say nothing."

February 25: Embracing Your Warrior Spirit

"Difficulties show what men are. Therefore, when a difficulty falls upon you, remember that God, like a trainer of wrestlers, has matched you with a tough opponent. 'Why?' So that you may be strengthened and made victorious. How then can you be proud of yourself if you have not faced any trial that makes you stronger? Show me a man who has been tried by affliction and yet remains resilient. That is the true warrior spirit." — Epictetus, Discourses (Book 1, Chapter 6)

There's no doubt that life demands a warrior's spirit. The Stoics believed that courage, discipline, and resilience are essential tools for facing the inevitable trials of life. Even when you're not looking for it, adversity will come your way. It's not something to be feared, but something to be confronted with strength and determination. I've eliminated the word "problem" from my dictionary and replaced it with "challenge." A challenge is something that will make you stronger, and a warrior's mindset embraces the challenges of life with the understanding that hardship is a pathway to growth. Courage means standing firm in the face of fear, and resilience is the ability to get back up after being knocked down.

Hacking Tip: Eliminate the word "problem" from your vocabulary and replace it with "challenge." A challenge is something that will make you stronger, and a warrior's mindset embraces the challenges of life, knowing that hardship leads to growth. Courage means standing firm in the face of fear, and resilience is the ability to rise after being knocked down.

February 26: Feminine Energy And Its Strength

Today's world is bombarded with separation and ideologies that don't serve us. One of these is the constant battle to define who is better, male or female. However, this comparison is unnecessary and detrimental. Each of us has our own unique strength, skills or qualities and our role in oru family and society, and there is no need for comparison or competition. So, there is incredible power in feminine energy—nurturing, intuitive, and resilient. When a woman recognizes this strength within herself, she steps into a life of balance and wisdom.

Biohacking Tip: Feminine energy isn't about being female; it's about following intuition, embracing love, care, and displaying incomparable strength. Embrace the balance of masculine and feminine energy through self-care, mindfulness, and intuition. Tap into your creativity, compassion, and connection to foster emotional balance and resilience.

February 27: Relationships In Your Life

"Remember that you are part of a larger whole, and that your duty in relationships is to support and love others. But this love should be rooted in wisdom, not in attachment or need. Every person is an individual, free to choose their own path. To be in a relationship, whether friendship or partnership, is to offer help and guidance when needed, but not to control or possess. Love is a partnership, not ownership."
— *Epictetus, Discourses (Book 2, Chapter 22)*

We are social beings, and relationships are vital for growth, resilience, and navigating the ups and downs of life. The Stoics believed that while we must cultivate inner strength, our connections with others offer the support we need through life's challenges. Strengthening your bonds with those around you brings respect, peace, and stability, while also providing emotional grounding when things get tough. True wisdom recognizes the value of strong relationships as a source of strength, mutual growth, and resilience.

Biohacking Tip: Prioritize quality time with your loved ones. Make friends, respect others, and engage in activities that foster deeper connections, whether through shared meals, meaningful conversations, or regular check-ins. Emotional connections are essential for life, and these moments of connection strengthen the emotional bonds that support overall well-being. They contribute to a balanced and resilient mindset.

February 28: Acceptance Of Others

I have this theory that each animal acts according to its instinct. You cannot be mad at a fly that lands on your meal or an ant that bites you. You can't be angry at a dog that barks or a shark that poses a danger to your life in the ocean. Each animal acts on its own instinct, and they can't differentiate between good and bad. The same applies to people. You can't judge others who don't act according to your expectations, nor should you hate them. Just accept it!

Stoic Insight: *"Begin each day by telling yourself: today I shall meet people who are meddling, ungrateful, arrogant, dishonest, jealous, and surly. They are like this because they cannot tell good from evil. But I have seen the beauty of good, and the ugliness of evil, and have recognized that the wrongdoer has a nature related to my own—not of the same blood or birth, but the same mind, and possessing a share of the divine. Therefore, none of them can harm me, for none can involve me in wrong. Nor can I be angry at my relative, or hate him, for we are made for cooperation, like feet, like hands, like eyelids, like the rows of the upper and lower teeth. To act against one another is contrary to nature." — **Marcus Aurelius, Meditations (Book 11, Section 18)**

True peace comes when we accept others as they are. The Stoics taught that judgment creates division and hinders genuine connection, while acceptance opens the door to love and unity. By embracing people for who they are, rather than who we think they should be, we cultivate deeper relationships and a sense of harmony with those around us.

Hacking Tip: Practice empathy, acceptance, and compassion by learning to see the world through the eyes of others. Mindfulness and active listening are powerful tools to help you better understand and appreciate others' perspectives. Also, do a self-evaluation: What bothers you about other people? Remember, people who are happy and in a joyful moment don't hurt others—only those who are facing frustration in life feel the need to act rashly toward others.

February 29: Activate Stem Cells With Hypoxic Exercise

Next time that you hit the gym try to breath out completely and hold your breath while keep repeating your sets, when you can not hold anymore slowly breath thru the nose and do 3 or 4 more reps more (or as much as you can). This type of breathing create a low oxigen environment in your body and besides encourage your parasympathetic activation, increase mitochondrial efficiency, stimulate Erythopoientin production which increate red blood cells production and oxigen transport in the body. Those are some benefits however, when you hold your breath afer full exhalation you create a hypoxic environment and stimulate the production and release of stem cell from the bode narrow.

Hypoxia exercises has been shown to trigger the release of Hypoxia-inducible factors, (HIFs), which can promote teh mobilization of steam cells. Stem cells are essential for tissue repair and celular regeneration which is a core principle in Biohacking for anti-ageing, Besides, stem cells repair damaged tissues and improves muscle recovery.

Biohacking tip: To doesn't matter your fitness level, if you have never done it before you must pay attention to safety first. You may want to start with very low weight (Maybe 40 to 50% of your normal exercise weight and increase it as you get used to.

This type of exercise require caution recommended for individuals with high risk of cancer. There's no strong evidence suggesting that this exercise can increase the risk of cancer risk for health individuals however, since cancer cells tend to grow on low oxygen environment, any activity of prolonged hypoxia could, theoretically encourage cancer cells survival and growth. To avoid any risk, or even for the amazing benefits it's strongly recommended that you learn and practive Soma breath or other breathing technique to balance the effect of hypoxia on the body after each set or after your workout routine.

March

Introduction
March 1: **Truth vs Reality**
March 2: **Dance For Emotional Expression**
March 3: **Sunlight For Well-Being**
March 4: **Red Light Therapy For Healing**
March 5: **Biohacking For Spiritual Well-Being**
March 6: **Visualization Of Your Passions**
March 7: **Chakra Balance**
March 8: **Letting Go Of Limiting Beliefs**
March 9: **Living With Freedom And Authenticity**
March 10: **Speaking The Truth In All Things**
March 11: **Using Fear As A Tool**
March 12: **Rejoicing In Challenges**
March 13: **Handling Success Gracefully**
March 14: **Handling Failure With Resilience**
March 15: **Forgiveness Of Self And Others**
March 16: **Accepting Your Emotions**
March 17: **Do Not Judge**
March 18: **Release Of Past Trauma**
March 19: **The Little Child Needs Your Support**
March 20: **Hack Your Longevity And Exceptional Health With Resveratrol**
March 21: **Our Thought Patterns**
March 22: **Trusting Your Intuition**
March 23: **Perseverance In The Face Of Obstacles**
March 24: **Creating Your Own Rituals**
March 25: **Biohacking Your Sleep**
March 26: **Embodying Passion**
March 27: **Finding Balance Between Emotion And Action**
March 28: **Compassion For Self And Others**
March 29: **Never Comparing Yourself to Others**
March 30: **Building Resilience Through Challenges**
March 31: **Mental Toughness In Adversity**

Introduction:

March brings a unique blend of intuition and passion, thanks to the combined energies of Pisces and Aries. This month is about listening to your inner voice and letting it guide you toward growth and self-expression. It's a time of emotional exploration, creative energy, and spiritual alignment. You're invited to dive deep, discover what makes you come alive, and let your intuition lead the way.

Your emotional health is at the forefront this month. Taking time to understand yourself—to really sit with your thoughts and emotions—will give you clarity and strength. When you can navigate your inner world, you'll feel more grounded and in control, no matter what life throws at you.

This is also a month for passion. What inspires you? What lights a fire in you? Find it, nurture it, and let it shine through in everything you do. Passion fuels creativity, and creativity helps us express who we are. Let March be the month where you create, express, and live fully.

On a spiritual level, take time to align with your purpose. Simple biohacks like breathwork or mindfulness can help you stay connected to that deeper part of yourself. When you're in tune with your spirit, everything else falls into place. March is your time to evolve—emotionally, creatively, and spiritually. Let this be a month of discovery and growth.

Mauro dos Santos

March 1: Truth vs Reality

What's true, if not your own perception of things? And what's reality or facts? *Knowing is the enemy of learning because those who believe they know everything end up closing their hearts to learning.* Mauro dos Santos

Our truth comes from our history, our perception of the world, and our limitations on learning. Unfortunately, most of us live this way, while the wise choose to be open to possibilities. Social truth, for example, is one of the most common. In order to feel accepted and fit in, we humans have a tendency to accept what the masses are doing.

What is true is not always popular, and what is popular is not always true. We are often swayed by the majority, who create their own collective truth, but we must focus instead on what reality actually demands of us.

"The wise man does not allow himself to be led by the crowd, nor does he seek validation in opinions, for only the truth found in reason and nature can guide him to live rightly."
— Seneca, *Letters from a Stoic*, Letter 78

In this letter, Seneca reminds us that social "truths" or collective beliefs often differ from reality. Reality, governed by nature and reason, should be our guide, not popular opinion or temporary trends.

Hacking Tip: Be open to possibilities; be open to learning from others, and you may end up seeing a world you never knew existed. We have a tendency to create walls around ourselves and close ourselves off to the possibility of a new reality or even seeing our own reality and knowledge in a different way.

When you are open to possibilities, you may discover that there's a world of opportunities that can shape your reality and concept of truth.

March 2: Dance For Emotional Expression

Movement is an expression of the soul. Through dance, we can articulate emotions that words often fail to capture, and it provides a way to express our freedom. When you dance, you connect with your inner self, releasing pent-up feelings and fostering a sense of liberation. Additionally, dance is a natural way to improve cognitive function, develop creativity, and bond with others. It is a holistic activity that balances the mind and soul.

Hacking Tip: Embrace dance as a powerful tool for emotional release and physical exercise. Engaging in rhythmic movement not only elevates your mood but also stimulates the brain, enhancing cognitive function. Whether it's a structured class, dancing with a partner, or simply dancing in your living room, let the music guide you. Don't focus on perfection, because there is no such thing in dancing. Remember, dance is not just about the steps; it's about expressing who you are and how you feel in that moment.

March 3: Sunlight For Well-Being

Exposure to sunlight is crucial for our health. Aim for 15-20 minutes of daily sunlight to boost Vitamin D levels, which support immune function, bone health, and overall vitality. Sunlight helps regulate circadian rhythms, and if you can do this barefoot in nature, it enhances the experience, as both are essential for quality sleep and mood stabilization. Early morning sun is particularly beneficial; it helps balance hormones, enhances alertness, sets a positive tone for the day ahead, and regulates your body's energy.

Additionally, natural light has a powerful impact on our mental health. It can elevate mood, reduce feelings of anxiety and depression, and foster a greater sense of connection to the world around us. Integrating sunlight into your daily routine—whether through a morning walk, gardening, or simply enjoying coffee outdoors—can lead to increased energy and improved emotional resilience.

Biohacking Tip: Prioritize daily sunlight exposure to reap these benefits. Consider setting aside time in the morning to allow nature to invigorate your mind and body. Remember, sunlight is not just a source of light; it's a vital element for nurturing your overall well-being. Embrace it fully and enjoy it!

March 4: Red Light Therapy For Healing

Red light therapy offers a wide range of benefits, especially for those looking to optimize health and performance. One of its key advantages is its ability to boost cellular energy production, which can improve overall vitality and reduce inflammation. This enhanced energy flow helps speed up recovery, making it ideal for anyone dealing with injuries or chronic pain. Additionally, red light therapy stimulates the production of collagen and creates healthier skin and can lead to a more youthful appearance, reducing wrinkles, scars, and blemishes. Surprisingly the red light therapy has been shown to help regulate circadian rhythms, improve sleep, and combat symptoms of depression. Over time, regular sessions can support overall physical and mental well-being, offering a natural way to enhance both recovery and performance. Also works by penetrating the skin and stimulating mitochondria in cells, which increases energy production and promotes faster recovery.

Incorporating red light therapy into your wellness routine can accelerate physical recovery and also contribute to mental rejuvenation. As the body heals, so too does the mind, as physical wellness is closely linked to emotional well-being.

Biohacking Tip: Set aside a few minutes each day for red light therapy sessions, focusing on areas of your body that need extra healing or care. Whether you're using a full-body red light panel or a handheld device, consistency is key. Regular sessions will help you maximize the benefits, supporting both short-term recovery and long-term vitality.

Embrace this process with the understanding that healing takes time, both inside and out. By integrating red light therapy into your routine, you're taking a proactive step toward holistic recovery, ensuring your body and mind stay resilient and healthy.

Mauro dos Santos

March 5: Biohacking For Spiritual Well-Being

Your spiritual well-being is not about religious devotion, but about aligning oneself with virtue, reason, and a sense of deeper purpose. True strength comes from within, and nurturing your spiritual well-being provides the foundation for resilience, clarity, and peace of mind and a better life overall. Stoicism teaches that the quality of our thoughts influences the quality of our lives, and maintaining inner harmony requires ongoing reflection and self-discipline. Just as we care for our bodies, our spiritual lives need intentional attention and growth. *"The happiness of your life depends upon the quality of your thoughts: therefore, guard accordingly, and take care that you entertain no notions unsuitable to virtue and reasonable nature."* — **Marcus Aurelius, Meditations** (Book 2, Section 2)

The Stoic pursuit of spiritual well-being comes from guarding your mind and cultivating resilience through reflection, mindfulness, and aligning with your higher purpose. It requires acknowledging the distractions that pull us away from inner peace and making a conscious effort to choose thoughts, think about what you are thinking, for example, and creating actions that nurture spiritual growth. In this way, the mind becomes stronger, better equipped to handle adversity, and more connected to what truly matters in life.

Biohacking Tip: To integrate this into your daily life, incorporate spiritual practices that foster clarity and connection. Practices such as meditation, mindfulness, and gratitude journaling help you nurture inner peace and strengthen your spiritual foundation.

Set aside time each day for spiritual reflection, whether through meditation, prayer, or journaling. Spend at least one day a week connecting with nature, walking in the park, hiking, or simply sitting in a quiet outdoor space. When you feel upset, anxious, stressed just make a self analyze. Think about what you are thinking. Think about what thoughts lead you to those specific feeling.

March 6: Visualization Of Your Passions

What we consistently focus on, we tend to manifest in our lives. Passion may drive our actions, but visualization sharpens our focus and aligns our mind with our goals. By imagining the outcomes we desire and reinforcing them in our thoughts, we create mental pathways that guide us toward success. Visualization helps us maintain clarity in our pursuits, even when obstacles arise, by keeping our attention on the bigger picture. *Your mind will be like its habitual thoughts; for the soul becomes dyed with the color of its thoughts. Soak it, then, in such thoughts as these: where life is possible at all, a right life is possible."* — **Marcus Aurelius, Meditations**

Use visualization techniques to mentally rehearse your ideal outcomes and goals. Visualization is more than daydreaming; it's an intentional practice that helps your mind and body prepare for success. Studies show that athletes and high achievers who visualize their performance often improve their real-life results. Close your eyes and vividly picture yourself achieving your goals. Imagine the details—how it feels, what it looks like, and how your life changes as a result. To enhance this practice, combine visualization with positive affirmations. Speaking encouraging words to yourself while imagining your success strengthens your motivation and builds confidence. This combination boosts your focus, ignites your passion, and helps you stay connected to your vision, making it easier to take the necessary steps to reach your goals.

Hacking Tip: Set aside a few minutes each morning and evening to practice visualization. Sit quietly and focus on your aspirations— whether they are related to personal growth, career success, or fitness goals. Combine this with positive affirmations that reinforce your belief in your abilities, such as "I am capable of achieving this" or "I am on the path to success." Doing this regularly can significantly improve your drive, clarity, and resilience as you work toward your passions.

March 7: Chakra Balance

Modern science is beginning to explore and validate the concepts behind ancient practices, including the role of chakras in maintaining overall well-being and not seen it as pure religion. Chakras are the energy centers in the body and are believed to influence both physical and emotional health. While rooted in ancient Hindu tradition, today's understanding of energy flow in the body aligns with emerging research in areas such as bioenergy, neuroplasticity, and even the body's electromagnetic fields. By balancing these chakras, we can promote physical vitality, emotional stability, spiritual growth and feel more energetic and alive.

You can balance your chakras through practices like yoga, breathwork, or meditation. Each chakra corresponds to different parts of the body and specific emotional and spiritual functions. For example, the root chakra influences feelings of safety and stability, while the heart chakra governs love and compassion. By focusing on these energy centers, you can release blockages that may be causing emotional or physical imbalances.

Practices such as yoga postures help to open and align specific chakras, promoting energy flow and reducing tension in the body. Breathwork, especially deep and rhythmic breathing, can clear emotional blockages, while meditation brings focus and intention to these energy centers. These methods support greater overall health by aligning the body's natural energy flow with mental and emotional clarity.

Hacking Tip: Incorporate chakra-balancing techniques into your routine. Combine breathwork and meditation, visualizing each chakra as an open, flowing source of energy. Regularly focusing on your chakras can improve your physical vitality, enhance your emotional balance, and promote a deeper sense of connection with yourself.

March 8: Letting Go Of Limiting Beliefs

"Do not conform to the pattern of this world, but be transformed by the renewing of your mind." — Romans 12:2

Limiting beliefs are the invisible chains that hold us back from reaching our true potential. These beliefs, often ingrained from past experiences or societal expectations, create barriers to growth. To move forward, we must break free from these mental constraints and transform both our mind and spirit. Growth is not possible without change—starting with the thoughts that shape our reality.

By challenging these limiting beliefs, you open yourself up to new possibilities, allowing your mind to embrace potential and opportunity. When you renew your mind, you step into a space where you can reimagine your life and take control of your future.

To release yourself from limiting beliefs, practice self-reflection and challenge negative thought patterns. Techniques from cognitive behavioral therapy (CBT) can help you identify and restructure harmful beliefs, transforming them into positive, empowering ones. Affirmations are another powerful tool to reprogram your mind. By regularly affirming statements like "I am capable" or "I am deserving of success," you begin to rewrite the narratives that have been holding you back.

Start by writing down any recurring negative thoughts or limiting beliefs. Ask yourself if they are true or if they simply reflect old fears and assumptions. Then, replace those thoughts with empowering beliefs that align with your goals and values. Over time, this practice will help shift your mindset, allowing you to approach challenges with confidence and resilience.

Practical Tip: Dream big and set aside time each day for self-reflection. Use a journal to track your thoughts and identify patterns of self-limiting beliefs that may be stopping you from realizing your dreams. Combine this practice with daily affirmations to reinforce positive thinking and reframe your perspective.

March 9: Living With Freedom And Authenticity

True freedom comes from living authentically and aligning with your core values. When you let go of external pressures and embrace your true self, you experience a deeper sense of liberation. Authenticity allows you to make choices that reflect who you truly are, rather than conforming to societal expectations.

"Is anyone free who is compelled to act against his will? No one is free who is not master of himself." — **Epictetus**

This Stoic insight emphasizes that true freedom is internal. If you are constantly swayed by the will of others or external pressures, you are not truly free. Mastering yourself—your actions, reactions, and choices—is the key to living a life of freedom. Freedom is about acting in alignment with your values and not being controlled by circumstances or external forces.

Biohacking Tip: Practice authenticity by setting boundaries and speaking your truth. Let go of the need for external validation and focus on self-expression.

March 10: Speaking The Truth In All Things

"If it is not right, do not do it; if it is not true, do not say it." — Marcus Aurelius

Truth is the foundation of character. The Stoics believed that speaking honestly, regardless of the consequences, is essential for integrity and personal growth. Truthfulness allows us to build trust, both in ourselves and in others.

When you practice clear and honest communication in all areas of life, avoiding gossip and half-truths, you embrace radical honesty. This not only reduces stress but also strengthens relationships and aligns you with your authentic self. When what you say is true, you don't have to remember what you said.

Hack Tip: Commit to speaking the truth, even when it's uncomfortable. Focus on delivering your message with kindness and clarity, but remain firm in your honesty. Over time, this practice will foster deeper, more authentic relationships and promote inner peace.

March 11: Using Fear As A Tool

"Do not be disturbed. For all things are according to nature, and in a little time you will be nobody and nowhere, like Hadrian and Augustus." — Marcus Aurelius

Fear is a natural part of life, but the Stoics taught that fear is a signal, not an obstacle. Rather than allowing fear to paralyze you, use it as a tool for growth. When you confront fear, you have the opportunity to strengthen your mind and spirit. Fear shows you where your limits lie, and by facing it, you expand those limits and move toward personal growth.

The book 12 Rules for life: *An Antidote to Chaos* by Jordan B. Peterson, teach us how fear is a powerful tool for growth when faced with courage and discipline. Instead of avoiding it, use fear to uncover your strengths, push beyond comfort, and pursue meaningful goals. By confronting fear directly, you transform chaos into order, gaining resilience, self-awareness, and the courage to act despite uncertainty.

Hacking Tip: The best way to overcome fear is by facing it. Confront your fears head-on using exposure therapy or gradual challenges that push your boundaries. Whether it's public speaking, cold exposure, or trying something entirely new, overcoming fear builds resilience and confidence.

March 12: Rejoicing In Challenges

Every time you face yourself in a difficult situation replace the word *problem* with **challenge**. When you use the word "problem," it can make you feel as though you are incapable of solving or facing it. However, a *challenge* is an obstacle that comes your way to make you stronger. Life's challenges are not setbacks but opportunities for growth. Every adversity you face provides a chance to cultivate inner strength, resilience, and wisdom.

To build resilience, actively seek out challenges. Incorporate hormetic stressors—small doses of controlled stress—that condition your body and mind to handle adversity with grace.

Hack Tip: Try introducing cold showers, extended fasting periods, or challenging workouts into your routine. These controlled stressors build the mental toughness needed to handle bigger challenges in life. By embracing discomfort in these small ways, you'll find greater ease in handling adversity when it comes.

Mauro dos Santos

March 13: Handling Success Gracefully

If you are reading this book, it means you are aiming for something big in your life, and eventually, you will be very successful. However, success is a double-edged sword. While it can elevate you, it can also be the very thing that leads to your downfall if not handled with humility. Arrogance blinds us to our flaws, makes us vulnerable to complacency, and distances us from others. True mastery lies in understanding that success is fleeting and external. What truly matters is the character we maintain in both triumph and defeat.

Success, like all external circumstances, is neither inherently good nor bad—it's how we respond to it that defines us. Use success not as a pedestal for pride, but as a reminder of the impermanence of all things. Handle your victories with humility and grace, knowing that fortune can change at any moment. Remain grounded, reflect on the effort it took to get there, and remember that you are always a student of life.

"Success is a dangerous thing. It can get you intoxicated, thinking you are invincible and immune to the laws of nature." — Epictetus (Discourses, Book 1)

It is very important that we always cultivate a daily practice of gratitude to stay grounded, even in moments of success. Recognize your achievements, but also acknowledge the support of others and the opportunities life has provided.

Hacking Tip: At the end of each day, reflect not only on what you've accomplished but also on the people and circumstances that contributed to your success. Practicing gratitude keeps you connected to reality, ensuring that you handle success with grace and wisdom.

March 14: Handling Failure With Resilience

Failure is a perception. No matter who you are or how successful you may be, you have experienced setbacks. If you replace the word "failure" with "setback," you'll realize that these moments are opportunities for evaluation and building something bigger and better. Failure is nothing more than how we respond to those moments. The Stoics understood that failure is not an end, but rather a stepping stone on the journey of growth. It is through failure that we learn our greatest lessons and cultivate resilience. Each setback is an opportunity to rise stronger, more focused, and more determined than before.

Your setbacks, like success, are just external events. They do not define your worth or capability. What defines a successful man or woman is their ability to rise, adapt, and keep moving forward. *"Our actions may be impeded... but there can be no impeding our intentions or dispositions. Because we can accommodate and adapt. The mind adapts and converts to its own purposes the obstacle to our acting. The impediment to action advances action. What stands in the way becomes the way."* — Marcus Aurelius, *Meditations* (Book 5, Chapter 20)

This shows that although external events may block our actions, they do not prevent us from maintaining our purpose or attitude. By adapting, we can turn obstacles into opportunities for growth. This passage emphasizes how challenges can become the path forward, which is central to Stoic thought. As Epictetus said, *"The greater the difficulty, the more glory in surmounting it. Skillful pilots gain their reputation from storms and tempests."*

Hack Tip: Use setbacks as fuel for self-improvement. After each setback, take time to reflect on what went right and how you can improve and recreate. Write down the lessons learned and visualize yourself overcoming the next challenge. This practice transforms challenges into a powerful tool for personal growth and resilience.

Mauro dos Santos

March 15: Forgiveness Of Self And Others

"Bear with each other and forgive one another.. " Colossians 3:13

When the Bible recommends that we forgive others, it's not because the other person needs our forgiveness, but because we need to free ourselves from the burden. Holding resentment is like punishing ourselves while hoping the other person feels hurt. Do you want a healthier physical body? Forgive. Do you want peace of mind? Forgive. Do you want a strong spiritual life? Forgiveness is essential. Wherever someone dide something that hurt you, **Set yourself free** and forgive immediately. Then, do a self-analysis: "What did I do to attract this event?" "Where is my responsibility in this?"

It's not worth carrying the weight of anger, bitterness, and regret, as it clouds our clarity, impacts leadership, and weakens emotional strength. Forgiveness is not about letting someone "off the hook," but about releasing yourself from the chains that keep you stuck in the past. It is an act of inner freedom.

For high-performing individuals—CEOs, executives, and leaders— the ability to forgive is even more crucial, as they face challenges on a daily basis. Forgiveness allows you to clear mental clutter and make better decisions from a place of clarity, purpose, and balance.

"He who does wrong does wrong to himself. He who does injustice acts unjustly to himself, because he makes himself bad." — Marcus Aurelius, *Meditations*

Hacking Tip: If you still feel resentment, pain, or discomfort when thinking about a particular event or person, it means you haven't fully forgiven yet. One way to work on your forgiveness is to write a letter to the person who hurt you, explaining how you were hurt and that you forgive them. Be specific. Then, write a letter to yourself, forgiving yourself for allowing this person or event to hurt you. **Set yourself free!**

March 16: Accepting Your Emotions

Emotions are a natural part of life, but they shouldn't control us. The Stoics believed in acknowledging emotions, but not allowing them to dictate our actions. Accept your feelings, but always act with reason and clarity.
"Make the mind tougher by a simple habit of ignoring the impulses of the body." — Marcus Aurelius

Many emotions are stored in the body, and practices like Kundalini yoga can be powerful tools to release them by bringing these emotions to the surface for processing. Similarly, Vipassana meditation, which focuses on observing bodily sensations, can be highly effective in gaining emotional control and self-awareness. It's also common for clients to experience deep emotional releases during a massage with Reiki energy, often recalling emotions linked to past events they no longer consciously remember but have stored in their bodies. Your sensations may reflect your personal history.

Biohacking Tip: Practice mindfulness to observe your emotions without judgment. First, accept them and recognize them without letting them control you. When emotions arise, label them and use techniques like deep breathing to process them in a healthy way. This approach helps you maintain control while allowing space for your emotions to be felt and released.

March 17: Do Not Judge

Judgment can be a complex concept. In the Bible, we see both a recommendation to judge and a warning against it. In 1 Corinthians 2:15, Paul writes, *"The spiritual person judges all things, but is himself to be judged by no one."* Yet in Luke 6:37, we are told, *"Do not judge, and you will not be judged."* This apparent contradiction leads some to believe they have the right to judge others.

However, examining the original Greek reveals two different words are used. *Diakrino* (διακρίνω) in 1 Corinthians means to discern or judge rightly, while *Krino* (κρίνω) in Luke 6:37 refers to judging or condemning, as if you are superior to the one being judged. This distinction shows that one form of judgment is about discernment, while the other involves condemnation, which we are advised to avoid.

The Stoic philosopher Epictetus offers similar wisdom on avoiding judgment:
"When you are offended at any man's fault, turn to yourself and study your own failings. Then you will forget your anger."
He teaches that judging others distracts us from our own flaws. Rather than focusing on others' faults, we should look inward and work on improving ourselves.

Hacking Tip: Judgment works against you. Next time you face a person or situation where you feel inclined to judge, ask yourself: *Why am I holding anger or resentment? What in me needs to change to be more accepting?* This reflection will help shift the focus back to your own growth.

March 18: Release Of Past Trauma

The past does not define who you are, but unresolved pain can create invisible barriers to your growth. Holding onto past trauma only keeps you a prisoner of suffering. By releasing what no longer serves you, you create space for healing and true transformation.

"Today I escaped anxiety. Or no, I discarded it, because it was within me, in my own perceptions—not outside." — Marcus Aurelius

Trauma often lingers in the body, manifesting as both physical and emotional blockages. Techniques like somatic therapy, breathwork, or energy healing can help release stored trauma, allowing for emotional and physical healing. By letting go of past pain, you unlock greater mental clarity, well-being, and the freedom to move forward.

During some of my practices with massage/Reiki, and energy healing, I noticed many clients becoming unexpectedly emotional. Through the blend of physical touch and energetic work, deep-seated emotions and old traumas began to surface and release. This confirmed to me how the body holds onto emotional pain in some tension points, and how touch and energy healing can open the path to true inner freedom.

Hacking Tip: Pay attention to your thoughts. Every time you notice yourself thinking unproductive, negative thoughts or feeling down, ask yourself: *Why am I feeling this way?* Don't judge your thoughts and feelings; instead, try to understand where they come from and what you need to do to release yourself from them.

March 19: The Little Child Needs Your Support

"The tongue has the power of life and death, and those who love it will eat its fruit." — Proverbs 18:21

Imagine your best friend, someone you love and respect, calling you every day to say: *"You're incapable of doing this," "You're an idiot,"* or *"You're a loser."* No matter how much you care about this friend, how do you think these words would affect you? While it's unlikely anyone has a friend like that, it's astonishing how many people speak to themselves this way. This kind of negative self-talk lowers your self-esteem, creates anxiety, and even impacts your physical health.

In the book *What to Say When You Talk to Yourself*, Dr. Shad Helmstetter highlights the power of self-talk and how our internal dialogue shapes our beliefs, behaviors, and life outcomes.

So, NEVER, under any circumstance, speak negatively about yourself. You are hurting your inner child and attracting negative results into your life. Instead, create a list of positive affirmations to replace those harmful thoughts.

Hacking Tip: One of the most effective ways to counter negative self-talk is to find one or two trusted friends and create an accountability group. Support each other in developing positive self-talk habits. You can even make it fun—at the end of each day, report your progress to a friend or the group. When you're together and hear someone speaking negatively about themselves, immediately counter it with a positive affirmation. Make it a game: whoever catches the negative self-talk first gets to shout a positive affirmation! This turns the process into something lighthearted and supportive, while helping you reinforce positivity.

March 20: Hack Your Longevity And Exceptional Health With Resveratrol

Resveratrol, a powerful antioxidant found in the skin of red grapes and berries, has gained attention for its potential to promote longevity and exceptional health. This compound supports cellular health by protecting your cells from damage caused by oxidative stress and inflammation. Research also suggests that resveratrol activates certain genes linked to longevity, including those involved in the body's natural repair processes.

By incorporating resveratrol into your diet, through foods or supplements, you can help boost heart health, improve brain function, and support metabolic well-being.

Hacking Tip: Add resveratrol-rich foods to your daily diet, like red grapes, dark chocolate, and berries. If you prefer supplements, look for high-quality resveratrol to maximize its health benefits. This small addition could be the biohack that helps you age gracefully while maintaining exceptional health.

March 21: Our Thought Patterns

Negative thought patterns, which often go unnoticed, influence our emotional and behavioral responses, leading to issues like anxiety, depression, or stress. These thoughts are usually irrational or distorted. Examples include catastrophizing (imagining the worst outcome), black-and-white thinking (seeing everything as all good or all bad), and personalizing (blaming oneself for things beyond control). We tend to stay within the limits of our own thinking, trapped inside a box of limitations.

In Cognitive Behavioral Therapy (CBT), individuals are encouraged to challenge these thoughts. For example, instead of thinking, *"I always fail at everything,"* you can start asking, *"Is that really true?"* This questioning helps reveal that our thoughts are often exaggerated.

Hacking Tip: The next step in CBT is replacing negative thoughts with more balanced ones. Instead of saying, *"I will never be good enough,"* try thinking, *"I may not succeed at everything, but I have strengths."* This shift helps reduce anxiety and directs you toward more positive emotional responses.

Do you know someone who might need to change their thought patterns? Take a picture of this page and share it with them.

March 22: Trusting Your Intuition

In our busy lives, it can be difficult to listen to and trust our intuition. We tend to rely heavily on logic and reason, but in many situations, our intuition—when aligned with clarity and self-awareness—can serve as a compass, guiding us toward our best decisions.The Stoics believed that intuition, when tempered by reason, is a powerful tool for making wise choices. By trusting your inner voice, you allow yourself to move more freely toward what feels true and right for you.

Have you ever felt that a decision, which seemed right at the time, would have been the best choice for a specific situation, but because you didn't act on it, you didn't get the outcome you expected? It's not always easy to listen to our intuition, especially when it seems to defy logic, but often your gut knows better than your logical mind.

Hacking Tip: Start a daily practice of reflection and meditation to develop your intuition. After your meditation, jot down any intuitive thoughts or feelings that arise. Over time, you'll strengthen your connection to your inner wisdom, making it easier to trust your intuition in key moments of decision-making.

March 23: Perseverance In The Face Of Obstacles

to overcome challenges when they arise.

Do you want to take it to the next level? Call that person who acts as your emotional personal trainer and thank them for helping you become a better As a personal trainer, I always studied my clients to understand their limits and how I could help them get the most out of each workout by pushing those limits forward. Sometimes our body complains, but when you lift a heavier weight than your last workout, you're preparing your body for the next level. Obstacles are not your enemy or setbacks—they are like your personal trainer pushing you to grow.

Challenges aren't meant to stop you; they're meant to strengthen you and make you better. In life, we often have someone who acts as our emotional personal trainer, pushing us to grow emotionally. Be thankful if you have someone like that in your life—they're helping you become emotionally stronger.

"The impediment to action advances action. What stands in the way becomes the way." — Marcus Aurelius

Focus on cultivating perseverance by engaging in practices that train your mind and body to endure discomfort. Cold exposure and intermittent fasting are examples of controlled stressors that build mental resilience. These practices not only condition your body to handle physical stress but also sharpen your ability to push through challenges in everyday life, all while offering numerous health benefits.

Hacking Tip: Introduce cold showers or intermittent fasting into your routine to build mental and physical toughness. By training yourself to embrace discomfort, you'll find it easier person.

March 24: Creating Your Own Rituals

Rituals are more than just routines—they are intentional practices that ground us, bringing structure, order, and peace to our lives. Marcus Aurelius, in *Meditations*, reflects on the importance of starting the day with purposeful thought. One of his daily "rituals" was to remind himself of the challenges he would face and to align his mind with the Stoic virtues of patience, humility, and resilience. He writes: ***"When you wake up in the morning, tell yourself: The people I deal with today will be meddling, ungrateful, arrogant, dishonest, jealous, and surly..."*** (Meditations, Book 2).

Though it may seem humorous to start your day with that statement, this ritual helped him prepare mentally and emotionally for the day ahead, serving as a reminder to maintain inner calm in the face of difficulties.

Rituals allow us to build consistency in our actions, fostering both mental clarity and emotional balance. Whether it's a morning routine that sets the tone for the day or an evening ritual that helps you unwind, these small practices provide a foundation of stability amidst life's unpredictability.

Biohacking Tip: Develop daily rituals that ground both your mind and body. Engage in activities like morning meditation, breathwork, or journaling—these practices enhance focus, discipline, and emotional resilience.

Practical Tip: Start small by incorporating one or two rituals into your day, and add more as you go. Some helpful rituals inspired by Stoic teachings include:

- Start your day early.
- Drink water first thing in the morning.
- Do some light exercise to loosen your muscles and prepare for the day.
- Practice meditation.

- Write in a journal.
- Plan your day with intention.
- Practice gratitude.
- Set aside a moment for reflection.
- Read something positive.
- Practice kindness.
- Bless someone by sharing something good or positive.

As you build consistency, these practices will become essential tools for your mental, emotional, and physical well-being.

March 25: Biohacking Your Sleep

Rest is crucial for maintaining clarity of thought and strength of body. The Stoics understood that a well-rested mind is better equipped to face life's challenges with reason and composure. Quality sleep is the foundation upon which resilience is built, allowing us to recover both physically and mentally for the tasks that lie ahead.

Hacking Tip: To optimize your sleep, create an environment that promotes deep rest:

- Avoid eating at least 4 hours before going to bed.
- Create a habit of going to bed early to ensure your deep, restorative sleep happens between 1:00 and 3:00 a.m.
- Make your room as dark as possible.
- Stay away from electronic distractions and blue light (computer, cell phone) two hours before bed.
- Stick to a consistent sleep schedule, aiming to go to bed and wake up at the same time every day, even on weekends.
- Consider supplementing with magnesium to support relaxation.
- Practice mindfulness or breathing exercises before bed to calm the mind and prepare your body for restorative sleep.
- Read a good book instead of watching TV.
- Avoid discussing important topics in bed to maintain a peaceful atmosphere for rest.

March 26: Embodying Passion

"Live with passion!" This is one of Tony Robbins' mottos. Passion is the driving force that fuels purpose, but like the Stoics taught, it must be aligned with wisdom and virtue. When passion is tempered with reason, it elevates our actions and connects them with a higher purpose. It's not about being carried away by emotion but about channeling that energy into meaningful and impactful ways.

Biohacking Tip: To embody passion in your life, focus on activities that bring you joy and fulfillment, and engage with them fully. Strive for flow states—those moments when you are so immersed in an activity that time seems to disappear. Identify what activities ignite your passion and make time for them regularly. Whether it's a personal project, physical exercise, or work-related tasks, approach them with intentionality and immerse yourself completely. By doing so, you not only increase your productivity but also deepen your sense of fulfillment.

March 27: Finding Balance Between Emotion And Action

We are emotional creatures, and emotions can either guide us or control us. Balancing emotional responses with measured action requires both awareness and acknowledgment. When emotions are recognized but not allowed to dictate our behavior, we make decisions rooted in clarity and reason.

As Epictetus said, emotions arise not from events themselves but from our judgments about those events. He famously stated, "It's not what happens to you, but how you react to it that matters" (*Enchiridion*, Chapter 5). According to his view, emotions like anger, fear, and sadness stem from irrational judgments. If we change how we judge a situation, we can see it differently and better control our emotional responses.

Hacking Tip: If your emotions become overwhelming, practice deep breathing techniques like the 4-7-8 method to calm your mind before taking action. Never make decisions or respond to someone when you're in a heightened emotional state. Give yourself space to regain composure first.

March 28: Compassion For Self And Others

Passion doesn't come solely from drive and ambition; it flourishes when we nurture ourselves and others with compassion.

We shouldn't be overly harsh on ourselves. When we judge ourselves too critically, we create barriers that stifle the passion driving our purpose. Constant criticism doesn't foster growth; passion thrives when we treat ourselves with kindness, just as we do with others. By forgiving ourselves and embracing our imperfections, we create space for creativity and motivation to flow.

Loving-Kindness Meditation for Passion. Loving-kindness meditation is a powerful way to cultivate compassion, which is essential for sustaining long-term passion. This practice nurtures empathy and emotional resilience, providing the emotional balance to pursue your goals with heart and energy.

Hacking Tip: Begin each morning by practicing loving-kindness meditation. Send warm thoughts to yourself and others, and notice how your compassion deepens your sense of purpose.

When faced with self-doubt or negativity, ask yourself: "Am I being too hard on myself?" Treat yourself with the same patience and encouragement you would offer to a friend. Compassion is the key that unlocks the energy needed for passion and success.

March 29: Never Comparing Yourself To Others

Our modern society has created a standard where everyone is expected to fit into others' expectations. Unfortunately, in the attempt to meet these expectations, we tend to lose our identity, self-expression, and freedom. Fulfillment comes from within, and comparison is the thief of joy.

In his *Meditations*, Marcus Aurelius was very clear about how we should live and act:

"Don't waste time thinking about what others are doing, how they are living, or what they are saying. Instead, ask yourself: 'Am I doing what I should be doing? Am I acting with the integrity that aligns with my nature?' Focus on your own path and work, and do not let the distractions of comparison pull you from your purpose. Life is short, and the time we spend comparing ourselves to others is time lost in pursuing our true purpose." — Marcus Aurelius, Meditations (Book 6, Section 51)

In this passage, Marcus Aurelius emphasizes that comparison to others is a distraction from living with purpose and integrity, or even living your own life. By worrying about others' actions, possessions, or achievements, we divert energy and attention away from what truly matters—our own progress and actions. The Stoic practice is to focus on what we can control: our thoughts, actions, and how we live in accordance with our values.

Biohacking Tip: Prioritize self-improvement by setting your own goals and tracking your progress against them. Avoid the trap of social comparison, which only adds unnecessary stress and pulls your focus away from your personal growth.

March 30: Building Resilience Through Challenges

Do you want to build your resilience? Face your life's challenges head-on. Every trial you encounter isn't meant to break you but to shape you into someone stronger, more capable, and unshakable. Challenges are the stepping stones to strength and character. Our tendency to stay in our comfort zone often keeps us from embracing opportunities for growth. But every challenge strengthens your ability to persevere, and with each test, you build the resilience needed for life's greater obstacles.

The Stoics believed that resilience comes from training the mind to handle adversity. Each difficulty or setback is an opportunity to practice patience, strength, and wisdom. Keep moving forward, even when things get tough, and trust that the process will make you stronger.

Hacking Tip: Each challenge is a chance to prove your strength. Persevere, and you'll emerge stronger, ready to take on whatever comes your way. The more you embrace difficulty, the more resilient you become.

March 31: Mental Toughness In Adversity

Adversity tests our mental strength, shaping us into stronger versions of ourselves. When faced with challenges, it's easy to fall into despair, but true growth comes from embracing these trials with determination.

Epictetus often described adversity as a training ground for character, viewing each challenge as an opportunity to live virtuously and wisely. He famously said: *"Difficulties show a person what they are. Therefore, when a difficulty falls upon you, remember that God, like a trainer of wrestlers, has matched you with a tough young man. For what purpose? So that you may become an Olympic conqueror; but it is not accomplished without sweat."* In this metaphor, we are like warriors in training, honing our strength through struggle.

Hacking Tip: Build mental resilience by engaging in cold exposure or challenging workouts. Training your mind and body to endure discomfort strengthens your ability to handle stress and adversity in all areas of life. Over time, you'll be more prepared to face life's challenges with confidence and grit. Learn to become comfortable in uncomfortable situations.

April

Introduction:

April is a month of power and stability, guided by the fiery energy of Aries and the grounded influence of Taurus. This is the time to focus on building both your physical and financial strength. It's about putting action behind your goals, but also ensuring you have the stability and resources to sustain that momentum.

Your physical health takes center stage this month. Take advantage of biohacking techniques to improve your vitality— whether it's optimizing your workouts, eating foods that fuel you, or getting the restorative sleep your body needs. The better care you take of your body, the more you'll be able to achieve in all areas of life.At the same time, April is about building wealth. Financial health is just as important as physical health, and this is the month to start thinking about long-term security. Whether it's learning more about investing, creating a budget, or setting financial goals, now is the time to strengthen your relationship with money. Remember, wealth isn't just about having more—it's about having control and freedom over your financial future. Finally, April reminds you to find balance. Yes, there's power in action, but there's also power in rest. With the strong energy of Aries pushing you forward, don't forget to balance that drive with the grounded, nurturing energy of Taurus. Rest, recover, and take care of yourself along the way. When you combine personal drive with self-care, you'll create sustainable success in every area of your life.

Mauro dos Santos

April 1: Activate mTHOR And Sirtuins

The Mechanistic Target of Rapamycin (mTOR) is a protein kinase that plays a crucial role in cell growth, proliferation, metabolism, and survival. Sirtuins, on the other hand, are a family of proteins that play a major role in cellular health, aging, and metabolism. According to Dr. StClair, they act as cellular guardians by regulating critical processes such as DNA repair, cellular stress responses, and energy efficiency. Due to their roles in longevity, both mTOR and sirtuins are popular targets in biohacking for promoting health and delaying aging.

Both groups share some similarities in how they can be activated and optimized. You can enhance their function through intermittent fasting or time-restricted eating, regular exercise, balanced protein intake, reducing simple carbohydrates and excessive calories, and incorporating resveratrol (found in red grapes, supplements, and berries) for its antioxidant properties. Other ways to activate these proteins include using curcumin, cold exposure, adequate sleep, and NAD+ boosters. These are among the many strategies you'll find throughout this book.

It's no surprise that a sedentary lifestyle, chronic stress, excessive alcohol consumption, and excessive caloric intake—especially from sugar and processed foods—can deactivate these proteins and lead to premature aging and even early death.

Biohacking Tip: Start activating mTOR and sirtuins by exercising regularly, incorporating intermittent fasting, avoiding overeating, improving sleep quality, and exposing yourself to cold (e.g., ice baths). I also incorporate polyphenols into my approach to activate sirtuins; these plant-based antioxidants are found in foods like berries, tea, coffee, dark chocolate, and wine. Additionally, I take resveratrol and an NAD+ booster supplement to support these pathways.

April 2: Sauna For Detox And Relaxation

A study conducted in Finland on May 12, 2003, and published in the National Library of Medicine (National Center for Biotechnology Information) shows that men who used a sauna two to three times per week were 27% less likely to die from cardiovascular diseases and 40% less likely to die from premature death. As shown in teh study, sauna therapy is one of the best ways to reduce the risk of cardiovascular disease, improve circulation, detoxify the body, strengthen the immune system, reduce muscle pain, and enhance brain function and muscle recovery.

But, sauna sessions offer more than just physical benefits—they help calm the mind, providing a sense of peace and restoration after periods of stress or exertion, and also support overall brain health.

Biohacking Tip: Incorporate sauna sessions into your routine for detoxification and muscle relaxation. The heat stimulates circulation, enhances recovery, and supports the body's natural detox processes. For an added boost, alternate sauna sessions with cold showers to improve circulation and build resilience. This combination sharpens both body and mind, making recovery a key part of your health regimen and leaving you unstoppable.

April 3: Inversion Therapy For Spinal Health

Insight:
Balance and alignment in the body often reflect the clarity and equilibrium we seek in our minds. When the body is aligned, we are better equipped to approach life's challenges with a clearer perspective, feeling more grounded and at ease.

Some benefits are:

- **Spinal Decompression:** Reduces pressure on vertebrae, discs, and nerves, relieving pain and discomfort.
- **Improved Posture:** Regular use helps correct misalignments caused by poor posture or repetitive strain.
- **Increased Circulation:** Promotes blood flow to the brain and body, improving oxygenation and potentially enhancing cognitive function.
- **Reduced Stress and Tension:** Gentle stretching of muscles reduces tension, providing a calming, restorative experience.

Biohacking Tip: Inversion therapy is an effective method to promote spinal health and alleviate back pain. By using an inversion table or simply hanging upside down, you decompress the spine, reduce tension, improve posture, and increase circulation. Regular use of inversion therapy can enhance physical alignment, relieve discomfort, and contribute to your overall well-being.

April 4: Red Light Therapy For Physical Recovery

Did you know you can use NASA technology to hack your body and improve your health?

Red light therapy is a cutting-edge technique that utilizes low-level wavelengths of red light to promote healing, recovery, and overall wellness. Initially developed by NASA to help astronauts heal wounds and maintain muscle health in space, this therapy has gained widespread popularity for its ability to penetrate deep into the skin, targeting cells at the molecular level.

The Science Behind Red Light Therapy: Red light therapy stimulates the mitochondria, the energy-producing centers of cells. By boosting cellular energy production, it accelerates tissue repair, reduces inflammation, and promotes regeneration. It's widely used for treating muscle soreness, joint pain, skin conditions, and even for speeding up recovery from injuries.

Key Benefits Include:

- **Enhanced Muscle Recovery:** Red light therapy reduces muscle soreness after intense exercise, speeding up recovery by promoting cellular repair.
- **Reduction of Inflammation:** It alleviates pain in joints and muscles by reducing oxidative stress and inflammation, making it effective for those with arthritis or chronic pain.
- **Skin Health and Rejuvenation:** Red light therapy stimulates collagen production, improving skin elasticity, reducing wrinkles, and healing scars or blemishes.
- **Improved Circulation:** It increases blood flow, delivering more oxygen and nutrients to tissues, enhancing overall healing.

Biohacking Tip: Incorporate red light therapy into your recovery routine, especially after workouts or physically demanding days. Aim for 10-20 minutes per session, focusing on sore or inflamed areas. Consistent use can significantly improve recovery time, reduce pain, and enhance skin vitality.

April 5: Spice UP. It's A Life Saver

Curcumin is the active compound found in turmeric, and it's known for its powerful anti-inflammatory properties, making it effective in reducing chronic inflammation, which is the root cause of many diseases like cancer, arthritis and some metabolic diseases.

By supporting gut health by reducing inflammation in the gastrointestinal track and improves the function of the endothelium (The lining of the blood vessels, which is crucial for regulating blood pressure and blood cloth. IT also reduces inflammation and oxidation.

Biohacking Tip: Some studies suggests that curcumin may be as effective as exercise or medication in improving health, specially following health surgery and also in helping your body lose weight.

You can easily incorporate curcumin in your nutrition by adding in almost everything you cook.

April 6: Breath High, Be Alive, Be Soma

Soma breath emphasizes rhythmic breathing to increase oxygen levels in the blood. It also increase mitochondrial function allowing the cells to produce energy more efficiently. This rhythmic breathing allow your body to balance oxygen and carbon dioxide Levens more efficiently.

Soma breath helps regulate blood flow to tissue and have anti-cancer properties as it inhibit growth of cancer cells by improving immune system. Soma breath emphasizes slow nasal breathing during recovery phases and activated the parasympathetic nervous system encouraging cellular repair and recovery, lower inflammation, balance oxygen and CO2 levels and also enhance the body ability to detoxify through oxygenation.

Biohacking tip: When I started to study for my soma breath certification, I tried different times of the day to see how it would work for me. When I did it at night I had difficult falling sleep since it increased the oxygen in the brain and put me in a "High" state. However, boing soma breath on the morning, right after my meditation, helped me have more energy and mental clarity during the day. Then I started to incorporate 5 to 15 min exercise during the day as way to increase productivity and activity efficiency.

I encourage you to do the same.

April 7: Courage To Take Action In Life

There are countless amazing ideas that never see the light of day: brilliant business opportunities that pass unnoticed, perfect relationships that never happen, life-changing trips that remain dreams, and impactful books that are never written. Why? Because ideas alone are not enough; we need courage to take action.

Millions of people have incredible ideas every day, but sadly, many of those ideas stay trapped in their minds. Courage is not the absence of fear but the ability to move forward despite it. We all feel nervous when thinking about asking someone to dance, we all fear failure, criticism, or judgment when starting a business, writing a book, traveling to unfamiliar places, or engaging with strangers. Yet, we all know that success in any area of life only comes from acting in the face of fear.

Biohacking Tip: To step out of your comfort zone, start small. For example, go to a public place, make eye contact with strangers, and bless them with a smile. Or, if you're ready for something more radical, head to a park or beach and dance in public. Close your eyes and dance like no one is watching—because trust me, everyone else is too preoccupied with their own lives to care. Dance to celebrate life, your freedom, and the joy of being alive.

April 8: Holistic Exercise For Better Fitness Efficiency

Holistic exercise is a comprehensive approach to fitness that addresses not only various aspects of the physical body but also mental, emotional, and spiritual well-being. It integrates a range of fitness modalities, movement practices, mindfulness, and healing techniques to promote overall health. Unlike traditional exercise routines, which might focus solely on muscle strength or cardiovascular fitness, holistic exercise aims to create harmony within the entire being—mind, body, and spirit—developing not only the best version of your body but also the best version of yourself.

Some lesser-known examples of holistic exercises include **yoga**, **Tai Chi**, and **Qi Gong**, where movement is combined with breath control, awareness, and meditative focus. Beyond the physical benefits, these practices enhance emotional and mental balance.

Holistic exercise often incorporates **natural movement patterns** that mimic the way the body is designed to move in daily life. This includes exercises that improve flexibility, balance, and coordination, with an emphasis on movements that support **overall functional strength** rather than isolated muscle groups.

Certain holistic practices focus on improving the **flow of energy** in the body, which is believed to support health and vitality. They are often geared toward promoting **long-term health** and vitality, as opposed to short-term fitness goals.

By approaching your fitness in a holistic way, you not only develop better and more efficient **physical health**, but also enhance your **mental** and **emotional well-being**.

Biohacking Tip: Pick one area of exercise that is not currently part of your fitness routine and start incorporating it slowly. Once it becomes a natural part of your routine, introduce another one to continue evolving your fitness practices for **high performance**.

April 9: Fasting For Better Life

Like ice baths, fasting is gaining popularity, especially among biohackers seeking the key to longevity in modern society. I'm frequently asked if fasting is safe, and my answer is, "It's 100% safe, but some precautions are necessary."

Benefits of Fasting: During fasting, our cells initiate a process called autophagy, where damaged components are removed, and cellular repair takes place. At the same time, the body lowers insulin levels, becoming more efficient at using stored energy. Besides aiding in weight loss, fasting helps balance hormones, boosting growth hormone levels, improving brain function by increasing the production of brain-derived neurotrophic factor (BDNF), and reducing inflammation.

At this point, I'm not telling you what to do, but I've personally done a 120-hour fast (5 days, from Sunday evening to Friday night) and felt completely safe with high energy levels. My regular fasting routine is to stop eating from Sunday at 2 PM until Tuesday at 10 AM, giving my body over 40 hours to detox and regenerate.

Women and Fasting: The approach I mentioned is, in my view, 100% safe for men of any age. However, due to hormonal variations, women should be more cautious, as aggressive fasting may disrupt menstrual cycles and affect fertility. The recommended approach is for women to engage in 12 to 16 hours of fasting, but to avoid fasting during their menstrual period due to potential low energy. During ovulation, when estrogen levels are higher, women may tolerate longer fasting periods more easily.

Biohacking Tip: Besides avoiding food for 4 hours before bedtime, start incorporating fasting into your daily routine by delaying breakfast by 2 hours, 3 to 5 days a week Drink plenty of water at room temperature or slightly warmer to soothe the stomach. If you enjoy coffee, like I do, sip on black coffee or the super coffee mentioned in this book on April 9, and enjoy a boost in ketones.

April 10: Life With Super Coffee

Imagine a coffee that not only boosts your alertness and focus but also supports fat metabolism and brain function by converting fat into ketones. This special blend helps with weight loss, enhances cognitive function and memory, and stimulates the production of nerve growth factor (NGF), while also offering powerful antioxidant benefits.

Your "Super Coffee" is more than just a morning beverage; it's a well-crafted biohacking tool. The unique combination of ingredients not only enhances your energy and focus but also provides cognitive, metabolic, and neurological benefits.

Some of the key benefits include:

- Boosts alertness and focus
- Rich in antioxidants
- Source of healthy fats
- Supports ketosis
- Natural energy booster
- Enhances cognitive function
- Provides neuroprotection: The medicinal mushrooms, backed by scientific studies, help protect against neurodegenerative diseases by reducing inflammation and oxidative stress in the brain.

The ingredients are:

- Organic coffee
- Organic butter
- Organic raw honey (optional)
- Lion's mane mushroom

You can enjoy all of these benefits with the Super Coffee formula I've created!

Biohacking Tip: How to Prepare Your Super Coffee

1. Brew a cup of strong organic coffee.
2. Add one tablespoon of organic butter (preferably grass-fed).
3. Add one tablespoon of organic raw honey for natural sweetness and additional health benefits (optional).
4. Blend everything for 15 seconds to achieve a smooth, frothy texture.

This Super Coffee will become a cornerstone of your daily routine, fueling both body and mind. It's a biohacker's dream blend that enhances performance, promotes mental clarity, and supports long-term brain health!

April 11: Magnesium For Muscle Recovery

Magnesium is essential to support the body's natural processes, allowing it to function at its peak. A lack of magnesium can lead to muscle cramps, spasms, fatigue, high blood pressure, muscle weakness, sleep disturbances, migraines, poor mental performance, and even chronic inflammation.

What magnesium can do for you:

- **Supports muscle and nerve function**, helping prevent cramps and tension.
- **Promotes heart health** by regulating blood pressure and heart rhythm.
- **Enhances bone health** by aiding calcium absorption.
- **Boosts mental health**, helping reduce anxiety and depression.
- **Improves sleep** by promoting relaxation and better sleep quality.
- **Increases energy production** through ATP synthesis.
- **Regulates blood sugar**, improving insulin sensitivity.
- **Reduces inflammation**, lowering the risk of chronic diseases.
- **Supports cognitive function**, aiding memory and brain protection.

Since it can be a challenge to find all seven essential types of magnesium and take several pills daily, I adopted **Magnesium Breakthrough**, which contains all seven forms of magnesium, each targeting specific health benefits:

1. **Magnesium Chelate**: Known for muscle recovery and overall health.
2. **Magnesium Citrate**: Helpful in reducing the risk of arterial calcification.
3. **Magnesium Bisglycinate**: Commonly used to improve digestion and reduce heartburn symptoms.

4. **Magnesium Malate**: Provides energy, especially useful for combating fatigue.
5. **Magnesium Sucrosomial**: Effective for boosting immune function.
6. **Magnesium Taurate**: Beneficial for cardiovascular health and blood pressure regulation.
7. **Magnesium Orotate**: Known for enhancing recovery and supporting energy production at the cellular level.

Biohacking Tip: Magnesium is essential for muscle recovery and relaxation. Supplement your diet with magnesium-rich foods like leafy greens, nuts, and seeds, or use **magnesium oil** or **Epsom salt baths** to support muscle repair and reduce soreness.

April 12: Sprint Running For Cardiovascular Health

Sprint running is a powerful tool for building cardiovascular strength and resilience, helping you endure life's trials. Sprinting challenges the heart and lungs, making them stronger and more capable of withstanding physical demands. According to scientists, it's also one of the most efficient ways to increase your VO2 max (maximum oxygen uptake), which is widely considered one of the best indicators of cardiovascular fitness and endurance.

Biohacking Tip: Incorporate sprint intervals into your workout routine by alternating short bursts of high-intensity running with rest periods. This method not only improves cardiovascular health but also boosts fat-burning and enhances metabolic function. Aim for 20-30 seconds of sprinting followed by 1-2 minutes of rest, and repeat for several rounds. This approach strengthens your heart, increases endurance, and accelerates fat loss efficiently.

April 13: Meat, Vegetarian, Or Vegan – Finding Balance

The debate around diet often leads to extremes, but balance is key. There is no one-size-fits-all when it comes to nutrition. Whether you choose to eat meat, follow a vegetarian, or adopt a vegan diet, it's important to find what works best for your body, lifestyle, and goals. I often hear from those who have adopted a vegetarian lifestyle that they feel more energetic and confident that it will contribute to a longer life. However, if you're considering making a transition, I highly recommend studying your approach carefully and proceeding with caution.

Biohacking Tip: Regardless of your dietary preference, focus on whole, nutrient-dense foods. Pay attention to how your body responds to different foods and adjust your intake accordingly. Whether it's adding more plant-based foods for energy or incorporating lean proteins for strength, listen to your body and prioritize quality. Balance is essential for optimal health and well-being, and when possible, choose organic foods to avoid unnecessary toxins.

April 14: Sleep Optimization For Recovery

Sleep is essential for physical health, mental recovery, cognitive function, and hormonal balance. It's the time when the body repairs itself and the mind processes the events of the day. Quality sleep is the foundation of strength, mental function, disease prevention, and longevity. Despite its importance, many people underestimate the impact that sleep has on their health.

Biohacking Tip: Optimize your sleep by creating a restful environment. Eliminate noise, reduce as much light as possible from your bedroom, and maintain a cool temperature. Avoid screens and stimulants like caffeine before bed to improve sleep quality. Small habits like sticking to a consistent sleep schedule and using relaxation techniques can also enhance recovery and support overall well-being. Additionally, while good sleep improves your fitness level, regular exercise also enhances your sleep quality.

By prioritizing sleep, you enhance every other aspect of your health—physical, mental, and emotional. It's a crucial part of any biohacking or wellness routine.

April 15: Blood Work And Knowing Your Health Markers

Understanding your body is a key aspect of maintaining optimal health, and regular blood work is an invaluable tool for monitoring your health, detecting potential issues early, and optimizing your well-being, especially when it comes to longevity. By regularly checking key biomarkers, you can make informed decisions about your diet, lifestyle, and health interventions to ensure you're on the right track. Your blood holds valuable insights into your physical well-being, helping you adjust and optimize for longevity and vitality. A few reasons why you should do blood work regularly instead of waiting for a disease or for your doctor to request it are: **early detection of health issues**, **prevention of chronic diseases**, **optimization of energy and vitality**, and **support for longevity and** **anti-aging**.
It's very important to know your **inflammation markers**, **cholesterol and vitamin levels**, **blood count and oxygen transport**, and **kidney and liver function**.

Biohacking Tip: Regular blood tests can provide a clear picture of your overall health. Keep track of essential markers and monitor the ones mentioned above to help you make informed decisions about your diet, exercise, and lifestyle. By knowing your health markers, you can take proactive steps to improve and maintain your well-being for the long term.

Mauro dos Santos

April 16: Super Power Ginger Tea

Have you ever imagined having a tea with anti-inflammatory properties that helps your digestive system, boosts your immunity, reduces muscle pain, contains prebiotics beneficial for your gut health, promotes ketosis, and protects your brain against neurodegenerative diseases by reducing inflammation and oxidative stress? Well, this can become your reality with my Super Power Ginger Tea. On top of that, you'll experience improved fat metabolism, which can aid in weight loss, while the MCT oil and Lion's Mane provide cognitive enhancement, improving mental clarity, focus, and memory.

The ingredients you need are:

- Organic ginger
- MCT oil
- Organic grass-fed butter
- Organic raw honey
- Lion's Mane mushroom powder

Preparation:

1. Cut the ginger into small pieces and boil for 5 minutes.
2. Add one tablespoon of MCT oil, one tablespoon of organic raw honey, one tablespoon of grass-fed butter, and one portion of Lion's Mane mushroom powder.
3. Blend for 30 seconds, strain, and enjoy. You may be surprised by how delicious it is!

Biohacking Tip: Try, test, and enjoy. Given your unique biology and nutrition history, you may want to start with small portions and observe how your body responds. Like most biohacking approaches, you are your own doctor and your own lab. If you feel that the results are positive, great! Add this to your morning routine.

April 17: Exercise For Your Brain

Every time you contract a muscle, your muscles release a protein called **irisin**. This hormone helps convert white fat into brown fat, which is more metabolically active, and promotes the growth of new neurons in your brain, especially in the hippocampus, which is crucial for learning and memory. Additionally, muscle contraction helps promote **BDNF** (Brain-Derived Neurotrophic Factor), which is a key molecule in brain plasticity.

In *The Revolutionary New Science of Exercise and the Brain* by Dr. John J. Ratey and research published in *The Lancet Psychiatry*, there's no mental health without an active lifestyle. Ratey explains that exercise is "the single most powerful tool" for enhancing brain function, boosting mood, and reducing anxiety, while sedentary behavior can lead to mental stagnation and increased risk of depression. The *Lancet* study supports this, showing that people who are physically active experience significantly fewer days of poor mental health each month compared to those who are inactive. Besides that, the brain releases **endorphins**, **serotonin**, and **dopamine**. No wonder physical exercise can be the best medicine for combating depression, reducing stress, and improving cognitive function.

Biohacking Tip: Do you want to live better and longer? Keep improving your fitness routine and engage in physical activity on a daily basis. Your body and brain will thank you!

April 18: Detoxing With Celery Juice And Cilantro

Celery juice combined with cilantro offers a powerful detoxifying blend that supports the body's natural ability to eliminate toxins and improve overall health. Each ingredient brings its unique properties, and together they form a synergistic duo that enhances detoxification, supports liver function, and promotes optimal digestion.

Some of the key benefits include detox properties, and when combined, they are rich in antioxidants, support hydration and electrolyte balance, improve liver function, and have alkalizing effects that help balance the body's pH. Additionally, they possess antibacterial and antifungal properties.

Biohacking Tip: To make this detox drink, simply blend fresh organic celery stalks with a handful of organic cilantro, then strain the juice. For the best results, drink this blend in the morning on an empty stomach to kick-start your detoxification process for the day.

Together, celery juice and cilantro offer a highly effective natural detox. By supporting liver function, aiding digestion, and removing heavy metals, this combination can help you achieve a cleaner, healthier body, making it a valuable addition to your daily routine for enhanced detoxification and overall well-being.

April 19: Building True Wealth

True wealth, according to the Stoics, isn't simply about accumulating money or material goods; it's about cultivating wisdom, discipline, and self-control. Building wealth is a reflection of the habits and mindset we consistently nurture. The Stoics emphasized that wealth, like life itself, should be approached with patience and sound judgment. It's not about short-term gains or fleeting success, but about building a strong foundation over time that supports both your material and inner well-being.

Mindset of Long-Term Growth:

Wealth-building is the result of a mindset focused on the future, rather than the temptations of quick profits or impulsive spending. Patience and discipline are essential to creating sustainable success. Like planting seeds in a garden, the habits you cultivate today will grow and compound over time. The Stoics taught that fortune can come and go, but when we live with wisdom, our wealth is secure in the balance and clarity we apply to every decision.

Hacking Tip: Focus on creating strong, healthy financial habits to set yourself up for long-term success. Avoid the temptation of quick financial fixes—invest in yourself and your future by practicing disciplined habits that lead to lasting financial security.

In the same way you invest in your physical and mental health, apply that level of commitment to your financial well-being.

April 20: Ten-minute Break

Some reports mention how Steve Jobs used to take 10-minute breaks to refresh during stressful moments. This rule is based on the idea that short breaks can help reset your mental state, improve concentration, and lower stress.

Some of the benefits of a 10-minute break include creating mental clarity, reducing stress, and increasing productivity.

Hacking   **Tip**:
When you feel stressed or stuck in your work or study, take a walk, preferably outdoors or in a park if possible. These 10-minute breaks can be highly effective for maintaining balance and focus.

April 21: Managing Personal Drive And Energy

"The impediment to action advances action. What stands in the way becomes the way." — *Marcus Aurelius, Meditations* (Book 5, Chapter 20)

Marcus Aurelius believed that inner strength and motivation are essential to living well. He emphasized that obstacles should fuel your drive, encouraging you to see challenges as opportunities to push yourself further rather than as roadblocks.

One of the most effective ways to improve focus, reduce burnout, and increase productivity is by using the **Pomodoro Method**, a time management technique developed by Francesco Cirillo in the late 1980s. This method is particularly useful for people who struggle with maintaining focus or need more structure in their work routine.

Hacking Tip: Using the Pomodoro Method

1. **Choose a task**: Select a specific task you want to focus on.
2. **Set a timer**: Set a timer for 25 minutes (one Pomodoro).
3. **Work**: Focus solely on the task without distractions until the timer rings.
4. **Take a short break**: Once the Pomodoro is complete, take a 5-minute break.
5. **Repeat**: After completing four Pomodoros, take a longer break (15-30 minutes) before starting the next cycle.

This method can help you maintain energy and drive throughout the day, ensuring sustainable productivity and reducing the risk of burnout.

April 22: Biohacking To Build Resilience

Stoic Insight: One of the best definitions of resilience comes from Seneca: "Difficulties strengthen the mind, as labor does the body." (Letters to Lucilius, Letter 78). Just as pushing yourself in physical exercise strengthens the body, enduring adversity strengthens the mind and spirit. Instead of fearing challenges, we should embrace them as part of life's process, knowing they will make us stronger and more capable of handling future obstacles.

There's also a popular phrase attributed to G. Michael Hopf from his post-apocalyptic novel *Those Who Remain*: "Hard times create strong men. Strong men create good times. Good times create weak men. And weak men create hard times."

Life's challenges not only forge our character but also impact society as a whole. The ability to endure adversity with grace is the true mark of resilience. In life, we shouldn't avoid difficulties but face them head-on, emerging stronger with each experience. Every obstacle is an opportunity to refine ourselves and grow.

April 23: Optimizing Your Morning Routine

The way you start your day sets the tone and energy for everything that follows. Positive thinking and a positive mindset in the morning shape your entire day, helping you approach challenges with optimism and clarity. Every morning, you have the opportunity to align your thoughts and actions with purpose and intention. It can dictate your reality, your productivity, and how you face challenges.

Hacking Tip: One of the best ways to start your day is by reminding yourself that your thoughts shape your reality. By beginning with positive intentions, you take control of your day from the very first moment. Upon waking, take a moment to express gratitude, set an intention for the day, or visualize a positive outcome. This practice helps prime your mind for success, keeping you focused and energized.

April 24: Developing A Healthy Relationship With Time

Time is the most precious resource we possess—far more valuable than money, yet often wasted and treated with far less care. In some quantum theories, we often hear about time bending, which is the art of altering your perception and experience of time.

On April 20, you learned about the Pomodoro Method, which is a way to increase your productivity with time. However, time bending goes beyond that. At its core, time bending suggests that time isn't fixed and can be shaped by our focus, awareness, and state of mind, depending on how present we are and how we create our focus and flow.

Hacking Tip: The best way to test time bending is if you have a set routine, like when you wake up in the morning until you leave for work. Most people have a set routine from the moment they wake up until they leave for work, often rushing to stay on schedule until you rush to the door.

To use time bending, during your meditation or a simple affirmation, set the intention to finish your routine 15 minutes earlier than the day before. For example: "When I finish brushing my teeth, taking a shower, fixing my hair, having my coffee, and getting dressed for work, I will finish by 7:15. You might be amazed by how this shift in focus can alter your experience of time.

April 25: Modify Training For Resilience

"Strength is born through challenge, not comfort. True resilience comes from pushing beyond our limits—both physically and mentally." Strength training isn't just about sculpting the body—it's about cultivating a mindset of discipline and perseverance that carries over into every area of life.

To build more resilience with your fitness routine, try making modifications outside of your usual exercises. Getting out of your comfort zone, even during workouts, will strengthen your mental and physical resilience.

Biohacking Tip: One effective method is to perform an exercise you're already familiar with, but use 25 to 50% less weight. Set your intention, then begin the exercise without counting reps. When you start feeling the burn, *that's when you start counting.* Keep going beyond what's comfortable. This approach not only helps you sculpt your body but also builds endurance and mental resilience.

April 26: Developing A Good Relationship With Relaxation Time

"When you arise in the morning, think of what a precious privilege it is to be alive—to breathe, to think, to enjoy, to love." (Meditations, Book 5). Though not directly about relaxation, this quote from Marcus Aurelius highlights the Stoic value of mindful appreciation in daily routines. I love this quote because it helps us embrace life and recognize that simply being present is a privilege. The Stoic approach is to live each moment, including relaxation, with awareness and gratitude, appreciating it without overindulgence.

In Ecclesiastes, we also find a reminder to enjoy life: *"So I commend the enjoyment of life, because there is nothing better for a person under the sun than to eat and drink and be glad. Then joy will accompany them in their toil all the days of the life God has given them under the sun." —* **Ecclesiastes 8:15.**

Hacking Tip: Take a morning to relax, enjoy a coffee or tea, and reflect on life. Clear your mind of work and commitments, and simply appreciate the present moment. In the present, you are free from problems and challenges—you just have life to enjoy.

April 27: Avoiding Burnout With Balanced Self-Care

Balance is key for good health and longevity. Continuous effort without rest and recovery does not lead to growth but to burnout and even mental health issues. The Stoics understood that pushing forward without moments of pause can wear down even the strongest individuals. True resilience is built by balancing effort with rejuvenation. Both the body and mind need time off to reset and grow.

Many highly successful people and billionaires make time for breaks, no matter how busy their schedules are. Some take weekends off just to think, while others take a week off every few months to refresh and reset. If they can do it, so can we.

Hacking Tip: To avoid burnout, schedule regular breaks and integrate self-care into your routine. During this time, disconnect from electronic devices and spend time with just your journal and your thoughts. Also, remember to take days off from your workouts to allow your body to fully recover. These restorative routines are essential for maintaining good health, long-term productivity, and mental well-being.

April 28: Building Wealth Through Mindset

Wealth is more than just numbers in a bank account—it is a reflection and result of the mindset you cultivate. Quantum science shows that money is energy, and like all energy, it must be treated with respect and positivity. To attract and build wealth, you must shift from a scarcity mentality to one of abundance.

Some of the key principles for building wealth are:

Celebrate When You Spend: Instead of feeling anxious when paying bills or spending money, shift your mindset to one of gratitude. Celebrate that you have the resources to meet your needs and the opportunity to contribute to someone. This creates a positive association with money flow.

Avoid Complaining About Costs: Complaining about prices or the cost of things anchors you in a scarcity mentality. It's like you're believing that you never have enough money and, as you believe, you become. So, every time you focus on what you don't have or what feels "too expensive," you limit the energy of abundance. Instead, embrace the cost of living as part of the flow of money and appreciate the value you receive.

Give Without Fear: When you help someone in need or support a cause, do so with a sense of abundance. Generosity opens the door for wealth to return to you in ways you may not expect.

Hacking Tip: Each time you spend money—whether paying bills, buying something, or giving to someone—do it with a mindset of gratitude and celebration. If you are spending, it's because you have. Remind yourself that money is energy, and as you allow it to flow through you while it brings you comfort and luxury, you'll attract more abundance. Focus on what you have, not on what you lack, and watch as your relationship with wealth transforms.

April 29: Know Your Genetic Makeup

We all have unique genetic blueprints that influence how our bodies function in various ways. Your genetic makeup affects how you metabolize nutrients, process fats and carbohydrates, and how sensitive you may be to certain foods. This is why one-size-fits-all diets don't always work—what works for one person may not work for another.

By understanding your DNA, you can create a personalized approach to nutrition and health. DNA tests can reveal how your body responds to lactose, gluten, caffeine, or alcohol, and even indicate if you need higher levels of nutrients like omega-3 fatty acids or antioxidants. This knowledge empowers you to optimize your diet and make choices that truly suit your biology, helping you maintain energy, improve digestion, and support overall well-being.

Biohacking Tip: Take a DNA test to unlock insights into how your body processes food and nutrients. Use this information to personalize your nutrition plan. Adjust your diet based on your genetic predispositions—whether it's increasing your intake of specific vitamins or avoiding foods that trigger sensitivities. This biohack ensures that you're fueling your body in the most efficient and effective way for long-term health and vitality.

April 30: Focus On What Matters For Success

We often feel the pressure to do everything, chase every opportunity, and please everyone. However, true success doesn't come from spreading yourself thin but from focusing on what truly matters. Most highly successful people spend 80% of their time on the one activity that will lead them to their goal.

When we channel our energy toward the things that matter most, we naturally increase our chances of success. But first, we need clarity—knowing what our highest values are—and be willing to let go of distractions that pull us away from them.

Biohacking Tip: First, find your true passion. Then, apply the Pareto Principle (80/20 rule) to optimize your time and efforts toward it. Focus on the 20% of activities that generate 80% of your results. This practice not only helps you achieve more but also ensures that your energy is directed toward what truly matters. By focusing on key areas that align with your values, you create a path to meaningful success.

May

Introduction

Introduction:

May is a month of both sensory pleasure and mental growth, guided by the grounded energy of Taurus and the curious, communicative energy of Gemini. It's a time to enjoy life's simple pleasures while also stretching your mind and building deeper connections with others.

With Taurus in the lead, this month encourages you to slow down and appreciate the world around you. Sensory biohacking is all about engaging your body's natural abilities to enhance well-being. Whether it's through enjoying a nourishing meal, taking a mindful walk in nature, or finding moments of relaxation and peace, May reminds you to be fully present and savor life's pleasures.

On the other side, Gemini brings the energy of learning, communication, and connection. It's the perfect time to focus on cognitive health—improving your memory, learning something new, and keeping your brain sharp. At the same time, this month is all about connection. Use the energy of Gemini to improve your communication skills, whether that's through more meaningful conversations with loved ones or building new relationships. The goal is to create a life where you feel both mentally stimulated and socially fulfilled.

May is about finding balance between enjoying the pleasures of life and growing intellectually and socially. By focusing on both your physical well-being and your mental sharpness, you'll create a month filled with joy, learning, and connection.

May 1: Cognitive Health And Memory Improvement

The mind, like the body, must be exercised to grow strong and stay active for a long time. Besides good nutrition, such as healthy fats, foods rich in antioxidants, and omega-3 fatty acids, your brain needs to be fed with knowledge and practice reflection to sharpen understanding. Keeping your brain active with new challenges and learning helps create new neural pathways that strengthen cognitive abilities and memory.

Dr. Joe Dispenza explains that every time you learn new information, your brain creates 10,000 new synapses, illustrating how powerful learning can be for brain health.

Biohacking Tip: Engage in cognitive-enhancing activities like reading, learning new skills, and practicing memory techniques. By continuously stimulating your brain, you promote mental agility and strengthen your memory for long-term cognitive health.

May 2: Take Care Of Your Enzymes

Enzymatic depletion is often overlooked by many of us, usually because we aren't aware of its vital role in health and survival. Enzymes are responsible for over 25,000 different functions in our bodies, and as they become depleted, we begin to feel the impact on our health.

Factors that contribute to enzyme depletion include aging, chronic stress, poor diet, medication use, processed foods, and exposure to toxins. The effects of this depletion can manifest as digestive issues, weakened immune function, and a less effective liver detoxification process, as the liver relies heavily on enzymes to break down and eliminate toxins.

Biohacking Tip: To counteract enzymatic depletion, it's recommended to eat enzyme-rich foods like raw fruits and vegetables. Fermented foods can also support digestive health, along with beneficial herbs like ginger and turmeric.

Lifestyle Adjustments: Reducing stress, getting adequate sleep, and staying hydrated support enzyme production. Minimize exposure to toxins and limit medication use when possible to further preserve enzyme levels.

May 3: Enhancing Physical Well-Being Through Sensory Biohacks

We often overlook our senses. Our sight, smell, touch, taste, and sound aren't just there to help us navigate the world—they're also tools for improving our mental and physical well-being. Ever notice how the smell of fresh coffee in the morning instantly lifts your mood, or how hearing your favorite song can completely turn your day around? That's the power of your senses!

We must live fully in the present, and engaging our senses is one of the easiest ways to get there. When we tune into what we're experiencing, we're not just coasting through life on autopilot; we're truly connecting with it.

Biohacking Tip: Turn up the volume on your sensory experience! Try things like aromatherapy to boost your mood and focus, or slow down to actually savor your food with mindful eating. Being more in touch with your senses can improve your energy, clarity, and overall vibe. It's all about creating a stronger connection between you and the world around you.

May 4: The Benefits Of Drinking Coffee (With Balance)

Coffee is one of the most widely consumed beverages in the world, if not the most, and it's not just for its flavor. For many, it's a ritual that marks the start of the day. But coffee is more than just a caffeine boost; when consumed wisely, it can be a powerful tool for mental and physical performance. Caffeine is the active compound in coffee, and it stimulates the central nervous system, boosting alertness, concentration, and even reaction time. It works by blocking adenosine receptors in the brain, which keeps you from feeling drowsy. There's also evidence that coffee contains antioxidants, which help reduce inflammation and protect the brain from oxidative stress.

Biohacking Tip: Use coffee as a tool, not just a habit. You can transform your daily cup into a biohack that enhances brain function, stabilizes energy, and supports longevity. Stick to 1-2 cups a day, ideally in the morning, to avoid sleep disruption and enjoy the benefits without the negative side effects of overconsumption.

May 5: Avoiding Gluten For Gut Health

Gluten is a protein found in wheat, barley, rye, and related grains. While many people can consume gluten without noticeable issues, it doesn't mean it isn't causing harm to your health. Gluten sensitivity can silently wreak havoc on your gut, leading to bloating, fatigue, and inflammation. Even if you don't have celiac disease, gluten may still be damaging your intestines, leading to nutrient deficiencies, fatigue, and neurological problems.

By eliminating gluten, you might experience surprising improvements in digestion, energy, and mental clarity. The recommendation is not just to cut gluten but to also add fermented foods like sauerkraut, kimchi, and kefir, which are rich in probiotics that help restore healthy gut bacteria and reduce inflammation.

Biohacking Tip: Try a gluten-free diet and track how your body responds. Incorporate fermented foods to nourish your gut and improve overall health. Listen to your body and adjust your diet for optimal well-being.

May 6: Breathwork During Exercise

Breathing properly during exercise is key to increasing your performance, and each type of exercise benefits from specific breathing techniques that enhance efficiency, reduce fatigue, and keep your body functioning optimally. When running, for example, the key is to establish a breathing cadence that matches your stride. By coordinating your breaths with your steps—such as inhaling for two steps and exhaling for two—you create a rhythm that maximizes oxygen intake and helps you maintain a steady pace over longer distances. Many people, consciously or unconsciously, hold their breath when lifting weights, a technique called the Valsalva maneuver. While it may create a feeling of stability during heavy lifts, it comes with risks, such as dangerously raising your blood pressure and causing dizziness. Instead of holding your breath, practice a controlled flow of air: inhale during the lowering (eccentric) phase of the lift when you are relaxed, and exhale during the exertion (concentric) phase when lifting or contracting the muscles.

Biohacking Tip: By optimizing your breathing for each specific exercise, you'll improve oxygen delivery, reduce fatigue, avoid common issues like dizziness or unnecessary strain, and also enhance your overall performance fatigue, avoid common issues like dizziness or unnecessary strain, and also enhance your overall performance.

May 7: Fun And Brain Enhancement

A great way to enjoy free time while improving cognitive skills like concentration and problem-solving is by engaging in **memory games**. These games stimulate neural pathways and encourage **neuroplasticity**, which is the brain's ability to reorganize itself by forming new neural connections.

Science has proven that memory games **enhance working memory**, **improve attention and focus**, and **slow cognitive decline**, all while being a lot of fun.

Biohacking Tip: Incorporating memory games into your daily routine can be a fun way to keep your brain sharp. Just like physical exercise strengthens the body, memory games help train and strengthen the brain, improving **mental agility** and **cognitive longevity**.

May 8: The Power Of Taking Responsibility: No Blame, Justification, Or Excuses

Taking full responsibility for your actions is a crucial step in both personal growth and leadership. It frees you from victimhood and paves the way for growth and accountability. A powerful example of this principle is Ronald Reagan's response to the **Iran-Contra Affair**.

In 1987, after it became public that arms were sold to Iran and the funds were diverted to support Contra rebels, Reagan made a televised speech. Though he didn't fully admit personal involvement, he stated:

- *"I take full responsibility for my own actions and for those of my administration."*
  Reagan's acceptance of responsibility, without shifting blame or offering excuses, helped restore public trust. He could have deflected the scandal, but by owning it, he exemplified true accountability.

Blame and excuses hold you back and give away your power, hindering personal growth. Instead of blaming external factors, take control by owning your actions without trying to justify mistakes or finding excuses to avoid responsibility. True leaders and successful people, like Ronald Reagan, take full responsibility.

Epictetus said: *"Don't blame others for your misfortunes. Blame yourself, or rather, hold yourself accountable, because that is what you can control."*

By taking responsibility, you empower yourself to adapt and grow. Avoiding blame or justification allows you to fully own your life, which is key to both personal and professional development.

Taking responsibility isn't easy but builds trust and sets you on a path toward real growth.

May 9: Avoid Cell Phone Radiation: Preserve Your Health

Cell phones emit radiofrequency (RF) radiation, but few people pay attention to the potential risks involved. Constant exposure, especially when held close to the ear or kept in the pocket, has raised concerns about possible links to brain or testicular cancer.

Some studies suggest that holding phones to your ear for long periods may increase the risk of developing brain tumors like gliomas. The World Health Organization (WHO) has even classified RF radiation as "possibly carcinogenic."

Additionally, carrying your phone in your pocket may expose the testes to RF radiation, which could affect sperm quality and potentially lead to testicular cancer. Though research is ongoing, the warning signs are enough to encourage precaution.

Hacking Tip

- Use a speakerphone or earphones to keep radiation away from your head.
- Avoid carrying your phone in your pocket, especially when the signal is weak.
- Opt for airplane mode when you don't need connectivity to minimize radiation exposure altogether.

The long-term effects of RF radiation may still be uncertain, but these simple changes can dramatically reduce potential risks. Share this info with your friends and help them stay safe—small steps can make a big difference!

May 10: Rest And Recovery For Longevity

"When you arise in the morning, think of what a precious privilege it is to be alive—to breathe, to think, to enjoy, to love." — *Marcus Aurelius, Meditations, Book 5*

Marcus Aurelius emphasizes that while we need rest, we must also appreciate our ability to act and fulfill our duties each day. Just as exertion is necessary for progress, rest is essential for renewal. Balance is key—pushing forward without taking time to rest will eventually lead to burnout. True strength and achievement come from recognizing when it's time to step back and recover, ensuring long-term success.

Biohacking Tip: Often, we don't realize we need rest when we're deeply focused on an important project. However, prioritizing rest is crucial. Schedule recovery days and ensure you get adequate sleep. Engaging in light exercise or yoga can help rest the brain and support the body's repair process, all while maintaining mobility. Optimize your sleep environment for better recovery and well-being.

May 11: Emotional Control In Challenging Situations

Life constantly throws challenges our way, testing our patience, resilience, and emotional control. On a daily basis, we face difficult conversations, unexpected setbacks, or intense moments of stress, and your ability to manage emotions determines not just the outcome of that situation but your long-term mental and emotional well-being.

The Stoics and the Bible taught us that emotions are natural—anger, frustration, fear—these feelings will arise, but how you respond to them is where your power lies. As Marcus Aurelius said, "You have power over your mind—not outside events. Realize this, and you will find strength." Emotions are fleeting; they pass like clouds, but wisdom comes from mastering your reactions and maintaining composure.

True emotional control isn't about suppressing your feelings but recognizing them, understanding them, and then choosing your response with intention.

Hacking Tip: You have control over your emotions and reactions. Never respond to a difficult situation impulsively; instead, take your time, process your thoughts, and respond with wisdom, expecting a positive outcome. Your emotional reactions can often lead to regret or a worse outcome—avoid it!

Mauro dos Santos
May 12: Give Without Expectations

Giving is one of the most beautiful and profound acts of kindness, especially when done with no intention of receiving anything in return. It's a quiet way of adding brightness to the world. When we give freely, we tap into a deeper joy—the kind that comes from witnessing someone else's happiness, from the simple pleasure of seeing a smile.

Seneca once said, *"The wise man does not give for the purpose of receiving, but simply to do good. The joy of the recipient is enough repayment."*
In Acts 20:35, the Bible also teaches, *"It is more blessed to give than to receive."* This reminds us that true fulfillment doesn't come from what we gain, but from the simple act of giving itself. It turns ordinary moments into something deeply meaningful.

By giving, we're not only helping others, but we're also weaving stronger bonds that hold humanity together. It's not about rewards; it's about sending ripples of kindness into the world—ripples that carry far beyond our reach.

Hacking Tip: Next time you see someone in need, give with an open heart. The act of joyful giving signals to the universe that you are abundant, creating a chain of prosperity flowing back to you. Let go of expectations and simply be part of someone else's happiness—that's where the real magic lies.

May 13: Multitasking vs. Focus – When To Use Each

The Stoics emphasized the importance of single-minded focus, understanding that a divided mind is far less effective than one that is fully engaged. Marcus Aurelius wrote, *"Do every act of your life as though it were the very last act of your life."* (Meditations, Book 2, Chapter 5), instructing us to focus on one thing at a time.

Dr. Caroline Leaf, a cognitive neuroscientist, calls multitasking "milkshake thinking." When we try to juggle multiple tasks at once, our brains don't actually handle them simultaneously; instead, they switch rapidly between them, leading to mental fatigue, reduced productivity, and more errors. According to her, multitasking can even lead to mental health issues over time.

Biohacking Tip: Try to reduce multitasking, reserving it for easy tasks like household chores where focus isn't crucial. When it comes to creative or demanding tasks, dedicate uninterrupted blocks of time to focus. The brain works best when it can dive deep into one thing at a time, leading to more effective results and greater clarity.

This approach aligns with Dr. Leaf's emphasis on "mono-tasking" for tasks that require deep thinking, allowing you to avoid the chaos of constant task-switching and achieve sharper mental performance.

Mauro dos Santos
May 14: Self-Growth Through Communication

Communication is more than just speaking. Have you ever spoken to someone who wasn't really listening? How frustrating is it when someone is only listening to respond? Communication is a tool for personal growth, but this growth happens when it is rooted in true listening. Ralph Waldo Emerson said, "In my walks, every man I meet is my superior in some way, and in that I learn from him." This reflects the belief that everyone has something to teach, and that each interaction is an opportunity for growth and learning. It aligns with the spiritual idea of seeing value in every person and experience, recognizing that we can learn something from everyone we encounter.

Hacking Tip: Next time you meet someone, be fully present and do a self-analysis. Ask yourself, "Am I really listening?" and "What can I learn from this person?" Show interest and ask questions, making the person you are interacting with feel like the most important person in the world.

May 15: Teaching Others To Reinforce Learning

Have you heard that the best way to learn is by teaching others? When you teach something, it forces you to break down complex ideas, articulate them clearly, and explain them in a way that others can understand. Teaching engages multiple cognitive processes. Not only are you recalling the information, but you're also synthesizing it and reorganizing it in a way that makes sense to your audience.

Hacking Tip: If you want to solidify your learning, find opportunities to share your knowledge. The process of teaching challenges your brain to organize, understand, and retain information better. The more you teach, the more you learn—every time you explain a concept to someone, you're solidifying your own knowledge, making it harder to forget. Plus, this approach aligns with a key biohacking principle: improving your brain's neuroplasticity through repeated engagement with material in new ways.

May 16: Curiosity As A Tool For Cognitive Development

Curiosity is more than just a desire for answers; it's a driving force behind cognitive development and mental agility. Knowledge is the key to wisdom and personal growth. As Proverbs 18:15 says, "The heart of the discerning acquires knowledge, for the ears of the wise seek it out." In this context, curiosity is essential for anyone seeking to sharpen their mind and expand their understanding of the world.

From a cognitive perspective, curiosity improves memory, wisdom, problem-solving, and creativity. When we explore unfamiliar topics or ask probing questions with the desire to learn, we stimulate the parts of the brain responsible for learning and growth, and we also develop new synapse connections. Some interesting studies have shown that curiosity enhances dopamine release, which is linked to motivation and pleasure.

Hacking Tip: To harness the power of curiosity, engage in activities that challenge your mind and broaden your horizons. Read books across different genres, and explore subjects outside your comfort zone.

By adopting a curious mindset, you'll find yourself more open to opportunities, more adaptable in your thinking, and more equipped to handle the complexities of life. It can also make you a more interesting person when dealing with others.

May 17: Developing Social Harmony

Creating social harmony is key to building an environment where both individuals and communities can thrive. But let's be real—it's not always easy. It requires a conscious effort to coexist peacefully with people who may think differently, have contrasting philosophies, or see the world in ways that challenge our own. True social harmony doesn't mean agreeing on everything; it means finding mutual respect even when we don't. Empathy and compassion are at the heart of this, as they allow us to see past our differences and connect as human beings. Promoting tolerance and inclusivity means embracing those differences rather than letting them divide us.

Hacking Tip: Societies that foster social harmony are not only happier but also more stable and prosperous. By reducing tension and improving collaboration, we create spaces where businesses can flourish and economies thrive. More importantly, when people feel respected and included, they experience greater mental well-being. So, next time you're faced with a differing opinion, ask yourself—how can I create a bridge instead of a barrier?

May 18: Reading For Knowledge And Pleasure

Reading is one of the simplest yet most profound ways to enhance your knowledge, understanding, and emotional well-being. Self-education through reading serves as both a tool for personal growth and a source of joy. It allows us to see the world through different lenses, expanding our perspectives and deepening our empathy for others.
The Stoics understood that wisdom begins with knowledge, and reading is a gateway to that knowledge. I particularly like this text from Seneca's letter to Lucilius: *"As long as you live, keep learning how to live."* — Seneca, *Letters to Lucilius*.

From a hacking perspective, regular reading has tangible benefits for the brain. It improves cognitive function, reduces stress, and can even enhance long-term brain health by stimulating mental activity and fostering neuroplasticity.

Biohacking Tip: Make reading a daily ritual. Highly successful people rarely watch TV, so replace TV time with book time. For an extra boost, try reading a few pages of self-development or philosophy books to start your day with purpose.

Have you set aside time for reading today? Even just a few pages can be the catalyst for new ideas, greater clarity, and a more fulfilled life. If you have difficulty, share with a friend and invite them to read and discuss a book together—you'll be amazed by your progress.

May 19: Be Happy And Raise Your Testosterone.

Scientific evidence has shown that being motivated, happy, and enthusiastic elevates testosterone in men. However, if you are feeling down, it will lower this crucial hormone. Engaging in activities that make men feel motivated and enthusiastic, like setting and achieving goals and taking on challenges, can lead to increased testosterone levels. These positive emotions lower cortisol, and since cortisol (the stress hormone) suppresses testosterone production, when you reduce your stress levels through positive emotions, you can maintain elevated levels of testosterone.

Biohacking Tip: Positive emotions like enthusiasm and motivation influence the endocrine system to maintain or increase levels of testosterone and estrogen. Similarly, healthy levels of these hormones contribute to enhanced mood, energy, and emotional well-being, creating a feedback loop where positivity boosts hormones, and hormones support more positive emotions.

May 20: Balancing Personal Pleasure And Responsibility

Life is a delicate dance between seeking enjoyment and fulfilling obligations. Both are essential aspects of a meaningful existence, but true wisdom lies in knowing when to indulge and when to focus on responsibilities.

It's okay to enjoy life—whether through food, leisure, or entertainment—but it should never come at the cost of your health, personal growth, long-term goals, or reputation. Indulgence without awareness can lead to imbalance, weakening your discipline and focus.

Hacking Tip: Practice mindful indulgence by setting intentional limits and responsibilities for your pleasure-driven activities. By balancing your desires with your responsibilities, you can live a more fulfilled, disciplined, and harmonious life.

May 21: Gratitude For Sensory Experiences

Gratitude for the small things in life often leads to the most profound sense of contentment. Simple pleasures—the warmth of sunlight on your skin, the sound of wind rustling through trees, or the taste of a delicious meal—are often overlooked in our busy lives. Yet, these sensory experiences offer immediate ways to connect with the present moment.

Stoic philosophy emphasizes finding contentment in the present, which means fully appreciating the small joys that surround us. Gratitude for sensory experiences brings us back to the richness of now, inviting us to notice the beauty and wonder in everyday life.

Hacking Tip: Engage your senses mindfully by practicing gratitude for sensory experiences. Whether you're eating, walking in nature, or enjoying a conversation, slow down and focus on the sensations around you. Notice the texture, smell, sound, and visual aspects of your environment.

May 22: Practicing Mindfulness In Daily Activities

Mindfulness is about being fully present in each moment, and when applied to daily activities, it transforms even the most routine tasks into opportunities for reflection and inner peace. Whether you are eating, walking, or cleaning, mindfulness allows you to experience the richness of every action, no matter how mundane.

In Stoic philosophy, mindfulness serves as a way to clear the mind and bring focus. As Marcus Aurelius expressed, "Nowhere can man find a quieter or more untroubled retreat than in his own soul." Similarly, Seneca advised reflecting on one's day and actions, considering what went well and where improvements could be made. This reflection encourages self-awareness, which is a core component of mindfulness.

"When the light has been removed and my wife has fallen silent... I examine my entire day and go back over what I have done and said, hiding nothing from myself." — Letters to Lucilius, 83.2

Hacking Tip: To practice mindfulness in daily activities, start with breath awareness.

Engaging in mindful activities consistently can lead to long-term benefits like improved emotional regulation, increased creativity, and enhanced cognitive function, making this a valuable biohacking tool for both mental clarity and overall health.

May 23: Celebrating Small Wins

In the pursuit of long-term success, we often overlook the importance of celebrating small wins along the way. These incremental achievements are not just minor milestones—they serve as proof of progress and as motivation to keep going. Marcus Aurelius often wrote about the importance of daily progress, no matter how small, in building toward more significant accomplishments. Recognizing these small moments of success keeps us motivated and focused, reinforcing positive behaviors that ultimately lead to long-term success.

Hacking Tip: Like a sports player who celebrates every point scored, even when behind in the game, we should celebrate each small victory, even if the final result is not yet where we expect it to be. Whether you're improving your physical fitness, advancing in your career, or achieving personal growth, acknowledging even the smallest steps forward creates a feedback loop that enhances motivation. Each win releases dopamine, which elevates your mood and drives you to pursue more goals. You can create a simple reward system, like treating yourself to something you enjoy after achieving a small goal. This habit of positive reinforcement will keep you energized and increase your likelihood of sustaining progress over the long haul. This will set a foundation for bigger achievements.

May 24: Power Of Positive Reinforcement In Relationships

Positive reinforcement is a powerful tool not just for shaping behavior, but also for building strong and healthy relationships. When we focus on acknowledging the good in others, we nurture a culture of trust, respect, and encouragement. This approach works in both personal and professional settings—whether in marriage, friendships, or teamwork. However, it's very important to be 100% honest when you praise someone.

Hacking Tip: To strengthen your relationships, start offering genuine praise and appreciation regularly. This doesn't mean empty compliments, but rather acknowledging real efforts and qualities in those around you. When you notice someone doing something right—whether a friend, partner, or colleague—let them know. Expressing gratitude or highlighting someone's strengths not only makes them feel valued but also reinforces positive behavior. These actions release oxytocin, often called the "love hormone," which strengthens social bonds and increases feelings of trust and connection.

May 25: Embrace Changes With Grace

Change is an inevitable part of life, and how we respond to it determines whether we grow or remain stagnant. Whether we welcome it or not, change finds its way into our routines, relationships, and even our mindset. It can feel unsettling, but learning to embrace it with grace is key to personal growth and resilience. Embracing change is not just about accepting external circumstances—it's about learning from challenges, adapting, and evolving through discomfort. Growth comes when we step out of our comfort zones, even when that feels unsettling or unfamiliar.

Learning through change involves practicing curiosity, staying open to new experiences, and seeing discomfort as a necessary part of the process. It's normal to feel resistance or fear, but it's in these moments of discomfort where the most profound growth occurs. Allow yourself to learn from these moments rather than resisting them.

The Stoics believed that resisting change only leads to frustration. Instead, they taught that by embracing it, we open ourselves up to new opportunities for growth. The more we learn to adapt, the stronger and more resilient we become in the face of life's inevitable twists and turns.

Hacking Tip: Build adaptability by stepping out of your comfort zone regularly. Embracing change isn't about having everything figured out—it's about being open to whatever comes next and trusting that, with the right mindset, you'll come out stronger on the other side.

Take a few moments each day to reflect on what you're learning and to express gratitude for the new experiences. Even if it feels uncomfortable, staying curious and open will help you navigate transitions more easily and with grace.

May 26: The Movie Called Your Life

If you were to write a movie titled "Your Life," how would it unfold? What would each scene reflect? How do you see yourself in that movie? What moments would stand out as your defining moments? Are you the hero of this movie, or are you just cheering for someone else and making them the hero? In the movie of your life, you are both the hero and the author, each role contributing uniquely to your story.
Think of how the hero of a movie or book behaves. They face challenges, overcome obstacles, and push forward despite setbacks. As the hero, you're called to take action with courage and resilience, embracing challenges with a positive outlook. How would you, as the hero, act and accomplish great things in your life? Would you want to be the character weighed down by negativity, or one who radiates charisma, charm, and strength?

Yet, being the *author* of your story comes with a distinct responsibility. As the author, you make intentional decisions, directing each scene and each chapter. You're not just responding to circumstances but actively shaping your journey with choices that align with your values and goals. Every action you take, every decision you make, contributes to the narrative of your life. And like every great hero, your story has the potential for triumphs, lessons, and growth.
Creating your life movie is a powerful way to reflect on your journey, clarify your values, and envision your future. It's like crafting a personal guide that captures who you are, what you believe in, and where you want to go. Start by outlining the key chapters of your story. Think about what experiences have shaped you—your childhood, pivotal moments, challenges you've overcome, and achievements you're proud of. Each chapter represents a piece of your journey, and being honest and open will make this process truly meaningful.

Focus on your dreams and goals. What do you want to achieve in the coming years? What steps can you take to turn those dreams into reality? This section will serve as your roadmap, guiding you as you navigate your path ahead. Your life has meaning, and you are not just a passive observer in your story; you are the author. Every action you take, every decision you make, contributes to the narrative of your life. And like every great hero, your story has the potential for triumphs, lessons, and growth.

Hacking Tip: Set aside dedicated time to work on your lifebook in a comfortable space where you can think and write freely. Don't worry about making it perfect; just let your thoughts flow. You can always revisit and refine it as you grow.

By writing your lifebook, you're not just documenting your life; you're creating a meaningful narrative that empowers you to live intentionally and authentically. Embrace this opportunity to reflect on your past, celebrate your present, and design the future you desire. So step into your role as the hero and author of your life, and create a story worth living!

Mauro dos Santos

May 27: Physical Flexibility For A Better Life

Flexibility plays a crucial role in overall physical health and functionality. While it's sometimes overlooked in favor of strength or cardio, flexibility is a fundamental aspect of fitness that enhances both performance and daily life. Often ignored by fitness enthusiasts, flexibility improves posture, enhances mobility, increases muscle efficiency, and reduces pain. It's also a key factor in better athletic performance.

Biohacking Tip: Flexibility isn't just about stretching far or touching your toes—it's about enhancing your body's functionality and longevity. By improving flexibility, you're supporting better movement patterns, reducing the risk of injury, and promoting long-term physical health. Whether you're an athlete optimizing performance or someone aiming to stay mobile and pain-free, flexibility should be a core part of your fitness regimen.

May 28: Sensory Detox (Reducing Overstimulation)

We live our modern lives with constant notifications, media, and noise; our minds are continuously bombarded with stimuli, leading to mental fatigue and stress. Just as our bodies need rest to recover, so do our senses. Sensory overload clouds the mind, making it difficult to find clarity and peace. This idea is beautifully captured in Psalm 23:2: *"He makes me lie down in green pastures. He leads me beside still waters."* This metaphor reflects the importance of taking a break from the hustle of life to find calmness and clarity.

Overstimulation—whether digital or environmental—can lead to mental clutter, anxiety, and emotional strain. By reducing sensory input, we create space for deeper thought, reflection, and renewal.

Hacking Tip: Practice a regular "sensory detox" by intentionally stepping back from digital devices, media, and overstimulation. Spend time in nature, engage in meditation, or take part in calming activities that help you reconnect with the present moment. Sensory detoxes aren't just about disconnecting from screens— they involve reducing all forms of unnecessary stimulation and allowing your mind to reset. The result is enhanced focus, reduced stress, and restored mental clarity.

By clearing the sensory clutter, you allow your mind to function more efficiently, leading to sharper decision-making, greater creativity, and a renewed sense of calm.

May 29: Focus On What You Can Control

Wouldn't it be wonderful if we could water our garden once and it stayed perfect forever? Or clean our house once and never worry about dust again? Imagine if we lived in a world full of perfect cooperation, understanding, love, and justice—where everything aligned with our ideals and points of view.

But life, in its unpredictability, doesn't grant us that luxury. Despite our best efforts, the world spins outside of our control, demanding constant work and throwing unexpected challenges, injustices, and surprises our way. We often struggle with this reality, wishing we could steer the course of events.

However, the beauty of life doesn't lie in controlling every outcome but in controlling and mastering our action and reactions. While the world may remain chaotic, you hold the power to control how you perceive and respond to it.

Hacking Tip: Shift your focus from trying to control the outcome and the uncontrollable to nurturing what you can—your thoughts, emotions, and actions in the present moment. You can control your actions but you can't control the outcome.

May 30: Biohacking For Enhanced Brain Performance

Your brain is one of the most powerful tools you have, and optimizing its performance can lead to profound improvements in focus, memory, and creativity. Enhancing brain function requires more than just mental exercise—it's about integrating lifestyle changes that keep your mind sharp and adaptable.

Biohacking Tip: The recommendations I make can be **subjective** (this word works best here), meaning they are based on what works for me personally. Here's what I adopt in my routine:

I incorporate natural cognitive enhancers like **L-theanine** or **Lion's Mane Mushroom** to improve focus and reduce mental fatigue. These nootropics help elevate memory retention and clarity.

For brain fuel, I've added **omega-3-rich foods** like salmon and flaxseeds, which support cognitive function and combat brain aging. I also include **antioxidant-packed foods** like berries and leafy greens to reduce oxidative stress.

Physical activity is crucial for boosting blood flow to the brain, which enhances memory and mental sharpness. I stay engaged in regular, varied workouts that are particularly effective for cognitive health.

I aim for **6.5 to 8 hours of sleep** per night to promote memory consolidation and mental recovery. Lack of sleep impairs brain performance and cognitive function. (March 25)

Daily meditation, mindfulness, and prayer are practices that help reduce stress and improve focus. Just **10 to 30 minutes** a day can enhance mental clarity and resilience.

By incorporating these biohacking strategies, I sharpen my mind, reduce brain fog, and unlock greater cognitive potential. Take charge of your brain's health to perform at your best.

May 31: Building Connections Through Authentic Communication

When was the last time you truly connected in a conversation? At one time or another, we're all guilty of half-listening and mentally preparing our reply while the other person is still talking. But authentic communication is a different game—it's not about being perfect, it's about being present and real. That means ditching the mental script and genuinely listening, even to what's not being said.

Authentic conversations aren't just about what you say, but about how you listen—listening to truly understand. **Funny Insight**: Have you ever walked away from a conversation and realized you didn't actually hear a word the other person said? Or felt that you were totally disconnected? That's because most of us are pros at responding, but not at connecting.

Hacking Tip: In your next conversation, create real, authentic moments.

- Practice active listening. Less nodding, more eye contact. Just let them finish.
- Be vulnerable and treat the person in front of you as the most important person in the world, because at that moment, they are.

Challenge: Go a whole conversation without mentioning yourself. Just listen, and you might learn more than you expect.

June

Introduction

Introduction:

June brings together the energies of Gemini and Cancer, blending intellectual curiosity with emotional depth. It's a month to focus on communication, emotional growth, and family life. With Gemini's air energy, your mind is sharp and ready to explore new ideas, while Cancer's water energy encourages you to connect with your emotions and the people who matter most.

This is the perfect time to focus on mental agility and mastering your time. June invites you to experiment with time-bending hacks and multitasking strategies that help you get the most out of each day. Whether it's learning new skills or improving your focus, this month challenges you to stay curious and keep growing mentally.

But it's not just about productivity—it's about connection. With Cancer's nurturing influence, you're encouraged to turn inward and focus on your relationships, especially with family. Strengthening those bonds, showing empathy, and being present with the people you love will not only improve your emotional health but also create a sense of harmony in your life.

Finally, take time to create spaces that feel harmonious and supportive. Whether it's your home, your workspace, or your social circles, June is about finding peace and balance in your environment. When you harmonize your surroundings, you'll notice the positive impact it has on your relationships and emotional well-being.

June 1: Too Much Protein May Be Making You Old

We often hear that protein is essential for muscle building and overall health—and it is. But there's a hidden side to the high-protein obsession that many people overlook: consuming too much protein, particularly from animal sources, might actually be accelerating your aging process. In regions of the world known as the Blue Zones, where people live the longest, healthiest lives, protein intake is surprisingly modest and primarily plant-based. These centenarians in places like Okinawa, Japan, and Sardinia, Italy, don't gorge on steak, chicken, or eggs. Instead, their diets are rich in legumes, vegetables, and whole grains, with animal protein being a rare addition to meals. This low protein approach may be one of the secrets to their longevity.

How Too Much Protein Accelerates Aging

One of the key reasons behind this is the way protein, especially from animal sources, activates certain metabolic pathways in your body—namely, the *mTOR* (mechanistic target of rapamycin) pathway. While mTOR is important for growth and muscle building, when it's constantly activated by high protein intake, it can speed up aging at the cellular level. It stimulates growth, but at the expense of cellular repair and maintenance, processes that are crucial for longevity. Over time, this can lead to the faster development of age-related diseases like cancer, diabetes, and cardiovascular issues. In contrast, limiting protein intake (particularly animal protein) has been shown to downregulate mTOR activity, giving your body a chance to focus on repair, maintenance, and ultimately, longevity.

Blue Zones: Low Protein, Long Life

The lifestyles in Blue Zones offer a living example of this. In Okinawa, for example, where the population has one of the highest rates of centenarians, people consume very little meat. Instead,

Mauro dos Santos

their diets are rich in sweet potatoes, tofu, and vegetables. Similarly, the residents of Sardinia focus on legumes, such as beans and lentils, and whole grains, with only small amounts of animal products. This balance keeps them healthy and thriving well into old age.

The Science of Protein Restriction and Aging

Scientific studies have supported the idea that lower protein intake, especially from animal sources, can extend lifespan. By reducing protein, particularly animal protein, you lower levels of *IGF-1* (Insulin-Like Growth Factor), a hormone linked to aging and increased cancer risk. When IGF-1 levels drop, the body shifts from growth mode to repair mode, increasing longevity and improving overall health.

The Power of Plant-Based Protein

The good news? You don't need to cut out protein altogether—just focus more on plant-based sources. Beans, lentils, and legumes provide all the protein your body needs, without triggering the same aging pathways. These foods are also packed with fiber, antioxidants, and other nutrients that fight inflammation and oxidative stress, keeping your body younger and healthier.

Conclusion: Balance Is Key

While protein is essential for your health, too much of it—especially from animal sources—might be speeding up your aging process. Take a page from the diets of the world's longest-living people: emphasize plant-based proteins, eat in moderation, and let your body focus on repair and maintenance. After all, longevity is about balance—nourishing your body without overloading it.

Hacking Tip: Try reducing animal protein and incorporating more plant-based options like beans, lentils, and nuts into your meals. Your body—and your future self—will thank you for it.

June 2: Mental Health Through Physical Fitness

Physical exercise isn't just about building muscle or increasing endurance—it's also a powerful tool for mental health. Numerous scientific studies have shown that regular physical activity can sharpen cognitive function. By strengthening your body, you're also bolstering your mental resilience and intelligence, leading to better overall mental health and a stronger response to life's challenges.

Additionally, physical activity promotes the release of neurotransmitters like endorphins and serotonin, often referred to as "feel-good" hormones. It also increases blood flow to the brain, enhancing cognitive function, improving memory, and sharpening concentration. Furthermore, regular exercise trains your body to handle physical stress, which can translate into a healthier response to emotional stress as well.

Biohacking Tip: To maximize the mental health benefits of exercise, try incorporating a variety of workouts into your routine. High-intensity interval training (HIIT) sessions provide quick, intense mood boosts, while practices like yoga and Pilates support mindfulness and relaxation. Aim for at least 150 minutes of moderate exercise per week and make it a priority in your schedule to experience gains in both physical and mental well-being.

June 3: Do Not Gossip, EVER!

Gossip might seem harmless and fun at first, but it can create deeply negative behavior patterns that affect your character. Both Stoic philosophy and biblical teachings warn against the dangers of gossip and harmful speech, emphasizing how destructive it can be for both the speaker and those around them.

Marcus Aurelius wrote in *Meditations*: "The best revenge is to be unlike him who performed the injury." This teaches us that instead of speaking ill of others, we should focus on being virtuous in our own lives and actions. Engaging in gossip is often a sign of insecurity and jealousy, pulling you further from living a life of integrity.

Proverbs 16:28 says: "A perverse person stirs up conflict, and a gossip separates close friends." Gossip creates division and destroys relationships, pulling people apart rather than bringing them closer together. It also reveals a lot about your character.

Ephesians 4:29 also reminds us: "Do not let any unwholesome talk come out of your mouths, but only what is helpful for building others up according to their needs, that it may benefit those who listen."

Hacking Tip: Next time you feel tempted to engage in gossip, remember, you may be hurting someone else's feelings, damaging their reputation, and revealing **your** true character to others. Avoid walking that path and use your words wisely.

365 Days to biohack your life
June 4: Strength Of Character

Building strength of character is a lifelong process that involves cultivating integrity, resilience, and moral conviction. It's not about how you act when things are easy but how you hold yourself in the face of adversity, temptation, or conflict.

Speaking on integrity, Marcus Aurelius said, "Waste no more time arguing about what a good man should be. Be one." Strength of character is not about standing above others, but about understanding our place in the whole, remaining humble, and staying open to learning while we develop self-discipline and empathy toward others.

Hacking Tip: Just as Marcus Aurelius kept his *Meditations*, consider journaling your thoughts, actions, and reflections each day. Practice self-discipline, gratitude for both good fortune and adversity, and compassion in small moments. Over time, you'll watch as your character strengthens, enabling you to face life's challenges with grace and resilience.

June 5: Time Management For Family Life

We often believe that our friends will be there for us through thick and thin, but what I have seen over and over is that when life's storms hit hard, it's usually our family who remains by our side. The differences we have with our family members—whether in values, habits, or even outlook on life—are part of the beauty that makes family so integral. At the end of the day, when all else fades away, it's family who stands with us, not because of similarities, but because of shared history, unconditional love, and loyalty, even when you don't feel like it.

The Stoics believed in embracing life's impermanence and valued close relationships over fleeting ones. Marcus Aurelius knew that, while friendships come and go, family ties are enduring, even with their flaws. Accepting those differences within your family leads to greater peace and wisdom.

Biohacking Tip: Instead of striving for perfection, focus on acceptance within your family members and embrace the differences. When we accept the imperfections of those closest to us, we cultivate resilience and a deeper bond, something that no amount of outside friendship can replace.

In the end, when hardships come knocking, it's your family who will sit beside you. Cultivate peace within your home today, and tomorrow's difficulties won't seem so overwhelming

June 6: No More Excuses: Let the Shaking Machine Do the Hard Work While You Stand There

Vibration platforms, often referred to as "shaking machines," have gained popularity for their ability to deliver whole-body vibration (WBV) and offer various potential health benefits. The science behind these machines is based on mechanical vibrations that stimulate muscles, bones, and connective tissues. Some of the key benefits include improved muscle strength, promoting bone health, and enhancing circulation. Additionally, these machines can help reduce muscle soreness, especially after exercise, and some studies suggest they may even provide hormonal benefits.

However, if you don't have access to a vibration platform, you can use a mini trampoline, which not only offers similar advantages but also improves balance and coordination through playful, dynamic movement. What really stands out, though, is that trampolines have shown to be highly effective in promoting lymphatic drainage, which is vital for detoxification and overall health.

Biohacking Tip: Aim for 5 to 10 minutes of use, 2 to 4 times a week on either machine. However, if you don't have that time available or the patience to do small jumps for 15 minutes, 2 to 3 minutes can still be beneficial, especially if you learn to relax while jumping. Aim for 5 to 7 days a week to maximize your results.

June 7: Share Some Good New.

Reflection of the day: In the book of Isaiah 52:7, the beauty of those who bring good news is celebrated, and in the Sermon on the Mount, Jesus teaches us that those who spread hope are blessed.

On the other hand, spreading bad news fuels a cycle of stress and anxiety. This affects our body and mind by raising cortisol levels, which promotes fat accumulation, causes tension, increases heart rate, and harms sleep and the immune system. It also impacts leptin, leading to unhealthy eating habits.

Although negativity may seem overwhelming, about 95% of events are positive, and only 5% are bad. Studies show that when we spread bad news, we create a chain of negativity.

Hacking tip: Instead of sharing the next bad news, share something positive – a good story, a kind gesture, or a success. By doing this, you improve your own well-being and create a wave of positivity that transforms everyone's day!

June 8: Set Yourself Free

When Nelson Mandela shared his thoughts after being released from 27 years of unjust imprisonment on Robben Island, he highlighted a profound truth: while he endured harsh physical labor, the guards could never touch his mind. This powerful statement underscores the resilience of the human spirit and the profound truth that our thoughts and attitudes are within our control, regardless of external circumstances. Freedom of the mind is not merely the absence of restrictions; it is about reclaiming our thoughts from negativity, doubt, and fear. In moments of struggle, it's crucial to remember that our inner dialogue shapes our reality. By consciously choosing empowering thoughts, we can transform our experiences and navigate life's challenges with resilience.

Studies in psychology and neuroscience support this concept. Research shows that our thoughts directly influence our emotional states and overall well-being.

Hacking Tip: Doesn't matter what people around us do, nobody can take away your freedom. By evaluating our reactions to events, we can figure out if we are indeed free.

June 9: Live Without Fear

"For God has not given us a spirit of timidity, but of power and love and discipline." — 2 Timothy 1:7

Fear is a powerful emotion, but it was never meant to dominate our lives. Unfortunately, fear has become a tool in many areas of life, particularly within certain religious frameworks that use it to control or manipulate behavior. However, when we look deeper, both spiritually and philosophically, it becomes clear that fear is the opposite of how we are meant to live.

Fear not only undermines our mental well-being, but it is also linked to various psychiatric disorders, from stress to depression.

Even Marcus Aurelius, the Roman emperor who had every reason to live in fear—surrounded by enemies, conspirators, and threats—chose to focus on the quality of his thoughts, rather than fear. He famously wrote, *"The happiness of your life depends upon the quality of your thoughts."* (Meditations, Book 2, Chapter 16). In this reflection, he emphasizes that it is our mindset, not our circumstances, that truly shapes our experience of life.

Hacking Alert: Break free from the cycle of fear by adopting practices that strengthen your mental and emotional resilience. Always challenge your fears. Is this fear based on reality, or is it rooted in hypothetical "what-ifs"? Focus on the present moment, instead of dwelling on the future or the past. Staying grounded in the now reduces fear's influence.

Reframe negative thoughts, and surround yourself with empowering people. Fear feeds on negativity, while confidence and courage flourish in positive environments. Fear is natural, but it doesn't have to lead you. Live with power, love, and clarity—because a life without fear is a life filled with possibilities.

June 10: Wake Up With Passion

"Wake up with passion." That simple phrase, one day, changed everything for me. Living with passion isn't about merely surviving the day—it's about embracing every single moment. When passion drives you, suddenly, every moment is filled with purpose and joy. Challenges turn into opportunities, setbacks become stepping stones for growth, and life feels richer.

Living with passion means you're not waiting for the weekend or some perfect moment to celebrate. You don't need Christmas to enjoy life—you live in the present, finding happiness in every step of your journey. It pulls you out of bed, excited for what the day holds, because every day is a fresh opportunity to move closer to your dreams.

Hacking Tip: Start each morning by asking yourself: *What excites me today?* Let passion guide your choices, and watch as your life transforms. Passion isn't just a fleeting emotion; it's a conscious decision to live with the fuel that makes life truly worth living.

Mauro dos Santos

June 11: Mastering Mental Clarity In Emotional Storms

Emotions have a way of distorting our judgment, often pulling us into knee-jerk reactions. But the true key to navigating those intense moments is finding mental clarity—a skill that transforms impulsive decisions into wise, deliberate actions. The Stoics knew this well, teaching that power lies in the pause, the space between emotion and response.

When emotions run high, stepping back—whether it's through a deep breath, a brief moment of reflection, or even a short break—can bring your mind into focus. This pause dissolves the fog of stress, giving you the space to respond with thoughtfulness rather than letting raw emotion drive your choices.

Hacking Tip: The next time you're overwhelmed, try this: take a deep breath, count slowly to ten, or step outside for a quick walk. That small act of resetting your mind can shift everything. With a clear head, you'll always make better decisions.

June 12: Embracing Gratitude For Family And Relationships

In the hustle of everyday life, it's easy to take those closest to us for granted. But when you intentionally practice gratitude for your family and relationships, it can spark something profound—deeper connections that thrive on appreciation. By expressing your thanks, even for the small things, you nurture bonds and start to see the beauty in the simplest moments.

Gratitude isn't just about making others feel valued; it enriches your own life by shifting your focus from what's missing to what's already present. It cultivates a mindset of abundance and joy in your relationships.

Hacking Tip: Make a habit of showing gratitude to your loved ones. A simple, heartfelt "thank you" with specifics on what you appreciate can uplift them and strengthen your connection. By regularly sharing what you admire about them, you create moments that foster love, respect, and a more fulfilling relationship.

June 13: Learning A New Language For Brain Health

Learning a new language does far more than simply expand your ability to communicate; it impacts your brain health in a very deep way. We often forget how vital it is to stretch our mental capacities, and one of the most effective ways to do this is by immersing yourself in a new language. Just as physical exercise strengthens the body, learning a language rewires your brain, enhancing cognitive function and mental agility, and helps avoid cognitive diseases in the future.

The Neuroscience Behind It: By learning a new language, your brain engages in neuroplasticity and forms new neural connections and pathways. Studies have shown that bilingualism or multilingualism boosts memory retention, improves problem-solving skills, and even delays the onset of neurodegenerative diseases like Alzheimer's.

Learning a language increases your attention, memory retention, and your ability to juggle between different linguistic systems, which keeps the brain young and adaptable to new situations as well. Additionally, when you're learning a new language, you're actively working both hemispheres of the brain, which enhances overall cognitive balance and can help increase your emotional intelligence, making you more adaptable and open to new perspectives.

Biohacking Tip: Learning a new language isn't just a hobby; it's a powerful tool to enhance brain health. Set aside 15-20 minutes a day for language learning, as consistency is key to building and maintaining new neural connections.

June 14: Mindfulness In Emotional Responses

Trust and faith are more than religion; they're guiding principles for navigating the unknowns of life. They teach us that life's meaning extends far beyond any single moment, victory, or hardship. When we practice trusting the process, even in the middle of a storm, we're choosing to believe that something is greater than the immediate struggle. This trust brings us a quiet strength, allowing us to find peace in uncertainty and resilience in the face of doubt. By embracing faith in life's larger picture, we learn to move forward with a calm heart and an open mind, even when the way ahead isn't yet clear.

Trust and faith aren't just about religion; they reflect an understanding that life is greater than any single moment or challenge. Trusting the process, even when you're in the midst of a storm, allows you to find peace in uncertainty.

Mindfulness is the practice of observing your emotions without letting them control you. It creates a space between feeling and reacting, giving you the clarity to respond with calm and thoughtfulness. The Stoics knew that mastering this skill was essential to maintaining inner peace and wisdom, even in difficult times.

Biohacking Tip: Incorporate mindfulness techniques into your daily routine. When stress arises, take a pause, breathe deeply, and reflect before acting. This mindful moment will help you stay centered and respond with intention rather than react.

June 15: Developing Effective Study Habits

Effective study habits are essential for growing both mentally and personally. The Stoics believed learning wasn't just about collecting facts but about truly understanding and applying knowledge in life. When you learn with intention and curiosity, you sharpen your ability to think clearly, make better decisions, and keep evolving.

For the Stoics, learning was a lifelong journey — each bit of wisdom gained helps you navigate life's challenges with greater clarity and strength.

Biohacking   **Tip:**
If you want to supercharge your brain, the **Pomodoro Technique** is a simple yet powerful tool: focus for 25 minutes, then take a 5-minute break. This method helps you stay productive without burning out. Equally important is **active learning**—rewrite what you've learned in your own words or explain it to someone else. This strengthens your understanding and memory.

Also, don't forget that your body impacts your mind. Stay hydrated, stretch during breaks, and keep good posture to stay focused.

Bonus Hacking Tip: Consider adding nootropics like **Lion's Mane mushroom** or **MCT oil** to your routine for enhanced brainpower. These natural supplements can help improve memory, concentration, and overall cognitive function.

When you combine effective study habits with biohacking, you're not just learning better — you're setting yourself up for long-term growth and success.

June 16: Enhancing Sensory Experiences

When you engage your senses with intention, you open yourself up to fully experience and appreciate the present moment. The Stoics believed that by tuning in to what you see, hear, taste, and feel, you can cultivate gratitude and improve your overall well-being. By paying attention to your sensory inputs, you create a deeper connection to the world and live more fully in the here and now.

Biohacking Tip: One simple way to enhance your sensory awareness is through **mindful eating**. Slow down, and really savor each bite. Notice the different flavors, textures, and aromas of your food. This helps you stay present and truly enjoy the moment. Also, spend time outside. Take in the natural world around you — the colors, sounds, and smells — to engage your senses and reduce stress.

By consciously immersing yourself in sensory experiences, you'll not only boost mindfulness but also increase your sense of inner peace and well-being.

June 17: Drink Water

If there's one crucial habit many neglect, it's proper hydration. Dehydration comes with a huge health price—one that we often don't realize until it's too late. You don't have to feel thirsty to know it's time to drink water. In fact, by the time you feel thirst, your body has likely already lost about 1-2% of its water content, putting you in the early stages of dehydration.

We've all heard the classic "8 cups of water a day" rule, but this one-size-fits-all guideline doesn't work for everyone. The amount of water you need depends on several factors: your weight, activity level, climate, and overall lifestyle. A more accurate approach to water intake considers your body weight. The Institute of Medicine suggests drinking between 0.5 to 1 ounce of water per pound of body weight per day.

But here's a catch—men generally need 45-50% more water than women because they have more muscle mass, burn more energy, and typically run at a higher temperature. Here's a simple breakdown, but not a rule:

- A **160-pound woman** should aim for around **9 cups** of water per day.
- A **160-pound man** should aim for around **10 to 12 cups** of water per day.
- A **280-pound woman** should target **14+ cups** daily.
- A **280-pound man** should drink **17.5+ cups** per day.

Biohacking Tip: The next time you feel hungry, try drinking a glass of water first. Often, we confuse thirst with hunger, and staying hydrated can prevent unnecessary snacking while keeping you in balance. Water is your body's fuel—use it wisely!

June 18: Cultivating Patience In Communication

Patience is a crucial part of effective communication. Taking the time to really listen before jumping in with a response helps you better understand the other person and avoids unnecessary conflicts. When you pause and reflect before speaking, your words come across as more thoughtful and meaningful.

Biohacking Tip: To build patience in your conversations, practice **active listening**. Focus completely on the person you're talking to, avoid cutting them off, and take a moment to process what they've said before responding. This not only shows respect but also strengthens your connection with them.

By embracing patience and active listening, you can foster more meaningful, harmonious conversations and relationships.

June 19: Embracing Lifelong Growth

Growth doesn't stop with formal education — it's a lifelong journey. Continuously learning and improving keeps your mind sharp and opens new doors. When you care for both your body and mind, you not only enjoy life more but also stay capable of taking on new opportunities. Embracing growth at every stage of life allows you to adapt with resilience, welcoming challenges as opportunities to expand your potential. It's this commitment to constant evolution that fuels a life of purpose, vitality, and fulfillment.

Biohacking Tip: Set aside time each day to focus on your health and learning. Whether it's discovering something new about nutrition, practicing functional exercises, or picking up a hobby, these habits enhance both your body and mind. Staying curious and active keeps your brain engaged and your body in top shape, giving you a better quality life.

June 20: Building Healthy Routines For Success

Healthy routines are the foundation of sustainable success. They're not just about getting through the day; they're about setting yourself up to thrive in every area of life. By establishing daily habits that support your physical, mental, and emotional health, you create a strong foundation upon which success can be built and maintained over time.

When you consciously design your routines, you're creating a personal blueprint for resilience, focus, and sustained energy. The secret to effective routines isn't complexity; it's consistency. Small, intentional actions—like a morning stretch, setting clear daily goals, or taking moments of mindful reflection—have a cumulative effect that fosters sustainable growth and well-being.

Success Coach Tip: To establish routines that last, start by identifying areas in your life that will benefit most from structured support. Consider the following pillars:

- **Physical Health**: Prioritize routines that promote energy and longevity. Incorporate daily exercise, balanced meals, and restful sleep as non-negotiables.
- **Mental Clarity**: Daily habits like setting intentions, practicing gratitude, and visualizing success help train your mind to focus on priorities and stay centered amidst distractions.
- **Emotional Balance**: Healthy routines aren't only about physical and mental productivity—they're also about maintaining emotional well-being.
- **Professional Development**: Treat growth as a continual process by scheduling time each week to learn something new, whether it's reading a book, attending a workshop, or refining a skill.

Building Accountability and Consistency

Mauro dos Santos

To turn these routines into lasting habits, track your progress and celebrate small wins along the way. Accountability can come from a mentor, coach, or even a friend who supports your goals. Remember, routines don't have to be perfect to be powerful; the key is consistency, even on days when motivation is low.

Hacking Tip: Healthy routines do more than improve productivity; they build a lifestyle that supports your goals and well-being at every level. Over time, these routines will become the silent force driving your success, equipping you with the energy, clarity, and resilience you need to achieve and sustain high levels of performance and fulfillment.

June 21: Building A Foundation For Exceptional Health

Socrates once said that if you wait for a doctor to take care of your health, you're being foolish. Yet, when it comes to health, many people get confused. The overwhelming amount of information and lack of clarity often make it hard to stay motivated to pursue exceptional health. Research shows that eating around 25% less than the average person can promote longevity. This concept, rooted in caloric restriction, has been studied for its positive effects on aging and lifespan.

Some of the benefits include better insulin sensitivity, lower cholesterol, and reduced inflammation—all key factors for a longer, healthier life. When you consume fewer calories, your body prioritizes cellular repair, enhancing processes like **autophagy**, where cells clear out damaged components, a crucial aspect of longevity. It also helps prevent conditions like obesity, type 2 diabetes, and heart disease, which can cut life short.

But it's not just about eating less—it's also about what you eat. Focusing on nutrient-dense foods, rich in vitamins, minerals, and antioxidants, is even more important when you're eating fewer calories to make sure you're still nourishing your body properly.

One well-known study, the **CALERIE trial**, showed that people who practiced caloric restriction for two years had better metabolic health and signs of slower aging.

Biohacking Tip: Consider trying **intermittent fasting** or **time-restricted eating** as an alternative approach. These methods focus on *when* you eat, rather than strictly cutting calories, allowing you to gain some longevity benefits while still maintaining a balanced nutrient intake.

This way, you're setting up a strong foundation for both health and longevity.

June 22: Managing Stress Through Communication

Stress is a part of life, but how we handle it makes all the difference in our overall health. Chronic stress can take a serious toll on both your body and mind, contributing to issues like high blood pressure, weakened immune function, digestive problems, and even heart disease. Mentally, it can lead to anxiety, depression, and burnout, making it harder to think clearly and make good decisions.

A powerful way to manage stress is by practicing open and honest communication. When you bottle things up, stress builds and can become overwhelming. But when you share your worries with someone you trust, it often brings relief and helps you gain clarity.

Biohacking Tip: The next time you're feeling stressed, don't keep it to yourself. Talk to a close friend, family member, or a coach. Sharing your feelings not only lightens the emotional load but can also help you see things from a new perspective. Sometimes, just saying what's on your mind makes a problem feel more manageable.

Remember, communicating your stress isn't a weakness—it's an important tool for maintaining your health and staying grounded in today's fast-paced world.

June 23: Letting Go Of Anger

Biblical Insight: In **Ephesians 4:26**, we're reminded: *"Do not let the sun go down while you are still angry."* This verse encourages us to deal with anger before it has the chance to linger. Holding onto anger not only strains relationships but also impacts our emotional and physical well-being. The message is clear—address conflicts, seek peace, and don't let unresolved anger take root.

Hacking Tip: At the end of each day, make it a habit to **release anger**. Whether through journaling, deep breathing, or talking it out, find ways to let go. Unresolved anger increases stress and affects sleep, so processing your emotions helps you reset and approach life with a clearer, calmer mindset.

Letting go of anger daily strengthens relationships, improves mental health, and brings more peace into your life.

June 24: Letting Go Of The Need To Impress Others

We often fall into the trap of trying to impress others, seeking their approval as if it defines our worth. But the truth is, constantly striving for validation pulls us away from living authentically. When you're focused on impressing others, you're not being true to yourself—you're performing for someone else's expectations, which can leave you feeling unfulfilled and disconnected.

The key to breaking free from this is **awareness**. By becoming more aware of why you're seeking approval, you can start to shift your focus inward. Realize that your value doesn't come from what others think of you but from living in line with your own values and goals. The more self-aware you become, the less power the need for external validation has over you.

Hacking Tip: Practice self-awareness daily. Take a few moments to reflect on your actions—are you doing things to impress others, or because they align with your true self? Journaling or meditation can help you stay grounded in your own sense of worth, reducing the need to seek approval from outside sources.

By becoming aware of the urge to impress others and choosing to live authentically, you reclaim your personal power and find peace in being exactly who you are.

June 25: The Power of Authenticity Over Love

There's an idea that **authenticity** is an even higher energy than love. Why? Because when you live in complete alignment with your true self, it creates a deep and unfiltered connection with life and those around you. Authenticity is about being fully aware of who you are, acting in accordance with your core values, and freeing yourself from societal expectations. It's a level of being that transcends love because it strips away the masks, fears, and insecurities, allowing you to be fully transparent—not just with others, but with yourself.

When you live authentically, you naturally enhance the love you give and receive. This state removes barriers, leading to relationships that are based on truth rather than expectation. In this way, **authenticity becomes the foundation** for genuine, unconditional love.

Some spiritual teachings suggest that authenticity holds the highest energy frequency. This is because it aligns you with your true purpose and creates a sense of harmony within yourself. By living authentically, you open the door to deeper connections and experience love in its purest form—unencumbered by fears or conditions.

Biohacking Tip: Start by practicing self-awareness. Reflect on your actions and decisions—are they coming from a place of truth, or are they influenced by outside pressures? The more you align your actions with your core values, the more authentic you become. This not only deepens your relationships but also strengthens your connection with yourself, fostering a life rooted in truth and purpose.

In the end, while love is a powerful force, it's authenticity that lays the groundwork for real, lasting love and connection. When you are true to yourself, the love you give and receive is free of conditions, allowing for the deepest, most meaningful connections in life.

June 26: Fostering Creativity

When we let go of fear and trust in our innate strengths, we unlock the ability to truly create, innovate, and express ourselves. Creativity thrives when we step away from fear and lean into the unique talents and abilities we've been given. The Stoics saw creativity as more than artistic expression—it's a reflection of the mind's power to solve problems and innovate. Tapping into your creative side allows you to grow personally. It helps you look at challenges from fresh perspectives, pushing you to think outside the box and navigate life with greater flexibility and resilience. Creativity isn't limited to the arts; it shows up in how you approach problems, make decisions, and build relationships. By embracing creativity, you pave the way for personal growth, fulfillment, and a deeper connection to your true potential.

Hacking Tip: Incorporate short, creative sessions into your day. Even 15 minutes of doodling, writing, or brainstorming can lead to breakthroughs in other areas of your life. Step away from the grind occasionally, and give yourself the space to explore ideas without fear of judgment or failure.

By fostering creativity, you're not just enhancing your ability to innovate—you're nurturing your own personal growth. Whether it's through artistic expression, problem-solving, or simply thinking in new ways, creativity empowers you to live a more fulfilling, authentic life rooted in self-expression and purpose.

June 27: The Power Of Travel For Wellbeing

Travel isn't just about going to new places—it's about stepping out of your usual routine and giving your mind and body a much-needed break. There's something about exploring new surroundings that just melts away stress. Whether you're sitting on a quiet beach or walking through the streets of a new city, you can feel your brain switch off from the everyday grind, and suddenly, everything seems lighter.

Travel also pushes you to grow. Being in unfamiliar places, meeting new people, and trying things outside your comfort zone builds confidence and gives you a fresh perspective on life. You come back home feeling recharged and often with a new outlook on things that once seemed overwhelming.

Physically, travel gets you moving without you even realizing it. Whether it's hiking in nature, strolling through markets, or just exploring the local sights, you naturally stay more active, and it feels fun and effortless. It's a great way to keep your body moving and energized.

But maybe the best part is how travel affects your emotions. It's those moments of awe, the deep conversations with loved ones, and the memories that stay with you long after the trip is over. You return home feeling more connected, not just to the world, but to yourself.

Hacking Tip: Incorporate travel into your routine, even if it's just a weekend away or a local adventure. Choose places that offer relaxation and nature to really boost your mental and physical wellbeing.

Travel isn't just an escape—it's a way to reconnect with yourself, refresh your spirit, and come back to life feeling better in every way.

Mauro dos Santos

June 28: Mindful Listening For Deeper Connections

In a world full of distractions, truly listening is a rare and powerful tool for building stronger relationships. The Stoics knew that listening deeply fosters respect and creates meaningful connections.

Mindful listening is about being fully present in the conversation—focusing not just on the words, but the emotions behind them. When you give someone your full attention, it shows you care, and that can completely change the quality of your interactions. It's a simple but impactful way to build trust and empathy.

Hacking Tip: To practice mindful listening, eliminate distractions. Put away your phone, focus on the speaker, and really absorb what they're saying. Reflect back their thoughts to show you understand. This deepens your connection and helps you engage in more meaningful conversations.

June 29: The Benefits Of Learning New Skills

Learning new skills is key to personal growth and resilience, perfectly aligned with Stoic values. The Stoics believed in always striving for self-improvement. By learning something new, you develop discipline, perseverance, and adaptability—traits that lead to a more fulfilling life.

Expanding your abilities also enhances **mental agility**. Engaging in the learning process keeps your mind sharp and flexible, encouraging you to think critically and solve problems from new angles. Marcus Aurelius himself highlighted the need for keeping the mind sharp, as it allows you to navigate life's challenges with more confidence.

Hacking **Tip:**
Make it a habit to regularly learn something new, whether it's a hobby, a language, or exploring a new subject. Doing so boosts cognitive function, improves mental flexibility, and keeps your brain engaged and resilient.

Embracing new skills is not just about growth—it's about building a mindset that helps you thrive in every area of life.

June 30: Reflecting On Personal Growth

Stoic Insight: Taking time to reflect on your life is essential for growth. The Stoics believed that regular reflection helps you see both your progress and the areas where you can improve. It's not about being hard on yourself—it's about learning from your experiences and using those lessons to live with more purpose and intention.

When you reflect, you recognize how far you've come and where you still want to go. It builds resilience by showing you that even your setbacks offer valuable insights, and it helps you move forward with clarity and direction.

Hacking Tip: Each week, set aside time to reflect on your personal growth. Think about the challenges you've faced, how you handled them, and what you've learned. Are you closer to your goals, or do you need to make adjustments? This practice helps you stay on course, keep improving, and feel more fulfilled as you track your progress and growth.

By making reflection a regular habit, you create the space to better understand yourself, stay focused on your goals, and grow continuously in a way that feels meaningful and rewarding.

July

Introduction
July 1: **The Power Of 10,000 Steps a Day**
July 2: **The Power Of Weight Training For Lifelong Health**
July 3: **Why Mobility Training Is a Game-Changer**
July 4: **The Power Of Core Training**
July 5: **The Benefits Of Binaural Beats**
July 6: **The Power Of Aromatherapy**
July 7: **The Power Of Being Present**
July 8: **The Power Of Making Your Own Meals**
July 9: **The Power Of Gratitude Before A Meal**
July 10: **Why I Always Skip Airline Food (And You Might Want to Too)**
July 11: **Balancing Work and Rest**
July 12: **Emotional Balance in Difficult Situations**
July 13: **Strengthening Mental Clarity**
July 14: **The Practice of Acceptance**
July 15: **Step Back**
July 16: **Lets Talk Aminoacids**
July 17: **Balancing Emotion And Logic**
July 18: **Nurturing Your Creative Side**
July 19: **Setting Boundaries For Emotional Health**
July 20: **Inspiring Others Through Action**
July 21: **The Power Of Kindness**
July 22: **Harnessing Creative Energy**
July 23: **Building Confidence Through Mastery**
July 24: **Fostering A Positive Mindset**
July 25: **Encouraging Innovation**
July 26: **Reflecting On Personal Growth**
July 27: **Nurturing Your Passion**
July 28: **Developing Strategic Thinking**
July 29: **The Benefits Of Receiving A Massage**
July 30: **Healing Through Reiki**
July 31: **Avoiding People With Bad Habits**

Introduction:

July is a month of emotional connection and personal empowerment, guided by the combined energies of Cancer and Leo. This is the time to focus on the relationships that matter most, to dive deep into your emotional world, and to stand tall in your personal power. It's about finding a balance between nurturing your emotional bonds and celebrating the strength that comes from within.

With Cancer's water energy, July asks you to connect more deeply with your emotions and the people around you. It's a month to focus on love—whether it's in your romantic relationships, family life, or friendships. By nurturing these connections and opening up emotionally, you'll create deeper, more meaningful bonds with those who matter most.

At the same time, Leo's fiery energy encourages you to stand in your power. This is a month for self-love, confidence, and personal growth. When you embrace your strengths and celebrate who you are, you'll find yourself more resilient, more confident, and ready to take on new challenges. Remember, self-love is the foundation for all love. When you shine brightly from within, it reflects in all areas of your life.

July is about finding balance—between love for others and love for yourself, between emotional depth and personal strength. By focusing on both, you'll create a month filled with growth, connection, and empowerment.

July 1: The Power Of 10,000 Steps A Day

Walking 10,000 steps a day is more than just a number—it's a proven biohacking tool with numerous health benefits. Regular walking boosts cardiovascular health, improves circulation, and helps lower the risk of heart disease. It also keeps your metabolism active, making it easier to maintain a healthy weight and sustain energy levels without extreme measures. Beyond the physical benefits, walking is a powerful stress reliever. It triggers the release of endorphins, reduces anxiety, and activates your parasympathetic nervous system, helping your body recover and manage daily stress. Walking also helps regulate blood sugar levels, reducing the risk of metabolic disorders like diabetes. For mental performance, walking enhances brain function and stimulates neuroplasticity, improving memory and cognitive clarity. It's a simple yet highly effective way to optimize both body and mind.

Ultimately, 10,000 steps a day isn't just about staying active—it's a holistic approach to better physical, mental, and cognitive health. A small effort with huge rewards.

July 2: The Power Of Weight Training for Lifelong Health

Weight training, or strength training, is one of the best ways to improve your overall health, and it goes beyond just building muscle. Regular weight training strengthens your bones, supports joint health, and gives your metabolism a boost. Whether you're lifting heavy weights or doing more reps with lighter weights, strength training has benefits that can positively impact many areas of your life.

One major benefit is **improving bone density**. As we age, bone density decreases, increasing the risk of fractures and osteoporosis. Weight training puts stress on your bones, which makes them stronger and more resilient—a crucial biohacking strategy for healthy aging. Strength training also improves **joint health** by building muscle around your joints, giving them better support and reducing the risk of injury. It also helps with flexibility and mobility, keeping you active as you get older.

When it comes to your **metabolism**, weight training can be a game-changer. More muscle means your body burns more calories, even at rest, helping with weight management and energy levels. Strength training helps you burn fat more efficiently, which is great for staying lean and fit.

While lifting heavy weights builds muscle volume, using **lighter weights with higher repetitions** can be just as effective, especially for joint health and endurance. This approach provides strength without overloading your body.

Biohacking Tip: Try a combination of **heavy and lighter weight training**. Use lighter weights with more reps to improve endurance, strengthen your joints, and boost metabolism. Focus on compound movements that work multiple muscles and give your body time to recover for long-term success.

July 3: Why Mobility Training Is A Game-Changer

Mobility training might not be as flashy as lifting weights, but it's a crucial part of staying active and pain-free. It's all about improving how your body moves, making everyday activities and workouts smoother and easier.

A big benefit of mobility work is **injury prevention**. By keeping your muscles and joints flexible and moving properly, you're way less likely to tweak something, especially if you're physically active.

Plus, it can **fix your posture**. If sitting all day leaves you stiff and sore, mobility exercises help correct those muscle imbalances, easing those annoying aches.

Mobility training also keeps your **joints healthy**, which is key as we get older or sit for long periods. It helps reduce stiffness, keeping you agile and pain-free.

And don't forget, it speeds up **recovery** after tough workouts by boosting blood flow to your muscles, helping you recover faster and feel less sore.

Biohacking Tip: Incorporate dynamic stretching, yoga, or foam rolling into your routine. It's a simple way to improve posture, prevent injuries, and recover faster—all while keeping you flexible and strong.

July 4: The Power Of Core Training

Core training isn't just about getting abs—it's about building the foundation for balance, posture, and overall movement. A strong core gives you **enhanced stability**, improving your balance and coordination in everything from walking to lifting, and boosting athletic performance.

It also leads to **better posture**. When your core supports your spine, you stay aligned and avoid slouching, which helps prevent back pain, especially with today's screen-heavy lifestyles.

A strong core is crucial for **injury prevention**, particularly in your lower back. It stabilizes your spine and ensures your hips and shoulders move efficiently, reducing the strain on your body.

Finally, a well-developed core enhances **movement efficiency**. From daily tasks to more complex movements, everything feels smoother when your core is strong.

Biohacking Tip: Add core exercises like planks and Russian twists to your workouts to improve stability, posture, and movement efficiency while preventing injuries.

By strengthening your core, you're building a solid foundation that supports every move you make, both in workouts and in daily life.

July 5: The Benefits Of Binaural Beats

Binaural beats are a fascinating tool for enhancing mental states, boosting relaxation, and sharpening focus. When you listen to two slightly different sound frequencies in each ear, your brain perceives a third frequency—a "binaural beat." This unique sound can influence your brainwaves, helping you tap into states that improve well-being and awareness.

Boost Focus and Concentration: Binaural beats in the beta range (14–30 Hz) can help you enter a state of heightened alertness and concentration. If you're working on a project or studying, these beats can improve focus, helping you get more done with clarity and attention.

Reduce Stress and Anxiety: Listening to binaural beats in the alpha (8–14 Hz) and theta (4–8 Hz) ranges promotes relaxation and calm. These frequencies are great for easing stress, lowering anxiety, and helping you unwind after a long day. They're also beneficial for improving sleep quality, making them ideal for anyone who struggles to relax.

Enhance Meditation: If you're into meditation, binaural beats in the theta and delta ranges (0.5–4 Hz) can deepen your practice. These frequencies help your mind relax and enter deeper states of meditation more easily, allowing for a more mindful and focused experience.

Improve Creativity:mCreativity thrives when you're relaxed yet alert. Binaural beats in the alpha and theta ranges can boost imaginative thinking, making it easier to unlock new ideas and insights. Perfect for creative work or brainstorming.

Better Sleep: For deeper, more restful sleep, binaural beats in the delta range (0.5–4 Hz) can help. These frequencies are associated with deep sleep cycles and can improve the quality of your rest, helping your body and mind recover effectively.

Biohacking Tip: Match your binaural beats to your goals—use beta for focus, alpha for relaxation, and delta for better sleep. Regular listening helps your brain adapt, optimizing your mental performance and well-being.

Binaural beats are a simple, effective way to boost awareness and mental health. Whether you're looking to focus, relax, or sleep better, binaural beats offer a natural way to tap into the potential of your mind.

July 6: The Power Of Aromatherapy

Aromatherapy isn't just about pleasant scents—it's about using the natural power of essential oils to improve your mental and physical well-being. Whether you're looking to reduce stress, boost energy, or improve your sleep, essential oils can offer a simple, natural solution. The scents we inhale have a direct effect on the brain, especially the limbic system, which controls emotions and memories. This is why certain smells can instantly relax or uplift us.

How It Works: When you breathe in essential oils, the scent triggers responses in your brain that can reduce anxiety, improve focus, or even help you sleep better. It's a mindful way to tap into the connection between your senses and your emotional health.

Popular Essential Oils and Their Benefits:

- **Lavender**: Perfect for calming your mind and easing stress, especially before bed.
- **Peppermint**: Helps boost focus and mental clarity, making it great for a mid-day pick-me-up.
- **Eucalyptus**: Known for its refreshing, clean scent, it supports breathing and mental clarity.
- **Rosemary**: Enhances memory and concentration, great for studying or work.
- **Citrus (lemon, orange, grapefruit)**: Uplifting and energizing, these oils boost mood and bring a sense of positivity.

Biohacking Tip: Use a diffuser to spread calming or energizing oils in your home or workspace. Try lavender oil at night for better sleep or peppermint during the day to stay sharp. You can also add essential oils to a bath or apply them (diluted) to your skin for a more direct effect. Aromatherapy is an easy and natural way to improve your mood, reduce stress, and support your overall well-being. Whether you want to relax, recharge, or refocus, essential oils can help you feel your best.

July 7: The Power Of Being Present

In a world constantly pulling us in different directions, the real power lies in the present moment. When you're fully present, you connect more deeply with yourself, others, and life itself. Everything becomes richer—colors, sounds, emotions—all amplified because you're actually *there* to experience them.

Being present isn't about ignoring the past or future, but about understanding that the only real moment is *now*. It's the only space where we have true influence. By anchoring yourself in the present, you free yourself from the distractions of what's ahead or behind, and instead focus on how you're showing up right now.

Hacking Tip: Bring moments of mindfulness into your day. Take a deep breath, tune into your surroundings, and pay attention to your body. Whether eating, walking, or talking, engage fully in the experience. This simple shift grounds you in the present and makes life feel more vibrant and meaningful.

The present moment is where transformation happens—it's where life unfolds, and everything becomes possible.

July 8: The Power Of Making Your Own Meals

When you prepare your own meals, you're doing more than just feeding yourself—you're taking control of your health at a cellular level. What we eat directly impacts our longevity, energy, and overall well-being. By cooking your own food, instead of buying prepared food from unknown source, you have the power to choose nutrient-rich ingredients that support your body's natural repair mechanisms, enhance metabolism, and reduce inflammation.

Think of every meal as a chance to fuel your body with what it needs to thrive. Fresh vegetables, lean proteins, healthy fats—each ingredient you choose plays a role in how well your cells function and how long they stay healthy. When you make your own meals, you avoid harmful additives and ultra-processed foods that speed up aging and damage our biological systems.

Hacking Tip: Start small—make one meal a day at home, using fresh, whole ingredients. This simple habit can slow aging, improve energy, and increase your longevity. Every meal is an opportunity to support your body's long-term health.

July 9: The Power Of Gratitude Before A Meal

Taking a moment to be thankful before you eat goes beyond tradition—it's a way to slow down and bring more awareness to the moment. Whether it's through a prayer or just a quiet pause, expressing gratitude before a meal allows you to connect with your food and prepare your mind and body for nourishment. It helps shift your focus from the hustle of the day to appreciating the meal in front of you.

Gratitude also has physical benefits. When you're in a calm, appreciative state, your body responds better to the food you're about to eat—improving digestion and encouraging mindful eating, so you enjoy the meal without rushing or overeating.

Tip: Before your next meal, take a few seconds to pause and give thanks. Whether it's a prayer or simply acknowledging the effort behind the food, this small act can make the meal feel more meaningful and satisfying. It's a moment to reset and appreciate the nourishment you're about to receive.

July 10: Why I Always Skip Airline Food (And You Might Want To Too)

As someone who travels a lot and tries to take care of my health, I've learned that airline food is something I usually avoid. It's not just the fact that it doesn't taste great—because let's be honest, most of it doesn't—it's also about the low quality and lack of nutrition.

Airline meals are mass-produced, filled with preservatives, and loaded with salt and sugar to make them last and taste halfway decent at high altitudes. But the reality is, that food often leaves you feeling bloated, tired, and far from your best. And when you're traveling, especially across time zones, you want to feel energized and alert, not weighed down by processed meals.

I've found it's so much better to pack my own snacks or simple meals. Things like nuts, fruits, or a homemade sandwich are easy to bring along and way more satisfying. Plus, I feel a lot better during the flight and when I land.

Travel Hack: Next time you fly, try bringing your own healthy snacks—nuts, seeds, fruit, or a quality protein bar. Trust me, your body will feel better for it, and you'll skip the post-flight bloat and sluggishness that often comes with airline food. Plus, you'll know exactly what you're eating, and that's always a win.

July 11: Balancing Work And Rest

We live in a world that glorifies the grind, but the truth is, balance between work and rest is key to staying productive and avoiding burnout. Pushing yourself too hard without taking time to recharge eventually leads to exhaustion. Real growth happens when you recognize that rest is just as important as hard work. Rest isn't weakness—it's what keeps you going for the long haul.

The Stoics understood this. They knew that while working hard is important, knowing when to step back and take a break is what keeps you focused and resilient. When you give yourself permission to rest, you come back more energized and ready to take on the next challenge.

Biohacking Tip: Try the **Pomodoro Technique**: Work in focused bursts for 25 minutes, then take a 5-minute break. It's a simple way to keep your energy and focus steady. Make sure you also plan regular downtime—whether it's a walk, a stretch, or just a few moments to breathe. These breaks allow your mind to reset and your body to recharge.

Balancing work and rest isn't about being less productive—it's about being smart with your energy. When you give yourself time to recover, you'll find you can get more done, with less stress, and maintain your well-being in the process.

July 12: Emotional Balance In Difficult Situations

Emotional balance isn't about shutting down your emotions; it's about staying grounded and centered when life throws curveballs. True strength is not in reacting impulsively, but in stepping back, taking a breath, and rising above the situation. It's about knowing that patience and wisdom are key, and overlooking small wrongs doesn't make you weak — it shows maturity and self-control.

Finding emotional balance is crucial to living a good, fulfilling life. Staying calm in tough times means learning to control your inner world, no matter what chaos is going on around you. When you master your emotions, you give yourself the space to respond with thoughtfulness, patience, and clarity — instead of getting lost in frustration or anger. This inner calm helps you face challenges without losing your peace of mind.

And here's the thing: emotional balance isn't just a mental game. It's also tied to how well you take care of your body.

Hacking Tip: Whether it's through mindful movement, meditation, or even deep breathing, developing emotional balance can help you stay grounded, no matter what life throws at you. It gives you the tools to approach each challenge with calm and wisdom.

July 13: Strengthening Mental Clarity

Mental clarity is key to thinking clearly and making good decisions. When your mind is clear, you can handle challenges with calm and focus instead of getting overwhelmed by distractions. But mental clarity doesn't just happen—you have to cultivate it through mindfulness and focus.

The Stoics believed that mental clarity leads to better judgment. By practicing stillness and cutting out distractions, we can make choices that align with our values and goals. In our fast-paced world, finding mental clarity takes effort.

Hacking Tip: Incorporate daily meditation or deep-breathing exercises to clear your mind. To go even further, schedule dedicated time for focused work and reflection—turn off distractions and create a space where you can think clearly.

With regular practice, mental clarity will help you make better decisions and move through life with more confidence and calm.

July 14: The Practice Of Acceptance

Life doesn't always go the way we want, and trying to control everything can leave us feeling stressed and frustrated. Practicing acceptance doesn't mean giving up—it's about recognizing what's beyond your control and finding peace with it. When we stop resisting what we can't change, we release a lot of unnecessary tension and open ourselves up to growth and new possibilities.

Acceptance lets you shift your focus to what *can* be changed—your mindset, your actions, and how you choose to respond. It's about letting go of the need to control everything and putting your energy into what truly matters.

Hacking Tip: Next time you're faced with a situation that's out of your hands, take a deep breath. Acknowledge what's happening, accept it, and then focus on how you can respond in a way that benefits your peace of mind. Acceptance isn't passive—it's an active choice to direct your energy toward what you can control.

When you practice acceptance, life feels less like a fight and more like a flow, giving you room for peace, clarity, and progress.

July 15: Step Back

Have you noticed how easy it is to spot solutions for someone else who's in a conflict? You can be a certified armchair therapist when it comes to other people's dilemmas. But when it's your turn to deal with a sticky situation, suddenly you're as confused as a cat at a dog show! That's why stepping back can be a game changer.

Taking a step back allows you to view your life from a different angle, like changing your perspective on a painting by moving to the other side of the room. Instead of getting lost in the details of your daily grind, this moment of pause can help you assess the bigger picture. Are you truly happy with where you are? Are your choices aligned with your values? Or are you just going through the motions, like a robot on autopilot?

When you create space for reflection, you're giving yourself a chance to think critically. This is especially important during stressful times when life can feel overwhelming. Instead of feeling like you're swimming upstream, stepping back helps you catch your breath and figure out your next move—preferably without the flailing!

Tip: Schedule regular "step back" moments for yourself—whether it's sipping your morning coffee in peace, going for a stroll, or jotting down your thoughts in a journal. Ask yourself the important questions: What's working? What isn't? What changes should I make?

By stepping back, you gain valuable insights and can navigate your life with a clearer mind. So, take a breather, laugh at the chaos, and remember: sometimes all you need is a little distance to see the way forward!

July 16: Let's Talk Aminoamides

Amino acids are small molecules that form the foundation of all proteins in the body, influencing everything from muscle growth to brain function. These amino acids are classified into three categories: **Essential** (such as leucine, lysine, and tryptophan), which cannot be produced by the body and must come from food sources; **Non-Essential**, which the body can produce on its own as long as it has the proper nutrients; and **Conditionally Essential**, which include glutamine and arginine. Although they are generally non-essential, they become necessary during periods of stress, illness, or intense physical activity.

Amino acids are responsible for muscle repair, hormone regulation, immune function, and neurotransmitter production, impacting how you feel, perform, and recover.

Biohacker Tip: Consider supplementing with specific amino acids, such as **Branched-Chain Amino Acids (BCAAs)**, which are critical for muscle synthesis and can be beneficial around workouts.

L-Glutamine supports immune function and gut health, while **L-Theanine** is known for enhancing mental clarity and relaxation, helping to balance the effects of caffeine and promote focus.

You can also optimize digestion with **digestive enzymes** to help break down proteins, especially if digestion issues hinder your ability to absorb amino acids.

Timing: Consider having protein-rich meals throughout the day to maintain consistent amino acid availability for muscle repair, mental function, and other bodily needs.

July 17: Balancing Emotion And Logic

Emotions play a crucial role in guiding our experiences—they give us insight into how we feel about a situation. However, when it comes to making decisions, relying solely on emotions can sometimes cloud our judgment. From a psychological perspective, it's important to strike a balance. Emotions provide valuable information, but decisions grounded in logic and reason lead to more consistent and ethical outcomes.

Hacking Tip: When you're navigating a decision, acknowledge your emotions without letting them take over. Take a step back, analyze the situation objectively, and then allow logic to guide your final choice. This balance helps you make decisions that are thoughtful, grounded, and in line with your long-term goals.

July 18: Nurturing Your Creative Side

Creativity isn't just about art—it's about giving your mind space to explore, express, and unwind. Whether you realize it or not, engaging in creative activities helps reduce stress and offers a much-needed break from the routine. The Stoics believed that nurturing your creative side feeds the soul and brings balance to our busy lives.

Hacking Tip: Take some time today to do something creative. Whether it's doodling, writing, or trying a new recipe, these small acts of creativity help refresh your mind, lower stress, and boost your overall well-being. Creativity isn't just a hobby—it's a way to keep yourself grounded and inspired.

Mauro dos Santos

July 19: Setting Boundaries For Emotional Health

Setting healthy boundaries is crucial for taking care of your emotional well-being. It's not just about saying no; it's about creating a space where you feel respected and supported. The Stoics recognized that boundaries allow for healthier relationships, ensuring that interactions are positive and enriching rather than draining.

Hacking Tip: Don't hesitate to assert your needs. Whether it's stepping back from certain commitments or having an honest conversation about what works for you, clear boundaries help prevent burnout and protect your peace. Remember, setting limits isn't selfish—it's a vital part of self-care that ultimately benefits both you and the people in your life. Embracing this practice can lead to more meaningful and respectful connections.

July 20: Inspiring Others Through Action

Actions really do speak louder than words. When you live by your values and act ethically, you inspire those around you to do the same. The Stoics understood that by demonstrating virtuous behavior, you create a ripple effect of positivity in your community.

Tip: Think about how you show up in everyday situations. Whether it's lending a helping hand, standing up for what's right, or simply treating others with kindness and respect, your actions can motivate others to follow suit. Remember, you have the power to influence the people around you just by being your authentic self and living with integrity. Your example can inspire meaningful change and uplift those in your life.

July 21: The Power Of Kindness

Kindness is a simple yet powerful way to enrich both your life and the lives of those around you. When you choose to be kind, you not only lift someone else's spirits but also boost your own psychological and emotional well-being. Every act of kindness, no matter how small, can spark a wave of positivity that creates deeper connections with others.

When you do something nice for someone, your brain releases feel-good chemicals like oxytocin and serotonin, which can help reduce anxiety and elevate your mood. This boost creates a cycle of positivity, making you more likely to seek out opportunities to be kind in the future. It's like a warm glow that brightens your day while lighting up someone else's.

Furthermore, kindness fosters stronger relationships. Being kind builds trust and rapport, allowing you to form bonds that can withstand life's ups and downs. Knowing you can make a positive impact on someone else's life gives you a sense of purpose and fulfillment, enriching your emotional landscape. In our busy lives, taking the time to show kindness can remind us of our shared humanity and the joy of helping others.

Hacking Tip: To cultivate more kindness in your life, start by setting a daily intention to perform at least one act of kindness, whether it's complimenting a stranger, helping a coworker, or simply listening to someone who needs support. You'll find that these small gestures not only brighten someone else's day but also enhance your own well-being, creating a cycle of positivity that benefits everyone involved. Embrace the power of kindness, and watch how it transforms your life and the lives of those around you.

July 22: Harnessing Creative Energy

Creativity is a powerful force within us, waiting to be unleashed. The Stoics understood that channeling this energy into meaningful projects not only brings personal fulfillment but also positively impacts your community. When you engage in creative pursuits that resonate with you, you find purpose and satisfaction in your work.

To harness your creative energy, start by identifying what inspires you—whether it's writing, art, music, or problem-solving. When you invest your time in projects that matter, you develop a sense of ownership and pride. This fulfillment comes not just from the end result but from the entire journey of creation.

Moreover, creativity connects people. Sharing your work invites conversations and collaboration, creating a sense of community. Your unique perspective can inspire others, encouraging them to express their creativity too.

Practical Tip: Set aside dedicated time each week to focus on your creative projects. Create a space that allows for free thinking and experimentation without fear of judgment.

By actively engaging in creative endeavors, you'll not only enrich your own life but also make a positive contribution to those around you. Embrace your creativity, and watch how it transforms both your world and the world of others.

July 23: Building Confidence Through Mastery

Confidence isn't something that magically appears; it grows through mastering skills and knowledge. When you dedicate time to developing your abilities, you empower yourself and lay a solid foundation for self-assurance.

The key to building confidence is repetition. Whether you're learning a new language, practicing an instrument, or improving a work-related skill, consistent practice is vital. The more you engage with a skill, the more comfortable you become. Over time, that familiarity turns into confidence, making it easier to tackle challenges head-on.

Hacking Tip: Make it a habit to set aside regular time for practice. Break things down into manageable steps and celebrate your progress along the way. Remember, mastery is a journey, and with each step forward, you're not just improving your skills—you're also boosting your confidence. Embrace the process, and watch how your self-assurance grows with your abilities.

July 24: Fostering A Positive Mindset

A positive mindset is a powerful ally in navigating life's ups and downs. It's not just about looking on the bright side; it's about using that outlook to overcome obstacles and keep yourself motivated as you work toward your goals. The Stoics understood that cultivating positivity can help you find solutions even in tough situations.

Having a positive mindset doesn't mean you ignore challenges or pretend everything is fine when it's not. Instead, it's about acknowledging those difficulties and choosing to focus on what you can learn from them. When you see setbacks as opportunities for growth rather than failures, you build resilience and determination to keep pushing forward.

Plus, embracing a positive mindset can do wonders for your emotional well-being. It encourages you to practice gratitude, recognize your strengths, and celebrate your progress, no matter how small. These small shifts in perspective can really boost your mood and reinforce your belief in your ability to achieve great things.

Hacking Tip: Start your day with a moment of reflection. Surround yourself with uplifting influences—whether it's inspiring books, podcasts, or friends who lift you up and support your growth.

By nurturing a positive mindset, you prepare yourself to tackle challenges with confidence and grace. This outlook not only helps you move closer to your goals but also enhances your overall enjoyment of life. Embrace the power of positivity, and watch how it transforms your journey.

July 25: Encouraging Innovation

Innovation is the engine of progress, and it thrives in environments that embrace experimentation and new ideas. The Stoics recognized that to truly innovate, we need to explore the unknown and challenge the status quo. This mindset encourages creativity and helps us see setbacks as opportunities for growth rather than failures.

Creating a culture that promotes innovation starts with fostering curiosity and openness. When people feel safe sharing their ideas without fear of judgment, they're more likely to take risks and think outside the box. This freedom allows everyone to contribute their unique perspectives, making the process richer and more dynamic.

It's also important to accept that not every idea will succeed—and that's perfectly okay. Innovation often comes from trial and error. By viewing failures as lessons, you motivate yourself and others to keep experimenting and refining ideas.

Hacking Tip: By nurturing an atmosphere that values innovation and experimentation, you inspire creativity and pave the way for breakthroughs. Remember, some of the best ideas come from those who dare to think differently and push boundaries.

July 26: Reflecting On Personal Growth

Taking the time to reflect on your personal growth is key to understanding how far you've come and where you still want to go. Reflecting on personal growth is a transformative process rooted in psychological and neuroscientific principles. Regular self-reflection helps you assess your progress, celebrate your achievements, and identify areas where you can improve.

From a neuroscience perspective, self-reflection activates specific areas of the brain, such as the prefrontal cortex, which is responsible for higher-order thinking, self-awareness, and emotional regulation. When we reflect on our experiences, we create new neural pathways, essentially "rewiring" the brain. By regularly practicing self-reflection, you teach your brain to become more adaptable and open to change, making personal growth an ongoing, dynamic process.

Psychologically, self-reflection helps you break free from automatic thoughts or self-limiting beliefs, which Tony Robbins often refers to as the "stories" we tell ourselves. Developing the habit of setting aside time for reflection is a powerful "Hacking Tip" that trains the brain to slow down, reducing stress and promoting clarity. Clarity is essential not only for reducing mental clutter but also for allowing creativity and inspiration to flow—both of which are necessary for a fulfilling personal growth journey.

Self-reflection isn't just about looking back; it's a powerful tool for shaping your future. When you pause to evaluate your experiences, you gain insights that can guide your next steps. This practice allows you to recognize patterns in your behavior, understand your motivations, and clarify your goals.

Hacking Tip: Set aside a few minutes each week for self-reflection. You might choose to journal, meditate, or simply sit quietly with your thoughts. Ask yourself what you've learned, what challenges you've overcome, and what you want to focus on moving forward.

Mauro dos Santos

By making self-reflection a regular habit, you empower yourself to grow and evolve continuously. Embrace this practice, and watch how it enhances your journey toward personal development.

watch how it enhances your journey toward personal development.

July 27: Nurturing Your Passion

Nurturing your passions is one of the most rewarding things you can do. Engaging in activities that light you up not only brings joy but also gives you a sense of purpose. The Stoics believed that pursuing what you love with dedication is essential for personal and professional growth. When you channel your energy into your passions, you create a powerful drive that pushes you toward excellence.

Passion fuels motivation and creativity, making challenges easier to overcome. When you're passionate about something, it feels less like work and more like an exciting adventure. Plus, nurturing your passions can enhance your well-being, reduce stress, and help you connect with like-minded people.

Hacking Tip: Make it a priority to set aside time for your passions, whether it's a hobby, a project, or joining a group. Even small steps toward nurturing what you love can lead to significant growth and fulfillment.

By dedicating time to your passions, you not only cultivate joy but also lay the groundwork for a more vibrant and successful life. Embrace what you love, and let it guide you to personal and professional excellence.

July 28: Developing Strategic Thinking

Strategic thinking involves planning and foresight, helping you make informed decisions that align with your long-term goals. The Stoics recognized the power of this approach; by carefully considering your actions and their potential outcomes, you can navigate life with purpose and clarity.

Embracing strategic thinking activates the prefrontal cortex, the part of the brain responsible for executive function, decision-making, and impulse control. This shift helps you stop reacting impulsively and instead start anticipating challenges and seizing opportunities. By consistently practicing this, you can begin to rewire your brain, prompting yourself to ask essential questions: "What do I really want to achieve?" and "How will my choices today shape my future?" Such reflection helps you prioritize what truly matters.

Hacking Tip: Consistency is key. Making strategic thinking a habit is crucial for lasting transformation. Dedicate time to reflect and plan: create a vision board, outline your goals, and map out the steps needed to reach them. Regularly review your progress and adjust your strategies as needed.

By developing strategic thinking, you empower yourself to make choices that are both thoughtful and aligned with your aspirations. Embrace this mindset, and watch how it transforms your journey toward success.

July 29: The Benefits Of Receiving A Massage

Receiving a massage is more than just a luxury; it's a vital practice for enhancing your physical and mental health. As a specialist in human biology, I can tell you that regular massages provide numerous benefits that can significantly improve your well-being.

First, let's talk about stress relief. Massage therapy helps reduce cortisol levels in the body while increasing the production of neurotransmitters like serotonin and dopamine. This combination promotes relaxation, lowers anxiety, and creates an overall sense of calm. In today's fast-paced world, where stress can lead to a variety of health issues, taking time for a massage is a proactive step towards maintaining your mental health.

On a physiological level, massages improve circulation by stimulating blood flow. This enhances the delivery of oxygen and nutrients to your muscles and tissues, which aids in recovery and reduces soreness. Improved circulation also helps flush out metabolic waste, promoting faster healing and increased energy levels.

Moreover, receiving a massage can enhance your emotional well-being. The power of touch fosters a sense of connection and belonging, releasing oxytocin—the "love hormone"—which can improve mood and strengthen emotional resilience. This aspect of massage is crucial for reinforcing self-care and self-acceptance.

Hacking Tip: Make massage a regular part of your wellness routine. Whether you visit a professional therapist or practice self-massage techniques, prioritize this time for yourself. Remember, investing in your body is investing in your health.

Incorporating massage into your life not only helps alleviate tension and discomfort but also supports your overall health and vitality. Embrace the healing power of touch, and witness the positive changes it brings to your mind and body.

Mauro dos Santos
July 30: Healing Through Reiki

Reiki is a gentle yet powerful healing practice that promotes balance and wellness by channeling energy to help the body heal itself. This non-invasive technique works on physical, emotional, and spiritual levels, making it effective for reducing stress, relieving pain, and enhancing overall well-being. During a Reiki session, the practitioner lightly places their hands on or near the recipient, allowing energy to flow. This process helps release blockages and restore harmony, often resulting in deep relaxation. Many people leave a session feeling a sense of peace and clarity, making Reiki a wonderful tool for emotional healing and stress relief.

For a long time, I resisted this approach due to my religious beliefs. I had been misinformed that Reiki wasn't aligned with a divine source. This limiting belief prevented me from recognizing the healing opportunities around me and even from fully embracing the gift God gave me—to bless others with my own hands.

Hacking Tip: Consider adding Reiki to your self-care routine. Whether you choose to visit a trained practitioner or learn some self-Reiki techniques, this practice can support your healing journey and bring greater balance to your life.

Your hands hold power; embrace this power and see how this holistic approach can enhance your health, promote healing from within, and bring deeper well-being into your life.

July 31: Avoiding People With Bad Habits

Surrounding yourself with positive influences is essential for your personal growth and well-being. While it's important to show compassion to others, consistently being around people with negative habits can drag you down and hinder your progress. When you spend time with individuals who engage in unhealthy behaviors—like excessive drinking, constant negativity, or procrastination—it can be all too easy to fall into those same patterns.

The people we associate with often serve as mirrors. If you're around someone with a growth mindset, you're more likely to adopt one yourself. But if you're frequently exposed to individuals with self-limiting beliefs, those attitudes can subtly seep into your mindset. On the other hand, being around people who embody success, resilience, or even just positive thinking makes you more inclined to adopt those qualities.

Interestingly, our brains are wired to seek connection, and mirror neurons play a significant role in this. Mirror neurons, discovered in the 1990s, are brain cells that activate both when we perform an action and when we observe others performing it. This neural mimicry makes the behaviors around us feel familiar and acceptable, regardless of whether they're positive or negative. Spending time with positive people essentially primes your brain to adopt similar thoughts and actions, reinforcing pathways associated with positivity, motivation, and self-discipline. If someone consistently drains your energy, it's not only wise but essential to limit your interactions with them. Your energy is sacred, and, as spiritual teachers often advise, surrounding yourself with those who nurture your energy rather than deplete it allows for deeper growth and personal peace.

Bad habits can be contagious. The more you're around people who make poor choices, the more those choices start to feel normal, making it harder for you to stick to your goals. It's crucial to recognize how your social circle influences your mindset and behaviors.

Hacking Tip: Assessing your social circle may feel challenging, but consider it a self-care practice. Take a moment to evaluate your relationships. Seek out friends and acquaintances who inspire you and support your ambitions. Building a network of positive influences not only reinforces your resolve but also creates an environment where you can truly thrive. By intentionally distancing yourself from negative influences, you make room for positive growth and a healthier, more fulfilling life. Embrace the power of your environment, and watch how it shapes your journey.

August

Introduction
August 1: **Fat Doesn't Deserve This**
August 2: **Eating Delicious Food While Getting Fitter**
August 3: **Ocular Vestibular Exercises**
August 4: **The Power Of 15 Minutes Of Focus**
August 5: **Building a Strong Foundation for Health**
August 6: **Embracing A "No To-Do List"**
August 7: **Getting Clear On What You Want**
August 8: **Biohacking for Mental Clarity And Focus**
August 9: **Daily Plan And Preparation For Achieving Your Goals**
August 10: **Eating Delicious Food While Getting Fitter**
August 11: **Embracing Practical Wisdom**
August 12: **Busting Emotional Walls**
August 13: **Developing Organizational Skills**
August 14: **Practicing Mindful Decision-Making**
August 15: **Fostering Harmonious Relationships**
August 16: **Energy Blocks Create Diseases**
August 17: **Don't Overthink**
August 18: **Building Emotional Stability**
August 19: **Maintaining Physical Health**
August 20: **Practicing Self-Discipline**
August 21: **Creating Your Positive Happy Statement**
August 22: **Forgive Yourself And The Past**
August 23: **Say Yes To Yourself**
August 24: **Goals And Mission Statements**
August 25: **Embracing Change With Flexibility**
August 26: **Enhancing Focus Through Minimalism**
August 27: **Building Resilience Through Adversity**
August 28: **Developing Strategic Thinking**
August 29: **The Power Of Routine**
August 30: **Mindful Consumption**
August 31: **Developing Healthy Boundaries**

Introduction:

August is a month of self-expression, health optimization, and organization, guided by the bold energy of Leo and the practical, grounded influence of Virgo. It's a time to focus on enhancing your mental clarity, creating better systems for your life, and tapping into your creativity to express who you truly are.

With Leo's fire driving you forward, this is the perfect time to focus on leadership and self-expression. Whether it's in your work, your relationships, or your personal growth, August encourages you to step into your power and let your authentic self shine. Use this time to engage socially, share your ideas, and find creative outlets that bring you joy.

Virgo's earth energy, on the other hand, invites you to get organized. This is the month to focus on structure—whether that's in your time management, your health routines, or your physical space. By streamlining your life and decluttering both your mind and environment, you'll feel more grounded and clear-headed, allowing you to make better decisions and achieve your goals with ease.

August is all about finding balance—between drive and order, between creativity and practicality. By focusing on both self-expression and health optimization, you'll create a month that not only helps you grow but also sets you up for long-term success.

August 1: Fat Doesn't Deserve This

In the world of good eating, it has long been misunderstood and suffered blame for too many calories. However, truth be told fats are at the foundation of everything we eat. As one of the three major nutrients-indeed, they are a primary substance that provides us with energy; they keep us alive through cell growth; and support our body's hormonal balance in its various functions on which our life depends. More importantly, omega-3 fatty acids are essential to brains functioning, cognitive health, and heart health.

Another little known fact is that over 60% of your brain is made from fat. Essential fatty acids such as omega-3s and -6s are key to maintaining the integrity of cell membranes, thus allowing neurons to communicate effectively with one another. Omega-3s, especially as DHA (docosahexaenoic acid), are the key for our cognitive ability and memory. Research has shown that higher intake levels of omega-3 fatty acids is closely related to enhanced cognitive performance and less chance of neurodegenerative diseases like Alzheimer's or Parkinson's-Two versions derivable only by chance counsel like Chinese whispers at best, perhaps their flavor as well.

In the 1950s,the hero was an American physiologist named Ancel Keys who transformed dietary fats into a cold-hearted enemy. This led to the US government promoting low-fat dietary guidelines by 1970s. The production of low-fat foods soared in response, even though a few scientists were already warning that this could damage public health. But recent research has emphasized the importance of healthy fats--especially unsaturated like omega-3s -- for best possible health.

Fat as the enemy concept began largely with Keys' research, worked later through public policy measures and the food industry's development of low-fat products line on which it flourished-like a blood stain on white linen. However, more recent research underscores that integrating healthy fats into your diet helps you maintain cognitive function, heart health and your overall good looks.

Biohacking Tip: Make Healthier Fats a Priority

For Ocean-3 Fatty Acids: Have omega-3 rich foods on hand to support brain and heart health as well as reduce inflammation, such as fatty fish (salmon, mackerel, sardines), flaxseeds, chia seeds, walnuts and supplements if necessary derived from algae extracts.-

For Monosaturated Fats: These fats have great research backing from food such as olive oil, nuts and avocados, so that they can be an ally in the fight for your heart health to improve health overall.-

Polyensa tura ted Fats: Omega-3 and 6 fatty acids are found in seeds, nuts and vegetable oils. Be sure you balance your intake of omega-6 with plenty to omega-3s for optimal health beginning from infancy.-

Restrict Saturated Fats: Although not as harmful as once thought, saturated fats from sources like full-fat dairy products are still best eaten in moderation (red meat, however should be limited even more). When possible, opt for lean meats or sources of plant proteins such as soybeans and lower-fat dairy selections and don't limit yourself to health food only.

Avoid Trans Fats: The worst fat for you is trans fats, which are found in processed foods and partially hydrogenated oils. They are connected with heart disease and inflammation. Carefully monitor ingredients whenever shopping so as not to accidentally eat something with either type of fat.

Balancing Fat Intake: You should moderate because fats are energy dense. Instead of shooting for a "low-fat" diet, target a range (recommended by many health authorities): about 20- 35 percent of your calories come from healthy fats.

Include Whole Foods:

Focus on organic food sources for fats like nuts, seeds fatty fish, and plant oils. These foods supply beneficial compounds including fiber and minerals that will not be found in a more processed oil-containing product.

Cook with Healthy Oils:

Cook using olive oil and avocado oil, which are rich in monounsaturated fats and stable at higher temperatures.

By knowing the important of healthy fats and adding these to your diet, it can support both your physical well-being and your look. Fat isn't the enemy--it's an essential part of balanced nutrition.

August 2: Eating Delicious Food While Getting Fitter

Eating well doesn't have to mean giving up flavor or enjoyment. In fact, finding and incorporating delicious, nutritious foods into your diet can completely transform your fitness journey. You can absolutely nourish your body while still savoring every bite!

Focus on whole, unprocessed foods that not only taste great but also fuel your body. Fresh fruits, vibrant vegetables, lean proteins, and healthy fats can be incredibly satisfying. Don't shy away from using herbs and spices to elevate your meals—well-seasoned dishes can turn simple ingredients into something truly delightful.

When you genuinely enjoy what you eat, sticking to healthy habits becomes much easier. It's all about creating a positive relationship with food. Exploring new recipes and ingredients keeps your meals exciting and varied, making healthy eating feel less like a chore and more like a fun adventure.

Hacking Tip: By focusing on tasty food that supports your fitness goals, you'll create a sustainable approach to health that feels both satisfying and enjoyable. Embrace the journey, and enjoy the delicious foods that nourish your body and soul!

August 3: Ocular Vestibular Exercises

"Ocular Vestibular Exercises," also known as "Eye-Head Coordination Drills," are commonly used in vestibular therapy, vision training, and certain movement practices like Feldenkrais and Z-Health. These exercises focus on enhancing the connection between the eyes and the rest of the body, especially the neck.

Purpose: The primary goal of these exercises is to improve eye control and coordination with head movement, which is essential for balance, spatial orientation, and reducing neck tension.

Mechanism: These exercises challenge the vestibulo-ocular reflex (VOR), responsible for stabilizing vision while the head is in motion. By training the eyes to move independently of the head, these exercises also enhance proprioception and improve nervous system efficiency.

Process: In these exercises, eye movements lead, followed by the neck. This approach enhances brain-body coordination. Typically, you begin by moving your eyes in specific directions (e.g., up, down, left, right) while keeping your head still, then add head movements after a few repetitions.

A More Specific Example: Ceiling Eye Tracking (Ocular Gymnastics):

1. Start by looking up at the ceiling without moving your head.
2. Move your eyes to one side, then down, and then to the other side in a circular motion.
3. Gradually, begin incorporating gentle neck movements after your eyes shift to enhance the neural link between eye and neck movement.
4. Alternatively, you can reverse this process by moving your head in various directions while keeping your eyes fixed on a single point, which offers a different level of challenge for the vestibular system.

Benefits:

- **Improved Spatial Awareness:** As the brain integrates visual input with head and neck movement, spatial awareness improves, helping reduce dizziness, increase focus, and prevent injury.
- **Tension Relief:** When performed correctly, these exercises alleviate neck and shoulder tension by training the body to respond efficiently to head movements without tensing up.
- **Neuroplasticity:** Training the vestibular and oculomotor systems can induce positive neuroplastic changes, enhancing the brain's adaptability.

How It Ties into Biohacking: From a biohacker's perspective, incorporating oculomotor drills into your routine can optimize brain function, enhance balance, and improve overall performance. These eye exercises engage the cranial nerves, contributing to parasympathetic activation (calming the nervous system) and helping reduce stress and improve mental clarity.

In summary, oculomotor and vestibular exercises challenge both eye movement and neck mobility in tandem, with applications for performance enhancement, stress reduction, and overall health.

August 4: The Power Of 15 Minutes Of Focus

In our busy lives, it's easy to get overwhelmed and lose sight of what truly matters. But what if I told you that dedicating just 15 minutes each day to your number one activity for success can make a world of difference? Whether it's working on a passion project, learning a new skill, or making progress toward a goal, that focused time can transform your journey.

When you commit to just 15 minutes of concentrated effort, you tap into a powerful sense of momentum. This short, dedicated burst allows you to dive deep into your task, unlocking creativity and enhancing your problem-solving abilities. By cutting out distractions and zeroing in on your priorities, you'll often achieve more in those 15 minutes than you might in an hour of scattered work.

Plus, this daily practice helps build a habit of discipline. Setting aside time for your most important task reinforces your commitment to your goals. Over time, you'll sharpen your skills and boost your confidence as you see the progress you're making.

HackingTip: Pick your top priority—your passion project or main goal—and set a timer for 15 minutes. Find a quiet space, eliminate distractions, and dive in. You might be surprised at how much you can accomplish in such a short time!

By making those 15 minutes a non-negotiable part of your day, you're laying the groundwork for long-term success. Embrace this practice, and watch how it propels you toward your goals and transforms your productivity. You've got this!

August 5: Building A Strong Foundation For Health

Creating a solid foundation for health goes beyond just eating right or exercising; it's about embracing a holistic approach that includes physical, mental, and emotional well-being. When you focus on these areas, you set yourself up for long-term vitality and happiness.

Start with nutrition. Fueling your body with whole, nutrient-dense foods provides the energy you need to thrive. Incorporate fresh fruits, vegetables, lean proteins, and healthy fats into your meals to support your immune system and maintain energy levels.

Physical activity is also crucial. Regular movement not only strengthens your body but also boosts your mood. Find activities you enjoy—whether it's dancing, hiking, or yoga—and make them part of your routine.

Fitness isn't just about building muscle, strength, and losing weight; it's also about cultivating the energy and vitality that enable you to face life's challenges with resilience and grace. In addition to boosting your health and energy levels, fitness enhances your overall appearance and presence. When you maintain a lean physique, particularly by reducing belly fat, it adds elegance and charm. A trim waistline is often associated with vitality, discipline, and elegance—qualities that are immediately noticeable to others. It also improves your posture, giving you a refined look that amplifies your physical grace.

Biohacking Tip: Belly fat is linked to a range of health issues and an increased risk of chronic diseases. It also drains your energy over time, impacting your daily vitality. Fluid retention or ascites can cause belly enlargement and may signal underlying conditions like liver or heart problems. Addressing this may require medical attention, a balanced diet, and regular activity to manage fluid and fat buildup effectively. Excess belly fat can affect your metabolic health, increase inflammation in the body, and impair circulation and oxygenation, all of which diminish energy levels.

Take a moment to evaluate your current habits and identify small changes you can make. By gradually building healthier routines, you'll create a strong foundation for lasting well-being. Investing in your health is one of the best gifts you can give yourself!

August 6: Embracing A "No To-Do List"

In a world where to-do lists seem never-ending, creating a "No To-Do List" can be a real game changer for your productivity and peace of mind. This idea is all about identifying what you *won't* do, allowing you to focus on what truly matters in your life.

Think about the tasks, commitments, or habits that drain your energy or don't serve your best interests. By consciously deciding to eliminate these from your daily routine—whether it's unnecessary obligations, distractions, or unproductive habits—you make space for the things that align with your goals and values.

Having a "No To-Do List" can significantly reduce overwhelm. When you take the pressure off trying to do it all, you can concentrate on the tasks that genuinely contribute to your happiness and success. It's all about reclaiming control over your time and mental energy, leading to a more balanced and fulfilling life.

Hacking Tip: Take a moment to jot down the things you want to avoid in your daily life. Reflect on how they affect you, and commit to letting them go. Embracing the freedom that comes with saying no can be incredibly empowering. By adopting a "No To-Do List," you're not just managing your time better—you're making a powerful statement about what truly matters to you.

August 7: Getting Clear On What You Want

Getting clear on what you truly want in life is a vital step toward reaching your goals. Without that clarity, it's easy to feel lost in the chaos of everyday life. When you take the time to define your desires and aspirations, you create a roadmap that can guide your decisions and actions.

Start by really reflecting on what matters most to you. What are your passions, values, and long-term dreams? This might involve journaling, brainstorming, or having meaningful conversations with friends or mentors. The key is to dig deep and be honest with yourself about what you truly want, rather than settling for what you think you should want.

Once you have a clearer picture, break your goals down into smaller, manageable steps. This approach makes your ambitions feel more achievable and keeps you motivated. Knowing what you're working toward helps you stay focused and say no to distractions.

Hacking Tip: Set aside some quiet time to write down your goals and desires. Be as specific as possible—it'll help solidify your vision. Revisit and adjust your list regularly, using it as a guide to keep you on track.

By getting clear on what you want, you empower yourself to take meaningful steps toward a life that truly reflects who you are. Embrace that clarity, and watch how it transforms your journey! You have the power to shape your future.

August 8: Biohacking For Mental Clarity And Focus

Mental clarity is crucial for staying productive, making sharp decisions, and performing at your best. When your mind is clear, you're able to focus, solve problems efficiently, and manage stress more effectively.

Biohacking involves using science, self-experimentation, and small lifestyle adjustments to improve both physical and mental performance. If you're looking to sharpen your focus and enhance cognitive function, biohacking techniques can make a real difference.

Cold Exposure. Ice baths are a biohacking method that's becoming increasingly popular. When you're exposed to cold, your body increases norepinephrine production, which boosts mood, alertness, and mental clarity.

Fasting and Intermintent fast. Fasting also enhances focus and mental clarity by regulating insulin levels and promoting brain health. In fact, Epictetus, a Greek Stoic philosopher, emphasized self-discipline and encouraged voluntary fasting to strengthen resilience and prepare for challenges.

Mindfulness Practices. Mindfulness techniques like meditation and deep breathing exercises are well-established methods for improving mental clarity. These practices help reduce stress, improve emotional regulation, and enhance focus. By training your mind to stay present and centered, you can improve both your short-term concentration and long-term cognitive function.

Nootropic Supplements. Nootropics, also known as "smart drugs," are supplements designed to enhance cognitive function. Popular nootropics like L-theanine, caffeine, and Lion's Mane mushroom have been shown to improve focus, memory, and mental clarity. Combining nootropics with other supplements like omega-3s, magnesium and biohacks, like mindfulness and cold exposure, can compound their effects, helping you stay mentally sharp throughout the day.

Soma Breath. Soma Breath combines rhythmic breathing techniques, breath retention, and meditation to enhance physical, mental, and emotional well-being. It increases oxygen efficiency, improves energy levels, reduces stress, and promotes relaxation. Regular practice of Soma Breath leads to more mental clarity, emotional balance, and resilience, while also boosting immune function and cardiovascular health.

Biohacking Tip: Incorporate cold exposure into your morning routine with a cold shower to kickstart your day. Pair it with a brief mindfulness session to ground your thoughts, add a nootropic supplement like L-theanine for an extra mental boost, and occasionally practice Soma Breath.

By embracing these biohacking practices, you'll take control of your mental clarity and focus, empowering you to perform at your highest level every day.

August 9: Daily Plan And Preparation For Achieving Your Goals

Creating a structured daily plan is crucial for making steady progress toward your goals. Here's a straightforward strategy to help keep you on track and motivated:

1. Define Your Goals

- **Write It Down:** Start by clearly defining your main goal. Be specific about what you want to achieve. For example, instead of saying, "I want to be fit," say, "I want to run a 5K in under 30 minutes."
- **Break It Down:** Divide your main goal into smaller, actionable milestones. This makes it easier to track your progress and stay motivated.

2. Establish a Daily Routine

- **Morning Ritual:** Begin each day with a positive routine. Consider starting with a few minutes of meditation, stretching, or journaling to set the right tone.
- **Dedicated Work Time:** Block out specific time each day that's just for working on your goal. Whether it's 30 minutes or a couple of hours, treat this time as sacred.

3. Create a To-Do List

- **Daily Tasks:** Each morning or the night before, jot down the tasks you need to complete that day to move closer to your goal. Keep it manageable—focus on 3-5 priority tasks.
- **Use a Planner or App:** Consider using a planner or productivity app to keep your to-do list organized and accessible.

4. Stay Focused and Minimize Distractions

- **Find Your Space:** Create a workspace that's free from distractions. Make sure it's comfortable and has everything you need to be productive.
- **Limit Interruptions:** During your dedicated work time, turn off notifications on your phone and computer to help maintain focus.

5. Review and Adjust

- **End-of-Day Reflection:** Take a few minutes at the end of each day to review what you accomplished. Think about what went well and where you can improve.
- **Weekly Check-In:** Set aside time each week to assess your progress. Adjust your plan and tasks based on what you've learned.

6. Celebrate Small Wins

- **Acknowledge Progress:** Celebrate your achievements, no matter how small. Recognizing progress keeps your motivation alive and reinforces your commitment to your goals.
- **Reward Yourself:** Treat yourself to something special when you reach a milestone to maintain that motivation.

By following this plan and making daily preparations, you'll stay committed to your goals and make consistent progress. Remember, success is a journey, and every step you take brings you closer to your dreams!

Mauro dos Santos

August 10: Eating Delicious Food While Getting Fitter

Eating well doesn't have to mean giving up flavor or enjoyment. In fact, finding and incorporating delicious, nutritious foods into your diet can completely transform your fitness journey. You can absolutely nourish your body while still savoring every bite!

Focus on whole, unprocessed foods that not only taste great but also fuel your body. Fresh fruits, vibrant vegetables, lean proteins, and healthy fats can be incredibly satisfying. Don't shy away from using herbs and spices to elevate your meals—well-seasoned dishes can turn simple ingredients into something truly delightful.

When you genuinely enjoy what you eat, sticking to healthy habits becomes much easier. It's all about creating a positive relationship with food. Exploring new recipes and ingredients keeps your meals exciting and varied, making healthy eating feel less like a chore and more like a fun adventure.

Hacking Tip: By focusing on tasty food that supports your fitness goals, you'll create a sustainable approach to health that feels both satisfying and enjoyable. Embrace the journey, and enjoy the delicious foods that nourish your body and soul!

August 11: Embracing Practical Wisdom

Practical wisdom is about making thoughtful and informed decisions in our daily lives. It involves stepping back to assess situations clearly and focusing on what you can control. The Stoics believed that by developing this skill, you can navigate challenges more effectively and maintain your inner peace.

When you embrace practical wisdom, you learn to respond thoughtfully instead of reacting impulsively. This approach helps you align your choices with your values and goals. By concentrating on what you can control—like your reactions—you empower yourself to manage life's ups and downs with grace.

Hacking Tip: Before making decisions, take a moment to pause. Ask yourself what is within your control and how your choices support your long-term goals. Reflecting on your experiences will strengthen your practical wisdom and guide you toward a more balanced life and when done consistently, can have profound effects over time. Regularly pausing and reflecting before acting helps you cultivate a calm, deliberate approach to life, making it easier to navigate challenges with resilience. As you build this habit, you'll find yourself responding to situations with greater balance and clarity, empowering you to make decisions that are truly aligned with your values.

By embracing practical wisdom, you cultivate the clarity and confidence needed to face challenges, leading to a more peaceful and purposeful existence.

August 12: Busting Emotional Walls

Our emotional walls seem like a safety net we have put up over the years to protect ourselves from pain or sadness. Although they may create the illusion of protective walls, in reality, these walls isolate us from truly living. They need to be broken down in order for us to grow and for us to have healthier relationships.

The trick to tearing those barriers down is acknowledging they exist in the first place.

Reflect on the origin of your stories: Which emotional wall did they come from? The why behind these defenses can help you understand how they affect your relationships and how you feel emotionally.

Then, consider the upside to being vulnerable. Being open and authentic is a catalyst for bonding and sharing with others. From there, share your opinions and emotions with someone who is likely to trust you. If you do it, I guarantee you will be surprised by how freeing that is and how much more connected it makes you.

Hacking Tip: With each step, you begin breaking down the wall and creating a new story in your life. You detach from old emotions, bringing a sense of freedom and opening up space for new dreams. Embrace the opportunity to create your new life.

By breaking down your emotional walls, you'll open yourself up to richer experiences and stronger relationships. Embrace vulnerability as a strength, and watch how it transforms your connections with others and your own sense of self.

August 13: Developing Organizational Skills

Developing strong organizational skills is key to reducing stress and boosting efficiency in your daily life. The Stoics recognized that having a well-structured approach to tasks creates a sense of order, which can significantly support your goals and overall well-being. Stoicism emphasizes internal control and order as a response to external chaos, valuing structure as a means to maintain inner peace even amid life's unpredictability.

When you take the time to plan and organize your tasks, you essentially lay out a clear roadmap for your day. This structure helps you prioritize what truly matters, making it easier to focus on the things that need your attention most. With everything laid out, you can avoid the chaos that creeps in when life gets busy.

Being organized also boosts your productivity. Knowing what needs to be done and when allows you to tackle your responsibilities more effectively, freeing up time for other things you enjoy. Plus, a tidy space—whether it's your desk or your home—fosters a calming environment that lifts your mood and keeps you motivated.

Hacking Tip: Try creating a daily or weekly planner to map out your tasks and priorities. Break larger projects into smaller, manageable steps, and set deadlines for each one. Regularly check in on your plans to adjust as needed and stay on track.

By honing your organizational skills, you'll not only lower your stress levels but also enhance your ability to achieve your goals. Embrace the power of structure, and watch how it transforms your daily life!

August 14: Practicing Mindful Decision-Making

Practicing mindful decision-making is an essential way to ensure your choices align with your values and long-term goals. In today's fast-paced world, it's easy to rush into decisions without fully thinking them through. The Stoics believed in taking the time to reflect on choices, as they saw thoughtful decision-making as a path to inner peace and resilience, even in the face of external pressures. This reflective approach often leads to more fulfilling outcomes.

When you pause to consider a decision, you give yourself the chance to weigh the pros and cons and see how each option fits with what truly matters to you. This mindfulness helps you avoid impulsive choices you might later regret. By connecting your actions to your core values, you'll feel more confident in your decisions and cultivate a greater sense of purpose, allowing your choices to reflect the life you aspire to create.

Hacking Tip: Before making an important decision, take a moment to breathe and reflect. Ask yourself how each option aligns with your values and long-term objectives. Writing down your thoughts or discussing them with someone you trust can also help clarify your perspective. Regularly practicing mindful decision-making can strengthen your self-discipline and emotional resilience over time, helping you stay aligned with your long-term growth.

Incorporating mindful decision-making into your daily routine will help you make more intentional choices that resonate with the life you want to create. Embrace this practice, and watch how it transforms your journey toward fulfillment!

August 15: Fostering Harmonious Relationships

Harmonious relationships are all about mutual respect and understanding. The Stoics believed that open communication and active listening are key to building strong connections. They saw listening as a path to understanding others' motivations, fostering compassion, and reducing conflict—essential elements for harmony. When you engage genuinely with others and value their perspectives, you create an environment that uplifts everyone involved.

Hacking Tip: Make a conscious effort to communicate openly with those around you. Focus on really listening to what others are saying without thinking about your response right away. Listening without judgment fosters trust and creates a safe space for others to share openly, strengthening the foundation of your relationships. This practice deepens connections, enriches relationships, and creates a space where everyone can thrive together.

August 16: Energy Blocks Create Diseases

Our bodies are more than just physical structures—they are intricate systems of energy constantly flowing and interacting with our thoughts, emotions, and environment. When this flow is disrupted, it can lead to energetic blockages that manifest as physical or emotional imbalances. Over time, these blockages can contribute to the development of diseases, both mental and physical.

Energy, in its natural state, is meant to move freely throughout the body. However, emotional traumas, unresolved conflicts, and even negative thought patterns can create "stuck" energy in specific areas of the body. This stagnant energy, when not addressed, begins to interfere with the body's ability to maintain balance and function optimally. Ancient Eastern practices, such as acupuncture and qi gong, are based on the principle that blocked energy leads to illness. Similarly, modern science is beginning to understand how stress, trauma, and emotions deeply affect our immune system, hormones, and overall health.

Negative emotions, when unprocessed, can activate the sympathetic nervous system—the body's fight-or-flight response—keeping the body in a heightened state of stress. While this response is beneficial in short bursts, chronic activation from unresolved emotions can disrupt the nervous system and weaken the immune system, ultimately contributing to issues like inflammation and disease. In fact, imbalances in energy flow are associated with certain conditions, such as energy imbalances in cancer cells or loss of energy balance in heart attacks.

For instance, when you experience prolonged stress or suppress emotions, your body continuously releases hormones like cortisol and adrenaline. These stress responses, when chronic, can contribute to conditions such as heart disease, digestive issues, and autoimmune disorders.

On an emotional level, repressed feelings like anger, grief, or fear often get lodged in the body as energetic blocks. You might experience tension in the shoulders, digestive issues, or unexplained fatigue, all of which can stem from emotional energy that hasn't been processed and released. People with chronic neck tension, for example, may be holding onto stress or responsibility, and releasing this tension through massage or breathwork can promote relief. Over time, this unresolved energy creates a perfect breeding ground for illness.

Healing Energetic Blocks: Releasing these blockages is key to preventing and even reversing some physical and emotional issues. Practices such as Reiki, acupuncture, yoga, and meditation work to release trapped energy, helping the body restore its natural flow and begin the healing process. Reiki and sound helps balance energy centers, while meditation promotes relaxation and nervous system regulation. For many, emotional healing—whether through therapy, breathwork, or simply acknowledging and feeling emotions—can also create profound shifts in physical health.

Hacking Tip: Tune in to your body. Notice areas of tension or discomfort—these are often signals of energetic blockages. Try incorporating energy-releasing practices like breathwork, meditation, or bodywork such as massage or acupuncture. Remember, healing happens when you acknowledge and release what no longer serves you, allowing your body's energy to flow freely, which supports your well-being.

August 17: Don't Overthink

Have you noticed how some incredibly smart and talented people don't always go far in life? Often, it's not a lack of ability but rather an inclination to overthink. When we become entangled in analyzing every detail, we can become paralyzed by indecision and fear of making mistakes. Overthinking activates the brain's "fight or flight" response, creating stress and often leading to inaction. This tendency can hold us back from seizing opportunities and taking action.

The Stoics believed in the power of simplicity and clarity. Instead of getting lost in endless possibilities, focus on what you can control and take decisive steps forward. Simplicity leads to clarity and frees up mental energy, allowing for focused action that enhances both productivity and satisfaction. Trusting your instincts and allowing yourself to move without overanalyzing can lead to growth and new experiences.

Hacking Tip: Next time you find yourself overthinking, take a step back. Ask yourself, "What's the next small action I can take?" Embrace the idea that it's okay to make mistakes along the way. By focusing on making progress over achieving perfection, you'll find that taking action often leads to better outcomes than endless deliberation. Remember, sometimes the best way to move forward is simply to take that first step. With each small step, you build confidence, creating momentum that carries you steadily toward long-term growth.

August 18: Building Emotional Stability

Have you ever noticed how some people seem calm and composed, even in tough situations? That's the power of emotional stability. It's about managing your emotions to respond thoughtfully, rather than react impulsively. Emotional stability improves relationships, enhances decision-making, and reduces stress, helping you lead a more balanced life. The Stoics understood that by staying grounded, you can navigate challenges without losing your cool, turning adversity into an opportunity for growth.

Hacking Tip: Practice mindfulness techniques, like deep breathing or meditation, to help you stay centered. Deep breathing, for instance, activates the parasympathetic nervous system, calming your body and mind. When emotions rise, take a moment to pause and reflect before responding. This simple practice can help you maintain inner peace and respond in a way that aligns with your values. With practice, emotional stability can become a source of strength and peace in your daily life.

August 19: Maintaining Physical Health

Physical health is the foundation for feeling good and living your best life. When you take care of your body, you give yourself the energy and vitality needed to pursue your goals. The Stoics understood that regular exercise, a balanced diet, and enough rest are essential for overall well-being.

Making time for movement—whether it's a workout, a walk, or even dancing—helps keep your body strong and your mind sharp. Pair that with nutritious meals and plenty of sleep, and you'll feel more energized and ready to tackle whatever comes your way.

Biohacking Tip: Start small by incorporating one healthy habit into your daily routine, like going for a 20-minute walk or adding an extra serving of veggies to your meals. Little changes can make a big difference in how you feel and function. By prioritizing your physical health, you're setting yourself up for success in every area of your life!

August 20: Practicing Self-Discipline

Self-discipline is key to reaching your goals. It's all about controlling those impulses and staying focused on what truly matters. The Stoics understood that by practicing self-discipline, you build the resilience needed to overcome challenges and keep moving forward. Self-discipline is more than just achieving tasks; it aligns you with your purpose, allowing you to be fully present in your actions without being distracted by fleeting desires or external pressures. This sense of presence connects you more deeply to each action, bringing a sense of meaning and intentionality to everything you do.

When you harness your self-discipline, you create a strong foundation for success. Whether it's sticking to a workout routine, managing your time better, or resisting distractions, each small act of self-discipline adds up to significant progress. Viewed through a spiritual lens, each step in discipline also becomes a pathway to personal mastery. Discipline is not just a practice but a tool for mastering oneself and one's reactions, empowering you to shape your life in alignment with your highest potential.

Hacking Tip: Start by identifying one area in your life where you want to improve your self-discipline. Set clear, achievable goals and create a plan to stay on track. Celebrate your small victories along the way, and remember that each step you take builds your strength and determination. Embrace self-discipline, and watch how it transforms your journey toward success!

August 21: Creating Your Positive Happy Statement

Creating a positive, happy statement is a great way to uplift your mindset and set a joyful tone for your day. This personal affirmation reflects your values, aspirations, and the happiness you want to cultivate in your life. It serves as a reminder of what truly matters to you, grounding you in positivity and purpose.

Start by thinking about what brings you joy and what qualities make you feel good. Craft a statement that resonates deeply and captures the essence of the life you aspire to live. For example, you might say, "I am worthy of love and happiness, and I embrace each day with gratitude and enthusiasm." This kind of statement not only reinforces your self-worth but also nurtures a positive outlook.

Hacking Tip: Take a moment to write down your positive, happy statement and keep it somewhere you'll see it often—like on your bathroom mirror, in your journal, or as a note on your phone. Repeating your affirmation daily, especially during challenging times, is key to its effectiveness. Consistency matters because repetition strengthens neural pathways, enabling positive beliefs to become default responses. This practice doesn't just provide a quick mood boost; over time, it can reduce stress and enhance emotional stability, helping to cultivate lasting mental well-being. Embrace this practice, and you'll be amazed at how it can shift your mindset and bring more joy into your life!

August 22: Forgive Yourself And The Past

We all have a history of pain and regrets—moments we wish we could change or words we wish we could take back. It's easy to get stuck in the cycle of guilt and self-blame, but holding onto those feelings only weighs us down. The truth is, we are all human, and part of that experience is making mistakes. Self-forgiveness is not about excusing your actions; it's about recognizing your humanity and allowing yourself to move forward. This practice of self-compassion can release self-judgment, shifting the focus from punishment to understanding. As you forgive yourself, you open the door to emotional healing.

Forgiving yourself is an act of self-compassion that can lead to profound healing and growth. Research has shown that self-forgiveness can reduce stress, improve mental health, and enhance resilience, reinforcing that this practice has tangible, long-term benefits for both emotional well-being and personal growth. To help you on this journey, consider making a list of seven things you need to forgive yourself for. This could be anything from missed opportunities to unkind words spoken in frustration.

As you write them down, take a moment to reflect on each one. This process can be emotional or even painful, so don't get discouraged. Once your list is complete, take a deep breath and consciously release the weight of each regret.

Hacking Tip: When you finish, read each item in front of a mirror, saying your name as if speaking to yourself, then forgiving yourself for each item on your list. By letting go of the past and forgiving yourself, you open the door to new possibilities and a brighter future. Embrace the idea that you deserve peace and growth, and allow yourself the freedom to move forward!

August 23: Say Yes To Yourself

How often do we find ourselves putting others' needs ahead of our own? It's easy to prioritize everyone else and forget to check in with ourselves. But today, let's shift that mindset and embrace the power of saying yes to yourself.

Saying yes to yourself means acknowledging and honoring your needs, dreams, and desires. It's about giving yourself permission to pursue what truly makes you happy. When you embrace this practice, you open the door to self-discovery and growth. This shift supports improved mental health, reduces stress, and builds self-esteem over time, creating a foundation for lasting well-being. It allows you to honor your passions, whether that means starting a new hobby, taking time for self-care, or simply allowing yourself to rest when you need it.

This doesn't mean you have to be selfish or neglect the needs of others. Instead, it's about creating a healthy balance where you also prioritize your own well-being. Setting healthy boundaries is an essential part of saying yes to yourself; it often involves saying no to obligations or relationships that drain your energy. When you say yes to yourself, you cultivate a sense of empowerment that not only benefits you but also positively impacts those around you. When you're happier and more fulfilled, you can show up better for others in your life.

Hacking Tip: Start small by incorporating one thing each day that feels like a yes to you. It could be treating yourself to your favorite coffee, saying no to an obligation that drains you, or dedicating time to a passion project. Celebrate these small wins as you learn to embrace the importance of saying yes to yourself. By consistently prioritizing what brings you joy, you'll strengthen your confidence and sense of self, building resilience for the challenges that lie ahead.

August 24: Goals And Mission Statements

Having clear and attainable goals can provide you with focus, motivation, and a sense of direction in your life. Goals act as a roadmap, helping you see new opportunities and guiding you toward your aspirations. Goals that connect to your core values are especially powerful, as they resonate with what truly matters to you, making the journey more meaningful and fulfilling.

Ensure that your goals are realistic and attainable. For instance, instead of vaguely saying, "I want to be in great shape," try, "I will exercise for 30 minutes a day, five days a week." This level of clarity makes tracking your progress much easier, and each small achievement releases dopamine, boosting your mood and confidence. These small wins contribute to emotional resilience and satisfaction, showing that goal-setting is more than just a productivity tool—it's a path to enhanced well-being. Next, break down your big goals into smaller, manageable steps. If your goal is to run a marathon, start by gradually increasing your running distance each week. Celebrate these small victories to keep your momentum and dedication going strong!

Hacking Tip: Use the SMART criteria—set goals that are Specific, Measurable, Achievable, Relevant, and Time-bound. Write them down and revisit them regularly to track your progress. Reflecting on your goals and adjusting them as needed helps keep them aligned with your values and evolving aspirations.

Mauro dos Santos

August 25: Embracing Change With Flexibility

Change is a part of life, and how we handle it can make all the difference. Embracing change with flexibility is key to adapting and thriving—even when life throws you a curveball. Instead of resisting, let's roll with it like a rubber band instead of being as stiff as a board!

When you suddenly face a change, like losing a job, it might feel overwhelming. But guess what? It could be your chance to explore a new career or dive into that passion project you've been putting off. Flexibility opens up new possibilities—like discovering that your favorite restaurant now serves breakfast all day. Yes, please!

Letting go of control can be tough, but accepting that change is part of the ride makes it easier. The best plans often come with a side of spontaneity, like finding a hidden gem of a coffee shop when you least expect it!

Hacking Tip: Step out of your comfort zone by trying something new—whether it's picking up a quirky hobby or chatting with that coworker you've never spoken to. Embrace the unexpected; you might just discover something amazing!

So let's embrace change with a smile and maybe a laugh, because life is too short to take too seriously!

August 26: Enhancing Focus Through Minimalism

Embracing minimalism can work wonders for your focus. By simplifying your environment, you eliminate distractions that often pull your attention away from what really matters. When your space is decluttered, it's much easier to concentrate on your tasks and reach your goals efficiently. Minimalism doesn't just provide a quick fix; over time, it supports cognitive efficiency, reduces mental fatigue, and strengthens your ability to focus.

Minimalism is also about promoting mental clarity. A tidy environment helps clear your mind, reducing stress and creating a sense of calm. When you're not overwhelmed by too much stuff, noise, or choices, you avoid decision fatigue, making it easier to focus and think more clearly. And minimalism isn't limited to physical space—digital minimalism, such as organizing files and reducing notifications, plays a significant role in reducing daily mental clutter.

Hacking Tip: Start small by decluttering one area of your space—whether it's your desk, a room, or even your digital devices. Notice how removing distractions improves your concentration and helps you feel more at ease. By adopting a minimalist approach, you can boost your focus, improve decision-making, and create a more productive environment that supports long-term clarity and well-being.

August 27: Building Resilience Through Adversity

Adversity can feel like that uninvited guest who crashes your party, but guess what? It often brings some unexpected benefits! Facing challenges head-on actually strengthens your character and builds resilience. Think of it as a workout for your soul—each tough experience helps you flex your inner strength, preparing you for whatever life throws your way next.

When you encounter difficulties, it's easy to feel overwhelmed. But remember, every challenge is an opportunity to grow. By tackling obstacles directly, you gain valuable insights that equip you to handle future hurdles. It's like collecting tools for your emotional toolbox—each challenge adds something useful for the next time you need to solve a problem.

So, the next time life throws you a curveball, don't back down. Embrace it! You'll come out stronger and more resilient, ready to take on whatever comes next.

Hacking Tip: Shift your mindset to see challenges as opportunities for growth. Over time, you'll be amazed at how resilient you've become! Building resilience through adversity isn't just about surviving; it's about thriving in the face of challenges. So gear up, tackle those obstacles, and watch yourself grow!

August 28: Developing Strategic Thinking

Strategic thinking is like having a GPS for your life; it helps you chart a course and avoid getting lost in the weeds. It involves planning and foresight, enabling you to make informed decisions that align with your long-term goals. Practicing this skill can enhance neuroplasticity by strengthening the neural pathways associated with complex problem-solving, making it easier to approach future challenges. When you develop this skill, you boost your ability to navigate complex situations, making it easier to see the big picture. Imagine you're playing a game of chess. Each move you make isn't just about the immediate situation; it's about anticipating your opponent's responses and planning several steps ahead. Strategic thinking works the same way in life, encouraging a balanced perspective that considers long-term goals and potential outcomes.

One of the key components of strategic thinking is the ability to analyze information critically. Think of it as being a detective in your own life, piecing together clues to make the best possible choice. This means gathering data, weighing your options, and considering the potential consequences of your decisions. This approach reduces emotional reactivity, as being well-prepared fosters a calm, grounded response to unexpected situations. Moreover, developing this mindset can boost your confidence. When you have a clear strategy, you feel more empowered to tackle challenges, knowing that you've thought things through. This proactive approach reduces the likelihood of being caught off guard, allowing you to respond to unexpected situations with poise and clarity

Hacking Tip: Start by setting aside time to reflect on your long-term goals. Don't be afraid to seek input from others, as collaboration can provide new perspectives and enhance your strategic thinking. By honing your strategic thinking skills, you'll not only make more informed decisions but also build a stronger foundation for achieving your aspirations.

August 29: The Power Of Routine

Establishing a consistent daily routine is one of the best ways to boost your discipline and well-being. Routines act like a roadmap, helping you avoid decision fatigue. Let's be real—who has the energy to decide what to do next when there's a cozy couch waiting?

When your day is planned out, you free up mental space for what really matters. Routines are your personal productivity cheat code! Whether it's a morning workout, a quick meditation, or dedicated work time, these habits create a rhythm that keeps chaos at bay.

Plus, having a routine reduces stress. Knowing what to expect gives you a sense of control, making you less likely to feel overwhelmed when life throws a curveball. It's like having a safety net made of good habits!

Hacking Tip: Identify key habits that align with your goals, and stick to a consistent schedule for waking up, working, and winding down. And remember, it's okay to adjust your routine—flexibility can keep things interesting!

By embracing a daily routine, you'll boost your productivity and set the stage for a happier, healthier life. So, wave goodbye to decision fatigue and say hello to the delightful predictability of your new routine!

August 30: Mindful Consumption

In today's fast-paced world, it's easy to get swept up in the endless choices we face every day. But have you ever stopped to think about how what you consume—whether it's food, information, or media—affects your well-being? Being intentional about consumption is crucial, as mindful choices lead to better health, clearer thinking, and a more balanced life. Over time, this practice supports sustained mental clarity, reduced fatigue, and improved decision-making.

Let's start with food. In a culture obsessed with convenience and quick fixes, we often prioritize speed over nutrition. Mindful eating encourages us to slow down, savor our meals, and truly consider what we're putting into our bodies. This goes beyond just choosing salads over fries (though that's a great start). It's about understanding how different foods make us feel. When we eat mindfully, we tune in with our bodies, allowing us to make choices that support our health and energy levels. Additionally, eating mindfully can recalibrate the brain's dopamine response, reducing the urge for quick-fix cravings in favor of healthier, fulfilling options.

Now, let's talk about the information we consume. With social media and constant news updates, it's all too easy to mindlessly scroll through feeds filled with negativity and sensationalism. Being intentional about the information you consume means curating your sources, seeking out uplifting and informative content, and critically evaluating what you read and share. This practice fosters clearer thinking, reduces mental fatigue, and helps you develop a more informed perspective on the world by minimizing overstimulation of the brain's fear center, which can trigger anxiety.

And then there's media consumption. Whether you're binge-watching the latest series or diving into a captivating novel, the media you choose can shape your thoughts and emotions. Mindful consumption here means selecting content that resonates with your values and enhances your life, rather than consuming mindlessly for distraction. Sharing your mindful consumption goals with friends or family can also create accountability, providing a supportive environment that strengthens your commitment to intentional choices.

Hacking Tip: Take some time to reflect on your eating habits, the information you read, and the media you watch. Ask yourself: Does this nourish my body and mind? Does it contribute to my well-being? Adjust your choices as needed, and embrace the positive impact of mindful decisions. By tuning into the long-term benefits of intentional consumption, you're investing in resilience, mental clarity, and emotional health.

So, let's commit to making choices that not only satisfy our immediate cravings but also nurture our long-term well-being!

August 31: Developing Healthy Boundaries

Setting healthy boundaries is crucial for protecting your time and energy, helping you maintain balance in both your personal and professional life. Think of it like putting a fence around your garden—boundaries keep out the weeds, allowing your beautiful flowers to thrive. When you establish clear limits, you not only safeguard your well-being but also foster mutual respect in your relationships. Boundaries are a form of self-empowerment, strengthening your confidence and showing yourself and others that your needs are valid and worth protecting.

Healthy boundaries help you communicate your needs and expectations, leading to less confusion and misunderstandings. This clarity reduces stress, creates emotional resilience, and fosters an environment where others know how to engage with you respectfully. This mutual respect strengthens trust and emotional security in relationships. From a quantum science perspective, boundaries manage the healthy flow of energy around you. When you set limits, you're defining where your energy stops and another person's begins. This intentional separation helps prevent energy depletion and burnout, allowing you to focus on what truly matters while managing your energetic space.

Moreover, maintaining healthy boundaries positively impacts your mental health. Research shows that those who set and enforce their boundaries experience lower levels of anxiety and stress. Protecting your time and energy creates space for self-care and personal growth, helping you flourish.

Hacking Tip: Identify areas in your life where you need clearer boundaries. Communicate your needs calmly and assertively, and don't hesitate to reinforce those boundaries when necessary. Remember, setting boundaries creates a safe space for you to flourish. By developing healthy boundaries, you enhance your well-being, foster respect, and reduce stress.

September

Introduction:

September brings a focus on health, balance, and harmony, guided by the grounded energy of Virgo and the social, relationship-driven energy of Libra. This is a month to fine-tune your physical health routines, bring more balance into your life, and create harmony in your relationships.

Virgo's earth energy asks you to focus on your physical well-being. It's not about working harder, but about working smarter. This is the time to refine your fitness routine, pay attention to your nutrition, and explore biohacks that help you maintain a balanced, healthy lifestyle. Whether it's through optimizing your sleep, staying consistent with exercise, or finding ways to boost your energy, September is about creating a health routine that supports you for the long term.

On the other side, Libra's air energy encourages you to find balance in your emotional and social life. This is a month to practice emotional awareness, mental clarity, and communication skills. Balance in your emotions leads to better decision-making and more harmonious relationships. Focus on building stronger connections, resolving conflicts with kindness, and creating environments where both you and your loved ones can thrive.

September is about finding that sweet spot between physical health and emotional well-being, between action and rest, and between personal and social life.

September 1: Physical Health Through Structured Routines

Habit and consistency are the keys to lasting physical health. By building structured routines around exercise and balanced nutrition, you create a foundation for long-term vitality. However, fitness isn't a magic pill. Developing the best version of your body requires consistent effort, and through that consistency, fitness becomes a habit—part of your regular routine that you stick to, even on days when motivation is low.

When you commit to a structured health routine, you're not just improving your physical fitness—you're also boosting your mental well-being. Exercise releases endorphins, improves cardiovascular health, and reduces stress.

But structure doesn't mean rigidity. Flexibility within your routine allows you to adapt to changes without falling off track. Incorporating variety, like switching up workout styles or trying new healthy recipes, keeps things fresh and engaging.

Hacking Tip: Instead of focusing on fitness and healthy habits just to lose weight, think of it as creating a new lifestyle. When fitness becomes part of who you are, being fit, healthy, and looking great become natural consequences of the person you've become.

September 2: The Importance Of Rest And Recovery

Your rest is just as crucial as activity when it comes to maintaining optimal health. Prioritizing sleep and recovery allows your body and mind to heal and recharge, sustaining your energy and resilience. When you do, you enhance your performance across all areas of life. Consistency in rest also aligns with your body's circadian rhythms, which are essential for balanced hormone production, immune health, and emotional stability.

It's easy to get caught up in the hustle, but neglecting rest leads to burnout. Quality sleep and intentional downtime are where the magic happens—your muscles repair, your brain processes memories, and your energy is restored. Rest also supports neuroplasticity, allowing your brain to consolidate new information and form new neural connections that enhance learning and problem-solving skills.

Intentional rest doesn't always mean complete inactivity. Active recovery techniques, such as gentle stretching, mindful walking, or yoga, stimulate blood flow, support muscle recovery, and maintain flexibility, reducing tension without adding stress to the body. This type of recovery not only refreshes the mind and body but also reinforces a healthy relationship with physical activity and rest.

Hacking Tip: Aim for a solid night of sleep or schedule a break during the day. Remember, you perform at your best when rested and recharged.

By committing to quality rest and recovery, you're investing in your long-term well-being, mental clarity, and resilience, allowing you to thrive in all areas of life.

Mauro dos Santos

September 3: Hack Your Longevity And Exceptional Health with Resveratrol

Resveratrol, a powerful antioxidant found in the skin of red grapes, berries, and peanuts, has gained attention for its potential to promote longevity and exceptional health. This compound supports cellular health by protecting your cells from damage caused by oxidative stress and inflammation. Research also suggests that resveratrol activates certain genes linked to longevity, including those involved in the body's natural repair processes, like the sirtuins family. By activating these pathways, resveratrol may mimic some benefits of caloric restriction, a proven method for extending lifespan in animal studies.

By incorporating resveratrol into your diet, through foods or supplements, you can boost heart health, enhance brain function, and support metabolism. Resveratrol has also shown promise in supporting mitochondrial health by promoting mitochondrial biogenesis, helping sustain physical energy and cellular resilience over time.

For even greater benefits, consider pairing resveratrol with synergistic compounds such as quercetin or pterostilbene. These combinations amplify antioxidant and anti-inflammatory effects, offering a more potent biohack for cellular health and longevity.

Hacking Tip: Add resveratrol-rich foods to your daily diet, like red grapes, dark chocolate, and berries. If you prefer supplements, look for high-quality resveratrol to maximize its health benefits. Optimal dosing may vary by individual, so consistent intake and, for some, experimenting with the right amount may yield the best results. This simple addition may be the biohack that supports graceful aging and exceptional health.

September 4: Biohacking for Balance In All Aspects Of Life

Creating balance is essential for a harmonious life and exceptional health. When your body, mind, and emotions are aligned, everything flows more easily. Biohacking practices support this alignment by optimizing essential areas of health in a way that promotes sustainable, long-term balance.

Sleep Optimization: The quality of your sleep is the foundation of your physical and mental health. Biohacking sleep means adjusting your habits to maximize deep, restorative rest. For example, minimizing blue light at night, keeping a regular sleep schedule, and optimizing your environment for better rest can enhance cognitive function and emotional stability. Aligning your sleep habits with circadian rhythms also reinforces natural cycles that regulate energy, hormone levels, and metabolism.

Diet Adjustments: What you fuel your body with impacts everything from energy and mood to cognitive function. Biohacking your diet might involve reducing processed foods and focusing on nutrient-dense options. Hydration is another key aspect here; even mild dehydration can affect mood, mental clarity, and overall physical performance. You can also experiment with intermittent fasting to stabilize energy levels and improve mental clarity, as fasting supports metabolic health and encourages cellular repair processes that reinforce cognitive resilience.

Stress Management: Stress disrupts balance. By incorporating stress-reducing strategies like mindfulness or relaxation techniques, you help your nervous system return to a state of calm and clarity. This also supports neuroplasticity, allowing your brain to maintain flexibility and emotional resilience. Adaptogens like ashwagandha can further support your body in managing stress by modulating cortisol levels and promoting balance in the hypothalamic-pituitary-adrenal (HPA) axis, which is crucial for long-term stress resilience.

Mauro dos Santos

Biohacking Tip: Start by choosing one area—sleep, diet, or stress—and apply a biohacking technique consistently. Watch how this simple change can shift your overall balance and well-being. Once you've mastered one area, move on to the next. Integrating these practices gradually allows you to align your habits with your body's natural rhythms, building a sustainable, balanced lifestyle that supports cognitive and physical performance.

September 5: Give Yourself A Foot Massage

Let's be honest—our feet do so much for us, and we rarely give them the attention they deserve. A good foot massage isn't just about instant relief; it's a small act of self-care that can have a surprising impact on your overall well-being.

For starters, foot massages improve circulation. If you've ever had cold feet or noticed some swelling after a long day, this simple routine promotes blood flow, bringing warmth and reducing that uncomfortable puffiness. **Stimulating circulation in the feet also activates the vagus nerve, which helps shift the body into a more relaxed, parasympathetic state**. Plus, it feels fantastic.

It's also a great way to reduce stress. **When you massage your feet, you trigger the release of endorphins**—those feel-good chemicals that calm your nervous system and help you relax. Physical touch, like a foot massage, also engages neuroplasticity, helping the brain reinforce relaxation pathways and creating a lasting resilience to stress over time.

Then there's pain relief. If you've ever dealt with foot pain—whether from plantar fasciitis or just general tension—a foot massage can work wonders. According to the gate control theory of pain, stimulating the nerves in your feet helps "close the gate" on pain signals, making massage an effective, non-invasive way to manage discomfort.

And let's talk about sleep. If you're someone who struggles to unwind at night, a foot massage makes an excellent bedtime ritual. It promotes relaxation, which naturally leads to better sleep. By calming the body and mind, foot massage activates the parasympathetic nervous system, creating a foundation for deeper, more restful sleep. Less stress, more balance, and a little foot rub might be all you need to drift off peacefully.

What's even more fascinating is how a foot massage can boost your overall well-being. Through reflexology, you can stimulate pressure points on your feet that correspond to different organs in your body, helping improve functions like digestion and immune response. Applying gentle pressure to specific acupressure points on the arch and heel is also believed to support detoxification pathways, stimulating the liver, kidneys, and lymphatic system, which can help eliminate toxins from the body.

Foot massages can even help relieve headaches by stimulating pressure points that release tension throughout your body. By pressing and massaging these points, you can ease stress and enhance overall balance, supporting both physical and mental clarity.

Biohacking Tip: I've already talked about how giving massages to my clients can release stored trauma and emotions, and the same principle applies here. When you give yourself a foot massage, you might notice more than just physical relief—it could unlock emotional blocks or even release limiting beliefs you didn't know you were holding onto. Regular foot massages reinforce neuroplastic pathways associated with relaxation, gradually helping you respond to stress with calm and clarity. So next time you take a few minutes for a foot massage, remember, you're not just soothing sore feet—you could be opening the door to deeper healing.

September 6: Emotional Balance Through Fitness

Exercise does more than just build muscles or improve endurance—it's a powerful tool for your emotional well-being as well. When you engage in physical activity, your brain releases endorphins, often referred to as the "feel-good" chemicals. These endorphins elevate your mood and create a sense of calm, helping you navigate emotional ups and downs with greater ease. Regular exercise also promotes neuroplasticity, allowing the brain to develop new neural pathways that enhance emotional resilience over time.

Also, by incorporating regular exercise into your routine, you actively reduce stress and tension, bringing a sense of balance back to your emotions. Consistency in exercise is essential for reinforcing this balance, as it stabilizes cortisol levels and enhances the brain's capacity for emotional stability.

Moreover, fitness has a meditative quality. Whether it's through rhythmic movements in running, the focus required in yoga, or the precision needed in weightlifting, exercise helps you stay present. This mindful aspect of fitness fosters clarity and grounding, allowing you to better manage negative emotions, reduce anxiety, and maintain emotional stability. Fitness activities done with others also promote social connection, creating a sense of community that further supports emotional well-being.

Hacking Tip: When you make exercise a regular part of your routine, you'll find it not only strengthens your body but also acts as a natural way to balance your emotions. By tapping into the emotional benefits of exercise, you create a reliable outlet for stress and a steady source of mood-boosting energy, helping you maintain emotional equilibrium in your daily life.

September 7: Enhancing Organizational Skills

Being organized is like giving yourself a roadmap for the day— it reduces stress, boosts efficiency, and helps you feel more in control. When you have your tasks planned out and structured, you're not just winging it; you're creating a sense of order that makes even the busiest days feel more manageable. Knowing what needs to be done and when makes it easier to stay calm and focused, freeing up mental space for creativity and decision-making as you're not weighed down by mental clutter.

Let's be honest—when you know what needs to be done and when, it's a lot easier to stay calm and focused. Organization helps you prioritize, so you're not juggling a million things at once. Instead of rushing to put out fires, you can move through your day with a clear plan, making steady progress on both the little tasks and the big goals. Organized systems provide a sense of predictability and resilience, helping you feel prepared for unexpected challenges rather than overwhelmed by them. And no, being organized isn't just about neat desks or pretty planners (though they do help!). It's about creating systems that make your life easier. Whether it's keeping a to-do list, using apps, or setting up a simple schedule, getting organized helps you manage your time and energy better. Over time, consistency in these habits reduces cognitive load and makes organization feel effortless, leading to greater long-term productivity and emotional resilience.

Hacking Tip: Start by organizing just one area of your life, like your workspace or daily routine. Break tasks into smaller steps and set clear deadlines. You'll feel less overwhelmed and more in control, making it easier to keep moving forward. Consistent organization also strengthens routines, creating a foundation for success by reinforcing neural pathways that support these habits over time.

When you get organized, you're creating a foundation for success. You'll stress less and get more done, which makes everything just a little smoother and a lot more productive.

September 8: Achieving Balance Between Work
And Health

Let's be honest with ourselves—finding balance between work and health sometimes feels like juggling flaming torches while riding a unicycle. But here's the thing: *You* can absolutely master that balance, and it doesn't have to be as impossible as it sounds. Sure, your work is important, but *You* know what's even more important? YOU. Prioritizing time for your health doesn't mean sacrificing productivity—it means enhancing it. When you carve out time for exercise, nourish your body with proper nutrition, and actually (dare we say) relax, you're setting yourself up for long-term success both at work and in life.

Imagine this: *You* start your day with a quick workout that fires you up, fuel up with something other than coffee and a donut, and actually take a few minutes to breathe in between meetings. What happens? You stay energized, focused, and less likely to melt down when the Wi-Fi drops during that important Zoom call.

Hacking Tip: You don't need to overhaul your life overnight. Maybe just a 10-minute walk after lunch or adding some greens to that takeout order.

Remember, *You* are the key to your own success. So why not invest in yourself by balancing work with health? When you feel good, *You* do good—and who doesn't want to be the superhero of both productivity and well-being?

September 9: Nurturing Emotional Well-Being

Taking care of your emotional well-being is just as important as looking after your physical health. In fact, it's the foundation of a balanced life. When you prioritize your emotional health, you're not just avoiding stress or sadness—you're creating a deeper sense of harmony within yourself.

It starts with acknowledging your emotions rather than brushing them aside. We all experience a range of emotions—some comfortable, others less so—but recognizing them is the first step to managing them. It's natural to feel frustrated, overwhelmed, or even a bit lost at times. What matters is how you handle these feelings. Are you bottling them up, or are you processing them in a healthy way? By processing emotions, you prevent "emotional buildup," which helps reduce both mental and physical tension over time, supporting cardiovascular health, immunity, and mental clarity.

Learning to manage your emotions creates a ripple effect throughout your life. You'll find yourself interacting with others more smoothly, with less conflict and more understanding. When you're emotionally balanced, you're better equipped to listen, empathize, and connect with those around you. This practice of emotional regulation supports neuroplasticity, building neural pathways that strengthen emotional resilience and adaptability, making it easier over time to respond calmly to stressors.

Hacking Tip: Set aside some time each day to check in with yourself. Whether through journaling, meditation, or simply sitting quietly with your thoughts, this habit helps you stay in tune with your feelings and allows you to handle emotions as they arise.

Prioritizing your emotional well-being isn't selfish; it's essential. When you nurture your emotional health, you're not just helping yourself—you're creating a healthier, more balanced life for you and everyone around you.

September 10: EFT for Mental, Emotional, And Physical Health

The first time I was introduced to EFT (Emotional Freedom Techniques), I'll admit—I thought it seemed a bit... quirky. I mean, tapping on different parts of your body to address emotional and physical issues? It felt more like something cozy or calming, but I wasn't sure how it could actually work.

But then, something shifted. After giving EFT a real chance and trying it out, I noticed changes—not just mentally, but emotionally and physically too. The process of tapping certain points on your body, combined with focused thoughts or affirmations, started to have a real impact. It wasn't just a distraction or a way to calm down temporarily; it felt like I was unlocking deeper layers of stress and tension I hadn't even realized were there. This deeper release may be linked to EFT's effects on the nervous system, as tapping activates the parasympathetic response, reducing cortisol and helping to lower overall stress levels.

EFT works by tapping on specific points, mostly on the head and chest, which are linked to your body's energy meridians (think acupuncture without the needles). As you tap, you're acknowledging and addressing emotions that may be blocked, whether it's anxiety, fear, or even physical discomfort. The act of acknowledging those feelings while tapping seems to calm the nervous system and help clear out the emotional clutter, and, over time, this repetitive process strengthens positive neural pathways, enhancing neuroplasticity and making it easier to respond calmly to stress.

And honestly, it's not just mental or emotional well-being that benefits—it can help with physical health too. Tension headaches, muscle stiffness, even sleep quality can improve when you incorporate EFT into your routine. The connection between mind and body is strong, and tapping helps to bridge that gap in a very practical, easy-to-apply way. By prompting you to identify and name emotions, EFT fosters self-awareness and self-acceptance, reducing the buildup of unprocessed emotions and promoting a healthy mind-body balance.

Tip: If you're new to EFT, start with something simple. Take a few minutes each day to tap through the basic points while focusing on an issue—big or small. Whether you're tackling anxiety before a big meeting or trying to relax after a long day, EFT can be a powerful tool for restoring balance to your mental, emotional, and physical health. Consistent use over time can help train your brain and body to respond more peacefully to daily stress.

Sometimes, the simplest methods can make the biggest difference, and EFT is one of those practices that's worth exploring.

September 11: Embracing Practical Wisdom

Practical wisdom is about making thoughtful choices in everyday life by focusing on what you can control. It's not about having all the answers but staying clear-headed and calm when facing challenges. Instead of stressing over things out of your hands, practical wisdom encourages you to focus on what's within your reach, which brings a sense of peace.

Practical wisdom involves cutting through emotional noise to see things clearly and make decisions that align with your values and goals. Whether it's in your career, relationships, or personal life, practical wisdom guides you toward smarter, more purposeful decisions. Neuroscientifically, this focus on the controllable activates the prefrontal cortex, which aids in emotional regulation and reduces stress by minimizing the brain's "fight-or-flight" response.

Self-reflection plays a significant role in cultivating practical wisdom. By regularly evaluating past decisions and outcomes, you build your capacity for clear thinking and emotional resilience, helping you apply these learned insights to future situations. This practice ultimately strengthens your ability to respond thoughtfully rather than react impulsively, enabling you to navigate challenges with a sense of balance and control.

Hacking Tip: Next time you face a challenge, stop and ask yourself, "What can I actually control?" Focus your energy there, and let the rest go. Over time, this mindset will help reduce stress and give you more confidence in dealing with life's ups and downs.

September 12: Practicing Mindful Decision-Making

In today's fast-paced world, it's easy to make snap decisions, but taking the time to pause and reflect can make all the difference. Mindful decision-making is about aligning your choices with core values and long-term goals so that today's actions create meaningful outcomes tomorrow.

Before jumping into any decision, ask yourself: "Does this choice reflect who I am and where I want to go?" By taking a moment to evaluate, you're not just avoiding impulsive actions—you're creating a life that feels more purposeful and fulfilling. Pausing to reflect also engages the prefrontal cortex, the part of the brain responsible for planning and rational thinking, while calming the amygdala, which handles emotional responses. This balance allows for clearer, more intentional choices, reducing the likelihood of reactive decisions that may lead to regret.

Hacking Tip: Next time you face a decision, slow down. Think about how this choice impacts your bigger picture. The more intentional you are, the more satisfied you'll be with the results. By making thoughtful decisions, you build emotional resilience and reduce feelings of regret, ultimately enhancing satisfaction and peace of mind.

September 13: Set Yourself Free

Our bodies are living archives, holding onto memories and emotions from past experiences—some we remember, and some that have long been buried. These physical memories often influence our feelings, behaviors, and how we perceive the world around us. Without realizing it, we carry the weight of these unresolved traumas, shaping how we interact with others and even how we view ourselves.

When you begin the process of healing your body, you are not just improving your physical well-being—you are opening the door to a deeper, more transformative healing. The body and mind are deeply interconnected, so by releasing tension, pain, and old wounds held within the body, you also start to release the emotional and psychological blocks that have been holding you back. You may find yourself letting go of traumas and suppressed emotions you didn't even know you were carrying. This shift is supported by neuroplasticity, as these healing practices help create new neural pathways that strengthen emotional resilience and support long-term balance.

This is the essence of holistic healing: when you heal your body, you heal your mind, and in turn, your spirit begins to flourish. By freeing yourself from the physical manifestations of past traumas, you allow your true, authentic self to emerge—lighter, more aligned, and ready to experience life in its fullest form. Engaging in regular holistic practices builds emotional resilience over time, creating a lasting "buffer" against future stressors and promoting sustained inner peace.

Hacking Tip: Start by incorporating practices like breathwork, yoga, or even massage to release stored tension in the body. These gentle forms of healing not only improve your physical health but also facilitate emotional and spiritual release, setting you on a path toward true freedom and transformation.

September 14: Tak Less About Yourself

In social encounters, it's common to feel tempted to start talking about our accomplishments, skills, and who we are. Very often, this reflects a need for admiration, recognition, or even low self-esteem and a need for validation. Not too long ago, I was involved in an investment business and found myself constantly talking about money—and let's be honest, no one enjoys hearing about a "Scrooge McDuck" swimming in cash. People don't want to listen to someone who seems to be showing off as a superhero, either. Interestingly, if you meet a billionaire or a world-class achiever, you'll notice they usually focus more on asking about *you* than on talking about themselves.

Here's the thing: when we take a step back and focus on others instead of ourselves, something powerful happens. Listening builds trust and connection, allowing others to feel seen and valued. This process can even lead to the release of oxytocin, the "bonding hormone," reinforcing that sense of connection and mutual respect. And there's another bonus: by giving others the spotlight, you're building an authentic rapport and showing humility—a quality people truly appreciate and admire.

Hacking Tip: Next time you meet someone, be willing to listen and get to know them. Look for clues about their passions and engage in their world. You'll notice people start to like you—even without knowing much about you. Empathy plays a big role here; try to understand their feelings and perspectives, not just their words. If you have a significant accomplishment, let others bring it up naturally—never talk highly about yourself. Listening, paired with empathy, sets the stage for real connections and lasting respect.

September 15: The Power Of Sharing

When we talk about sharing, it's more than just giving something away—it's an exchange of energy that deeply affects both the brain and the heart. From a neuroscience standpoint, sharing activates oxytocin, the "bonding" chemical that builds trust and connection. Every time you share, your brain releases oxytocin, reinforcing your bond with others. The ventral striatum, the part of the brain that controls feelings of reward, also lights up, making sharing feel fulfilling and joyful.

But it goes deeper than that. When you share, you activate your mirror neurons—the ones responsible for empathy and compassion. These neurons allow you to feel the joy of others, making giving just as rewarding as receiving. In fact, your brain is literally rewiring itself for more cooperation and emotional intelligence.

From a spiritual perspective, sharing is a reminder that we are all connected. It's not just about the act itself—it's about dissolving the ego and aligning with the flow of abundance in the universe. Sharing taps into unity consciousness, where you realize that someone else's well-being is directly tied to your own. Whether you're giving your time, knowledge, or resources, each act aligns your energy with a higher purpose.

The more we share, the more we reinforce the brain's natural capacity for joy and empathy, while also creating harmony in our energy field. When we align our hearts and minds through sharing, we're not just transforming ourselves—we're contributing to the collective consciousness, shaping a better world for everyone.

Hacking Tip: So, when you share, you're literally rewiring your brain for connection and rewiring your life for growth and contribution. It's a powerful act that bridges the mind and spirit, helping you step into your highest potential.

Mauro dos Santos

September 16: Spill Out Sugar

Let's be honest, sugar is like that charming friend who's fun to hang out with at first but leaves you feeling drained and full of regret afterward. Sure, it tastes sweet in the moment, but sugar's effects on your body and mind are anything but. It's time to spill it out for good.

When you eat sugar, it's like setting off a firework show in your blood sugar levels—big, bright, and fast—but then comes the crash. That short-lived energy boost? Gone. And what's left? Sluggishness, irritability, and a craving for more sugar, creating a vicious cycle. Here's where it gets interesting: sugar consumption triggers a dopamine release in the brain's reward center, which gives a temporary "high" and reinforces cravings. Over time, this dopamine effect makes it harder to break the habit. Your mood tanks, and forget about focus or energy. Spoiler alert: it's not pretty. But here's where it gets even trickier; sugar isn't just messing with your waistline. It's messing with your brain. Too much sugar can fog up your memory, leave you feeling anxious, and even lead to long-term cognitive decline. This is partly due to neuroinflammation, which sugar can exacerbate, affecting areas of the brain involved in mood regulation and memory. Stable blood sugar is crucial for mental clarity and emotional stability; when you keep it balanced, you're far less likely to experience mood swings, brain fog, and those dreaded energy crashes. Eating too much sugar is like putting junk fuel in a high-performance car—eventually, things start breaking down.

Biohacking Tip: Replace that sugary snack with something that actually fuels you—think fresh fruit, nuts, or even some good ol' veggies. No need to quit cold turkey (unless you're feeling bold!), but being aware of what you're putting in your body can lead to real change. Cutting out sugar isn't just about saying goodbye to that donut. It's about reclaiming your energy, mental clarity, and long-term health. So, next time you're eyeing that candy bar, remember: sugar may be sweet, but ditching it? That's sweeter.

September 17: Strengthening Problem-Solving Skills

Effective problem-solving is all about balance—using both logic and creativity to tackle challenges. It's not just about finding quick fixes but approaching issues with a clear, calm mind. When you take the time to analyze a situation from different angles, you open the door to solutions that are both practical and innovative.

Instead of letting stress cloud your judgment, try stepping back and breaking the problem down into smaller parts. Sometimes, the best way to solve a tough situation is to simplify it, focus on what's controllable, and let your creativity do the rest. This mental flexibility—the ability to shift seamlessly between logical and creative thinking—is essential for adaptive problem-solving, as it helps you adjust your approach when faced with new or unexpected information.

From a neuroscientific perspective, engaging both logic and creativity in problem-solving promotes neuroplasticity, the brain's ability to form new neural connections. This process strengthens pathways for analytical and innovative thinking, making it easier to approach future challenges with adaptability and resilience.

Perspective-taking—considering problems from multiple angles—also adds value by enabling you to break free from fixed assumptions. By looking at an issue from different viewpoints, you may discover insights that transform how you understand the problem itself, often leading to more comprehensive solutions.

Tip: Next time you face a challenge, slow down. Consider the problem logically, but don't forget to tap into your creative side for out-of-the-box solutions. The combination of both can lead to breakthroughs you didn't expect!

Mauro dos Santos

September 18: Use Your Other Hand

When you start using your non-dominant hand, it's more than just shaking up your routine—you're actually rewiring your brain and changing how you interact with the world around you. Let's take a look at what's really going on when you make this simple switch.

1. **Activating Neuroplasticity**: Your brain is an incredibly adaptable organ. By using your non-dominant hand, you step out of your comfort zone and force your brain to fire in new ways, triggering neuroplasticity—your brain's ability to form new pathways. The more you do this, the stronger those connections become, keeping your brain sharp and flexible.

2. **Harmonizing the Hemispheres**: Typically, your dominant hand is controlled by the opposite hemisphere of your brain. When you engage your non-dominant hand, you activate the other hemisphere, which is often linked to creativity, intuition, and spatial awareness. This practice creates better communication between both sides of your brain, bringing balance to your overall cognitive functioning— much like what happens in deep meditation or flow states.

3. **Boosting Creativity**: Switching hands takes you out of autopilot, forcing your brain to explore new ways of doing things. This unfamiliar experience opens the door to creative thinking and problem-solving. Breaking free from your usual habits allows fresh ideas and solutions to flow more easily, helping you tap into a deeper well of creativity.

4. **Heightening Mental Focus**: Using your dominant hand often requires little thought, but switching to your non-dominant hand demands focus. It's like learning a new skill, which forces your brain to concentrate. This mental exercise doesn't just improve dexterity—it builds your ability to focus and be present, strengthening your attention span over time.

5. **Protecting Cognitive Health**: Challenging your brain by using your non-dominant hand is like giving it a workout.

This type of mental exercise helps keep your brain adaptable and responsive, which neuroscientists agree is essential for cognitive longevity. By keeping your neural pathways flexible, you may even reduce the risk of age-related mental decline.

6. **Emotional Balance and Resilience**: The brain's hemispheres are also linked to different emotional processes. By stimulating the non-dominant hemisphere, you tap into emotional regulation, helping you build resilience. This practice allows you to respond to situations calmly, rather than reacting impulsively, fostering emotional balance.

Biohacking Tip: nStart your morning by brushing your teeth with your non-dominant hand. It's a small change, but it taps into all the benefits mentioned above.

When you challenge yourself by using your opposite hand, you're not just improving motor skills—you're training your brain to operate at a higher level, fostering emotional and mental resilience, boosting creativity, and ensuring long-term cognitive health. You're stepping into the unknown, and that's where true growth begins.

When we focus intently on new tasks, we reinforce neural connections, making skills learned with the non-dominant hand more ingrained over time and using the non-dominant hand helps refine motor skills, improving hand-eye coordination and physical control.

September 19: The Ego That May Lift You Up Can Be Your Worst Enemy

I was in a subway in a bustling city in Brazil, and as we approached a station near the soccer stadium, a huge group of fans flooded in—singing, screaming, and celebrating their team's victory in the national championship. Their energy was contagious. But in the midst of this joyful celebration, I overheard two guys talking, not about the win, but about how they ran into fans from the opposing team—and beat them up. It hit me hard: Why would someone, filled with the joy of victory, engage in such senseless violence?

The answer, of course, is ego. War, competition, fights, and people taking advantage of others—these are all driven by the ego. It's the ego that creates the illusion of separation, convincing us that we're better, stronger, or more deserving than others. And while the ego can momentarily lift you up, it often blinds you to the bigger picture, leading to destruction—both internally and externally.

But what if we could step beyond the ego? What if, instead of letting it control our actions, we learned to control it?

When we start to tame the ego, we open ourselves up to a deeper sense of peace. Ego wants us to win at all costs, to compete, to prove ourselves. But controlling it allows us to shift our focus to collaboration, compassion, and unity. By reducing the influence of the ego, we begin to see that we are not separate from others. We are part of something larger, connected to everything around us.

Here's the secret: When we control the ego, we don't lose anything. In fact, we gain everything. We gain freedom from unnecessary conflict, from the anxiety of comparison, and from the weight of always needing to be "better" than someone else. We step into a space where we can truly connect with others, without fear, without judgment. The more we align with this state, the more we access true joy and fulfillment, not the fleeting kind the ego offers.

Hacking Tip: Next time you feel the ego rising—whether it's in a moment of frustration or in a victory—pause. Take a deep breath and ask yourself: *Am I acting from a place of fear and separation, or from a place of love and connection?* By simply shifting that focus, you start training your mind to operate from a higher state of awareness.

Controlling the ego isn't about diminishing yourself; it's about rising above it. True power comes not from what the ego promises but from transcending it and embracing the unity of all things.

September 20: Practicing Self-Discipline

Self-discipline is the foundation for achieving any goal. It's about having the strength to control your impulses, stay focused, and push forward even when things get tough. As the Stoics believed, true freedom comes from mastery over oneself. By practicing self-discipline, you build resilience—the ability to overcome obstacles and keep making progress, no matter how challenging the path may seem.

Self-discipline doesn't mean being rigid or harsh with yourself; it's about understanding what truly matters to you and choosing actions that align with your goals, even when distractions or temptations arise. It's the quiet commitment to show up for yourself every day, regardless of how you feel in the moment. This practice reduces stress, builds inner peace, and gives you greater life satisfaction by helping you feel more in control of your path.

When you practice self-discipline, you're not just achieving external goals—you're strengthening your character. Each time you choose discipline over instant gratification, you're teaching your mind to focus on long-term success over short-term pleasure. By aligning your self-discipline with your core values and purpose, you're not only building habits but also creating a meaningful, sustainable foundation for growth.

Stoic Insight: The Stoic philosopher Epictetus once said, "No man is free who is not master of himself." Practicing self-discipline allows you to take control of your life, making choices that reflect your values, rather than being led by whims and impulses.

Hacking Tip: Start small. Commit to a single daily action that aligns with your bigger goal, whether it's a workout, writing, or meditation. Over time, these small actions will build momentum, helping you develop the discipline you need to achieve lasting success.

September 21: Find Your Inner Power

Stoic Insight: Within each of us lies a reservoir of untapped strength and potential. Often, we overlook this inner power, letting fear and doubt hold us back from reaching our true capabilities. The Stoics teach that true power comes from within—not from external circumstances or possessions. This inner strength, or *eudaimonia*, represents living in harmony with our true selves and flourishing in alignment with our values.

Elaboration:
Imagine the incredible power that resides inside you, waiting to be discovered. It's that unwavering resilience that gets you through tough times, the creativity that sparks innovative ideas, and the courage that pushes you to take bold steps towards your dreams. Yet, many of us remain unaware of this latent strength, constrained by self-limiting beliefs and societal expectations.

Hacking tip: Today, commit to exploring your inner landscape. Reflect on past challenges you've overcome and recognize the strength it took to persevere. Set aside time for self-discovery through journaling, meditation, or simply quiet contemplation. Neuroscientific research shows that activities like these strengthen pathways in the prefrontal cortex—the area of the brain responsible for self-regulation and resilience—helping us respond more thoughtfully to life's challenges. Embrace your unique talents and passions, and allow them to guide you toward unlocking your full potential. Remember, your inner power is your greatest asset—recognize it, nurture it, believe in it, and watch as it transforms your life.

September 22: Take Empowered Action Daily And Make Your New Action Your New Belief

If you want to change your life, it starts with one thing: taking empowered action. Every single day. When you take action, you're not just moving forward—you're telling yourself, "This is who I am now." You're shifting your belief system with every step you take.

Look, the key to real, lasting change isn't just about setting big goals. It's about the small, consistent actions you take every day that create momentum. Each time you complete an action, your brain releases dopamine, reinforcing the behavior and building a positive feedback loop. The more you act, the more you build that belief—the belief that you can do it, that you will do it, and that this is your new reality. Tony Robbins says, "Repetition is the mother of skill." So if you want to create a new belief, it starts with repeating the actions that support that belief.

Here's the deal: Action isn't just about doing things for the sake of doing them. It's about aligning those actions with the person you want to become. You want to be fit? Take that daily run, lift those weights, make it a non-negotiable part of who you are. You want to build a successful business? Show up, put in the hours, and take risks, even when it's uncomfortable.

Empowered action leads to empowered beliefs.

Hacking Tip: Start by identifying one small action you can take every day that aligns with the belief you want to cultivate. Stick with it, no matter what. When you make that new action a part of your daily life, you're transforming how you see yourself—and your life.

Remember, you are what you repeatedly do. Take action, build the belief, and watch how your life transforms. You've got this!

September 23: Avoid The 4 Major Killers—Sugar, Alcohol, Gluten, Dairy

If you want to optimize your health, you can't overlook the impact of four major dietary killers: sugar, alcohol, gluten, and dairy. These aren't just buzzwords—they are substances that, when consumed in excess, can lead to chronic inflammation, weight gain, and a host of diseases that can rob you of vitality and longevity.

Let's start with **sugar**—the silent killer. It's addictive, inflammatory, and a leading contributor to obesity, diabetes, and heart disease. When you consume sugar, especially in processed foods, your body experiences spikes in blood sugar, leading to insulin resistance over time. It's not just about gaining weight; it's about how sugar accelerates aging and fuels chronic disease.

Then there's **alcohol**. While moderate consumption might not be harmful, regular overindulgence can damage your liver, spike your blood sugar, and impair brain function. Alcohol can also disrupt sleep patterns and cause dehydration, all of which accelerate aging and slow down recovery processes in the body.

Gluten, found in wheat, barley, and rye, may not be harmful to everyone, but it's a major disruptor for many. Gluten can cause inflammation in the gut, leading to digestive issues, fatigue, and brain fog—especially for those with gluten sensitivities or celiac disease. Even if you don't have a sensitivity, reducing gluten intake can help support gut health and overall inflammation levels.

And finally, **dairy**. For some, dairy can be a good source of calcium and protein, but for many, it's a source of inflammation and digestive discomfort. Lactose intolerance is more common than we realize, and the proteins in dairy, especially casein, can trigger inflammatory responses that lead to skin problems, joint pain, and even respiratory issues.

But before you panic and start cutting out everything in your diet, here's the key: **you don't need to be extreme.** Life is about balance, and that's where the **80/20 rule** comes in. As I mentioned on April 20, the 80/20 rule is your guide to sustainability. Aim to eat clean and avoid these major killers 80% of the time, while allowing for some flexibility 20% of the time. You don't need to be perfect— just consistent. This way, you avoid being overly restrictive and still enjoy life, without letting these dietary offenders dominate your health.

Biohacking Tip: Start by reducing your intake of these four major killers gradually. Swap out sugary snacks for healthier options like nuts or fruits. Limit alcohol to social occasions, and explore gluten-free and dairy-free alternatives that suit your lifestyle. Use the 80/20 rule to make this sustainable—aim for progress, not perfection.

Remember, it's not about deprivation; it's about empowering yourself with knowledge and making choices that protect your health for the long haul. You've got one body—let's take care of it!

September 24: The Power Of Prayer

"Pray without ceasing.*" — 1 Thessalonians 5:17 (KJV)*

Prayer is more than just religion or a spiritual practice; it's a powerful tool for enhancing mental, emotional, and physical well-being. Whether you're praying for strength, guidance, or simply offering gratitude, prayer creates a space for reflection, calm, and connection. It's a moment to step back from the chaos and align yourself with something greater.

Neuroscience backs this up. When you pray, your brain releases chemicals like dopamine and serotonin, which promote feelings of peace and happiness. Studies show that prayer can lower stress, reduce blood pressure, and even strengthen your immune system by activating the parasympathetic nervous system—the body's way of shifting out of stress mode into relaxation. This means prayer isn't just calming for the mind; it's physically healing for the body too.

Prayer also helps in processing emotions, offering a safe, contemplative space to release and understand difficult feelings. By expressing these emotions in prayer, you allow yourself to approach situations with a clearer mind and a calmer heart. In this way, prayer can serve as a tool for self-reflection and emotional resilience, helping you navigate life's challenges with greater ease.

Beyond the science, prayer can be seen as a form of mindfulness, involving present-moment awareness. Like mindfulness, prayer reduces stress by focusing attention on the present and fostering a sense of calm. This mindful aspect of prayer helps you develop greater self-awareness and inner peace, connecting you to a more grounded perspective.

Prayer ultimately fosters resilience, offering hope in tough times and reminding us that we're not alone. By regularly praying or taking moments for quiet reflection, you can gain clarity and cultivate gratitude, giving you strength to navigate life's challenges with a grounded perspective.

Hacking Tip: Incorporate prayer or quiet reflection into your day. Whether it's a few minutes in the morning, during a tough moment, or at night, make it a habit to connect with your deeper self and express what's on your heart.

Prayer isn't always about finding answers—it's about finding peace and creating space for clarity. And the more we practice it, the more we align ourselves with a sense of inner calm and purpose.

September 25: Nurturing Creativity

Creativity isn't just about art—it's about expressing yourself and finding unique solutions in everyday life. When you nurture creativity, you invite mental flexibility and joy into your world. It's about breaking free from routines and thinking outside the box.

From a **Stoic perspective**, creativity is a key tool for problem-solving. As Marcus Aurelius said, *"What stands in the way becomes the way."* By using obstacles as opportunities, you turn challenges into chances for innovation. Creativity helps you focus on what you can control and find new paths forward.

Engaging in creative activities, whether it's cooking, brainstorming, or simply doodling, brings satisfaction and adaptability into your life. The more you tap into your creativity, the more joy and resilience you'll experience.

Hacking Tip: Set aside time each day for creative activities—small acts can spark big ideas. Creativity is about exploration and self-expression, so embrace it, and watch it transform how you see the world.

September 26: Practicing Mindfulness

Mindfulness is about being fully present, aware, and engaged in the moment. It helps you focus on what's in front of you, preventing distractions from pulling you away. By practicing mindfulness, you improve your clarity, reduce stress, and approach situations with calmness.

From a **Stoic perspective**, mindfulness aligns with the Stoic principle of focusing on what you can control. By staying present, you respond thoughtfully to life's challenges instead of reacting impulsively. It allows you to manage emotions and see things clearly.

Tip: Incorporate mindfulness into daily routines. Whether it's during a meal, a walk, or a conversation, stay fully engaged in the present. It helps you approach life with more clarity and balance, creating space for thoughtful responses.

September 27: The Power Of An Accountability Partner

Having an accountability partner can completely transform how you approach your goals. When someone's there to keep you on track, you stay more focused and motivated. When no one's watching, it's easy to let things slide, but knowing you'll have to check in with someone pushes you to follow through.

Studies show that people who share their goals with an accountability partner are significantly more likely to achieve them. It's not just about having someone to talk to—it's about having a structure. When you have that person to plan with and get feedback from, you're far more likely to succeed. This feedback provides perspective, guiding you to adjust and improve along the way.

Accountability also strengthens self-regulation. The external structure of accountability helps build your ability to self-monitor and stay disciplined over time, making it easier to cultivate long-term habits that support personal growth. Another huge benefit is the support they provide. When things get tough, having someone in your corner can make all the difference. They remind you that you're not in this alone and help keep you moving forward, even when your motivation dips.

Accountability also improves time management. You're more likely to prioritize tasks and break big goals into manageable steps when someone's expecting progress updates. Plus, it cuts down on procrastination—you're less likely to put things off when someone's waiting for results.

Hacking Tip: Find someone to share your goals with, even if it's just one check-in a week. That simple act of sharing keeps you committed and focused. It's not about perfection, but progress. An accountability partner helps you stay on track, gives valuable feedback, and provides the push you need to hit your goals.

September 28: Inspire Someone

True success isn't just about reaching your own goals; it's about helping others rise with you. The most successful people don't keep their insights and experiences to themselves—they share them and inspire those around them. Inspiring someone means igniting their potential, fueling their journey toward growth and success.

Take Oprah Winfrey, for example. She didn't just overcome adversity to build her own empire—she used her platform to lift others. By sharing her struggles and triumphs, she shows people that where you start doesn't define where you can go. Her story continues to inspire millions to tap into their own potential.

Then there's Elon Musk. Love him or hate him, there's no denying his ability to inspire through bold ideas. Musk's vision for the future, from electric cars to space exploration, pushes others to think big. He's shown the world that daring to dream and take risks can lead to groundbreaking innovation.

Inspiration isn't limited to celebrities or massive platforms. Each act of inspiration creates a ripple effect, influencing those around you to aim higher. You can inspire others every day—by sharing your knowledge, offering encouragement, or simply leading by example. The passion you bring to your actions can motivate others to reach for more in their own lives.

Hacking Tip: Today, consider inspiring someone by sharing a personal story or offering a few words of encouragement. True success is about more than just personal achievements; it's about lighting the way for others, creating a ripple effect of growth and motivation.

September 29: Embrace Discomfort To Get The Job Done

If you really want to grow and succeed, you've got to get used to being uncomfortable. The truth is, nothing great happens in your comfort zone. Life will throw you into situations that test you, challenge you, and push you to your limits—but it's in those uncomfortable moments that you make the most progress.

Whether it's a tough conversation you've been avoiding, a project that feels overwhelming, or pushing yourself physically, stepping into discomfort is where the magic happens. Successful people don't shy away when things get hard. They know that getting the job done often means pushing through those awkward, stressful, or difficult moments. Discomfort signals that you're growing, expanding beyond your usual boundaries.

Instead of retreating when things get tough, lean in. Take on that challenging task, have that conversation, or push yourself a little further in whatever you're doing. Each time you tackle discomfort, you're not only building resilience but also boosting your self-confidence and stress tolerance, reinforcing your ability to handle even bigger challenges in the future.

Hacking Tip: Success isn't about avoiding hard moments; it's about tackling them and growing in the process. Embrace discomfort, knowing that every uncomfortable step builds mental strength and clarity. With each challenge faced, you'll be amazed at how much you're capable of achieving.

September 30: Learn A New Language And Keep Your Brain Sharp

Learning a new language does more than just help you communicate—it keeps your brain in top shape. Research shows that people who speak more than one language tend to have better memory and sharper cognitive skills as they get older. It's like a workout for your brain, keeping it adaptable and engaged.

Learning a new language activates key brain regions like the hippocampus, which supports memory, and the prefrontal cortex, which enhances focus and problem-solving. This combination boosts problem-solving abilities, improves focus, and even lowers the risk of cognitive decline. And beyond cognitive health, language learning fosters emotional and social intelligence by encouraging cultural understanding and empathy—qualities that enrich relationships and build flexibility in thinking.

Plus, it's a fun, enriching way to challenge your mind, keeping you active and engaged as the years go by.

Hacking Tip: Start small. Spend a few minutes each day with a language app or watch shows in a foreign language. You'll be surprised at how quickly you pick it up—and your brain will thank you in the long run!

October

Introduction
October 1: **Auto-Suggestion for Good Health**
October 2: **The Power Of Your Gut Microbiome**
October 3: **The Profound Benefits Of Laughter**
October 4: **Reframing Your Limiting Beliefs**
October 5: **Reframing Yourself For A New Perspective**
October 6: **Creating A Balanced Approach To Health**
October 7: **A New Perspective Leads To New Growth**
October 8: **Aim To Fly High**
October 9: **Building Strong Support Networks**
October 10: **Reprogramming Your Mindset For Success**
October 11: **Biohacking For Emotional Resilience**
October 12: **Mental Clarity Through Balanced Routines**
October 13: **Enhancing Neuroplasticity With Meditation**
October 14: **Practicing Self-Compassion**
October 15: **Your Body Is A Temple**
October 16: **Strengthening Neuroplasticity With Learning**
Octuber 17: **Step Back**
October 18: **Biohacking For Energy Optimization**
October 19: **Physical Strength For Longevity**
October 20: **Embracing Solitude For Self-Reflection**
October 21: **Optimizing Brain Health With Omega-3s**
October 22: **Harnessing Breathwork For Mental Clarity**
October 23: **Enhancing Focus Through Ketosis**
October 24: **Enhancing Physical Health Through Movement**
October 25: **Enhancing Longevity with Anti-Inflammatory Foods**
October 26: **Strengthening Memory with Brain Games**
Octuber 27: **Developing Empathy**
October 28: **Optimizing Longevity Through Hormonal Balance**
October 29: **Improving Neuroplasticity With Novelty**
October 30: **Biohacking Emotional Balance with Gratitude Practices**
October 31: **Strengthening Focus with Meditation**

Introduction:

October is a month of love, transformation, and deep emotional connection, guided by the balanced energy of Libra and the intense, transformative power of Scorpio. This is a time to deepen your relationships, heal emotional wounds, and embrace personal growth.

Libra's influence brings love and harmony to the forefront. It's a time to focus on the relationships that matter most, whether romantic or otherwise. Emotional intimacy, trust, and connection are key. October asks you to be fully present in your relationships, showing up with empathy and love. Whether it's through heart-centered communication or simply spending quality time with those you care about, this is the time to nurture your bonds.

Scorpio, on the other hand, brings a powerful energy of transformation. This is a month to face your fears, let go of what no longer serves you, and step into a more empowered version of yourself. Whether through spiritual practices, meditation, or emotional breakthroughs, October invites you to evolve. Transformation isn't always easy, but it's through this process that you grow stronger, more resilient, and more in tune with your true self.

Finally, October is about healing—both within yourself and in your relationships. It's a time to address old wounds, resolve conflicts, and create harmony where there was once tension. When you bring love and transformation together, you not only heal your past but also create space for a brighter, more fulfilling future.

October 1: Auto-Suggestion For Good Health

Auto-suggestion is one of the most powerful tools available to us. We're constantly feeding ourselves with this quiet, internal voice that shapes not only how we perceive the world but also has a profound influence on our health and well-being.

Take, for example, cases during the AIDS epidemic in the 1980s. Tragically, many individuals who were misdiagnosed with AIDS began to display symptoms, and some even died, only to be discovered later that these symptoms were manifestations of the mind's belief in illness rather than the disease itself. Their bodies responded to the belief that they were ill, exhibiting symptoms associated with a disease they didn't actually have. Similarly, in recent years, the world faced a widespread impact from a disease called COVID-19—a real illness, but one that affected individuals differently, and in some cases, the fear and suggestion surrounding it amplified symptoms and responses.

Science today supports the idea that the body and mind operate as an integrated system, responding directly to the brain's directives. For instance, studies reveal that stress and fear weaken our immune system, while positive beliefs and affirmations actively enhance healing. When we harness the power of positive auto-suggestion, we guide our body toward resilience, creating a fertile ground for healing and a balanced immune system.

The Science Behind Auto-Suggestion: Our minds have a profound influence on our physical state, and this connection is not abstract—it's rooted in neuroscience. The brain communicates directly with the body through the release of hormones and neurotransmitters, which can affect immune function, energy levels, and even cellular health. Positive self-talk, or auto-suggestion, can reduce stress hormones like cortisol while increasing "feel-good" chemicals like dopamine and serotonin. This physiological response creates a ripple effect, enhancing overall health.

Mauro dos Santos

Socrates wisely stated, "If you rely on doctors to take care of your health, you are a fool." In today's world, where environmental factors and even some aspects of our food supply challenge our health, this truth is more relevant than ever. Auto-suggestion and positive beliefs are powerful tools we can use to improve well-being, aligning mind and body to work in our favor.

Biohacking Tip: Integrate auto-suggestion into your daily routine by linking it to a specific habit, such as a morning practice that reinforces health beliefs. Spend a few minutes repeating a positive statement and visualizing your body responding with health and vitality. You can further enhance this practice by pairing it with deep breathing exercises to calm the nervous system and strengthen the mind-body connection. This biohack amplifies the effects of auto-suggestion, helping you make it an ingrained habit that nourishes both mind and body.

October 2: The Power Of Your Gut Microbiome

Your gut microbiome—home to trillions of microorganisms—plays a pivotal role in your health, reaching far beyond just digestion. It impacts your immune system, hormone regulation, mental clarity, and even your mood. As I often emphasize, "Your body is an interconnected system, and your gut's health can determine how well your body functions."

When your gut microbiome is balanced, you absorb nutrients better, regulate stress more effectively, and maintain strong immune defenses. A healthy gut leads to sharper cognitive function and emotional stability. But an unhealthy gut—caused by processed foods, excess sugar, and antibiotics—can lead to inflammation, brain fog, anxiety, and chronic diseases. Science shows that gut bacteria influence neurotransmitters like serotonin and dopamine, meaning that an imbalanced gut can directly impact your mood, focus, and overall mental well-being.

Feeding your gut properly is key. Prebiotics from garlic, leeks, and oats feed beneficial bacteria, while probiotics in fermented foods like yogurt and sauerkraut help maintain balance. This kind of mindful nutrition supports not just your digestion but your body's entire network, from mental to immune health.

Biohacking Tip: Tune into how different foods affect you. Introduce more fiber-rich and fermented options, and limit processed foods that can harm your microbiome. Reducing stress also supports a healthier gut, as chronic stress can disrupt its balance and weaken immune response. This simple change can lead to clearer thinking, a more stable mood, and improved overall health.

Your gut's health is central to your well-being. Take care of it, and you'll see benefits ripple through both your mind and body.

October 3: The Profound Benefits Of Laughter

Laughter isn't just a moment of fleeting joy—it's a powerful tool for improving both mental and physical well-being. When you laugh, your brain releases a surge of endorphins, those natural chemicals that not only make you feel good but also reduce stress and anxiety. It's a biological response that has a profound impact on your health.

Laughter has been shown to boost your immune system by increasing the production of antibodies and activating immune cells. This means a good laugh doesn't just lift your spirits; it can also strengthen your body's defense against illness. On top of that, laughter improves circulation, lowers blood pressure, and supports heart health by improving blood flow. Practicing laughter regularly can even lower the risk of chronic illness, such as cardiovascular disease, due to its stress-relieving effects.

Emotionally, laughter helps us build resilience. In moments of stress or hardship, finding humor gives you perspective. It helps you step back and view problems in a lighter way, making challenges feel less overwhelming. It's no wonder that many therapists use laughter as a form of therapy—it helps you cope, see life with a fresh perspective, and even process difficult emotions. In fact, regular laughter can encourage neuroplasticity, helping your brain stay flexible and adaptable over time.

Hacking Tip: Incorporate laughter into your daily life, whether through sharing a funny story, watching something that makes you laugh, or simply allowing yourself to find humor in the little moments. Consider joining a laughter yoga session or setting a "laughter reminder" in your day—it's a fun and intentional way to bring humor into your life. It's not just a break from the seriousness of life—it's an essential practice for better health, stronger relationships, and a more resilient mindset.

October 4: Reframing Your Limiting Beliefs

We all have limiting beliefs—the stories we tell ourselves about why we can't do something or why success isn't meant for us. These beliefs aren't facts; they're just thoughts shaped by past experiences or fear. The good news? You can change them.

Limiting beliefs often stem from early conditioning or past failures. Maybe someone once told you that you weren't good at something, and you've carried that belief with you ever since. But here's the truth: these thoughts can be reframed. Instead of thinking, "I'm not good at this," shift your mindset to, "I'm learning, and I can get better."

Reframing means taking a limiting belief, questioning it, and replacing it with something more empowering. When you do this, you're opening yourself up to new possibilities. Your brain is adaptable—when you consistently repeat and act on new empowering beliefs, they become your reality.

Hacking Tip: Identify a belief that's holding you back. Write it down and reframe it with something positive. Repeat it daily, especially during challenges, and watch how your perspective and actions begin to change.

Reframing limiting beliefs is about taking control of your story. When you change those negative thoughts into empowering ones, you unlock new opportunities and possibilities for yourself.

October 5: Reframing Yourself For A New Perspective

We often get trapped in old stories about who we are—stories that keep us locked in habits, behaviors, and mindsets that don't serve us anymore. But as Joe Dispenza teaches, you have the power to rewire your brain, to break free from the past, and to see yourself from a completely new perspective.

Reframing yourself is about challenging those outdated beliefs and labels. Maybe you've always thought, "I'm not confident" or "I'm bad at handling challenges." These thoughts are just programs, repeating over and over, reinforcing your current reality. But the beauty of the human mind is that it's adaptable—neuroplasticity allows you to rewrite these old narratives and see yourself through a new, empowered lens.

When you start to shift your perspective, something incredible happens. You stop defining yourself by your past, and instead, you begin to focus on your potential. You start seeing the strengths and possibilities within you that were always there, just waiting to be tapped into. You're no longer limited by old habits or labels—you're free to step into the future you truly want.

Tip: Take a moment today to challenge one outdated belief about yourself. Maybe it's "I'm always stressed" or "I can't succeed." Reframe that belief into something more aligned with your potential: "I'm learning to manage stress" or "I'm capable of achieving anything I set my mind to." Repeat this daily and watch your brain start to align with your new reality.

Reframing yourself is the key to breaking free from your old patterns and stepping into a new, elevated version of you. As Dispenza says, "You are not doomed by your genes or hardwired to be a certain way for the rest of your life. You can change."

October 6: Creating A Balanced Approach To Health

True health isn't just about your body—it's about balancing physical, emotional, spiritual, and social well-being. When these aspects align, *you* create a sense of flow and vitality in your life.

Physical health is the foundation. Movement strengthens the body and releases energy, lifting your mood and clearing your mind. Keeping active helps create space for emotional and mental clarity.

Emotionally, health means balance and resilience. Practices like mindfulness and meditation help *you* manage stress, creating emotional stability and a steady center in the face of challenges.

Spiritually, health is about connection—whether it's to yourself, a higher purpose, or the universe. Nurturing your spiritual side opens *you* up to a deeper sense of peace and purpose.

Socially, health involves building strong, supportive relationships. Positive connections remind *you* that you're not alone, reinforcing your emotional well-being.

Hacking Tip: Develop Small daily habits—move your body, meditate, connect with those who uplift you—will help you create balance in every aspect of your health, unlocking deeper joy and fulfillment.

Track specific health metric, such as heart rate variability for stress management or sleep quality for physical health. This can provide real-time feedback on how well-balanced your physical health is and how other aspects may be affecting it.

Mauro dos Santos

October 7: A New Perspective Leads To New Growth

When you shift your perspective, you open the door to a whole new level of understanding about yourself. As Joe Dispenza teaches, "If you want to create a new personal reality, you must first create a new personality." That begins with how you see yourself and your world. The moment you step outside your old ways of thinking, you create the possibility for profound change and growth.

New perspectives lead to new learning. When you begin to see yourself not as the person defined by your past experiences or limitations, but as someone capable of evolving, you break the chains that hold you back. Suddenly, you're no longer stuck in old patterns—you're free to explore, to experiment, and to grow into the person you truly want to be. This is where real transformation happens.

By challenging old beliefs and seeing yourself through a new lens, you unlock doors to possibilities you hadn't even considered. You start to realize that the only limits are the ones you've been imposing on yourself. The more you embrace this, the more your brain rewires itself for growth, for success, for fulfillment.

Tip: Today, challenge yourself to adopt a new perspective. If there's something you've always believed about yourself—"I'm not good enough," or "I'll never be able to change"—ask yourself: *What if this belief is just a story?* Start seeing yourself as the person who can grow, who can change, who can succeed. This shift in perspective will create space for new opportunities and growth.

As Joe Dispenza often says, "Where you place your attention is where you place your energy." Place your attention on the possibility of who you can become, and watch as new growth and transformation unfold. It's time to embrace a new reality.

October 8: Aim To Fly High

Fly high and reach a new level. When we do not conform to the norm, we aim for something greater. Our lives were not meant to be ordinary. While we may be naturally inclined toward comfort, we are equally driven to soar. However, flying high is only possible when we detach ourselves from the ordinary. You'll start to notice that you're distancing yourself from those who choose to stay behind, and gradually, you'll connect with a smaller group on a new level. The higher you fly in life, the more you'll encounter those who are also reaching for greatness.

I enjoy playing online chess, and it's very noticeable that at the beginner level, around 1000–1200, there are many players. To move up to the advanced level, around 1600–1800, you must think more analytically, exercise greater focus, and connect with others on the same level. Reaching 1800 means you're at a pre-master level, where players are committed to becoming masters. At this level, you no longer connect with beginners or novices—masters compete only with other masters or higher-level players.

As you reach the elite level, you'll find yourself among a small group. Your level of achievement is high, your thinking sharper, and your mastery over the "game" of life more refined.

Hacking Tip: Aiming to Fly High. Jonathan Livingston Seagull, a seagull who refused to conform to the typical life of his flock, chose to fly beyond what others could understand or value. He followed his passion, defying societal expectations, mastering flight, and embracing his uniqueness with the courage to overcome limitations. Through continual improvement, he eventually met other enlightened seagulls who helped him explore life's true meaning, understand love, forgiveness, and purpose. By breaking free from limitations, he discovered his unique path.

October 9: Building Strong Support Networks

Human connection is vital for emotional and mental well-being. As the Stoics believed, we thrive when we're surrounded by supportive, like-minded individuals. Having a strong support network isn't just a comfort—it's essential for growth and resilience, especially during tough times. A solid network provides more than just emotional comfort. It offers perspective and clarity when you're facing challenges. People who share your values can remind you of your strengths and help you find solutions you might not see on your own. Marcus Aurelius said it best: "We are made for cooperation, like feet, like hands, like eyelids." The Stoics understood that real strength comes from the connections we build with others. But it's a two-way street. Supporting others in their moments of need not only strengthens your relationships but also creates a cycle of trust and resilience that benefits everyone involved.

Tip: Make a habit of connecting with people who share your values and goals. Schedule regular check-ins, offer your support where you can, and don't hesitate to ask for help when you need it. By nurturing these connections, you build a network of trust and resilience that sustains you through life's ups and downs.

No one gets through life alone. Building a strong support network of people who challenge, inspire, and lift you up is key to facing life's ups and downs with strength and confidence.

October 10: Reprogramming Your Mindset For Success

Your mind is the most powerful tool you have, but it's also the most underused. Most of us operate on autopilot, running the same patterns and beliefs we've held for years. If you want to achieve real success, you have to start by reprogramming your mindset. As Joe Dispenza often says, "Your thoughts create your reality." To change your life, you must first change the way you think.

The brain is highly adaptable, thanks to neuroplasticity. This means that by consistently shifting your thoughts and breaking old patterns, you can literally rewire your brain, creating new neural pathways that reinforce positive beliefs. Over time, these pathways become stronger and more automatic, enabling you to operate from an empowered belief system. If you've been carrying limiting beliefs like "I'm not good enough" or "I'll never be successful," it's time to replace them with empowering ones. Repetitive positive thoughts, combined with intentional action, can cement these beliefs and shift your self-image to align with your goals.

It's not just about thinking positively—it's about consistently aligning your thoughts with your goals and taking actionable steps to support them. Each time you challenge a limiting belief, you're not just thinking differently; you're actively reprogramming your brain to work for you, not against you. Psychologically, this process helps reduce stress, increases resilience, and cultivates a healthier, more confident self-image.

Tip: Start small by incorporating techniques like visualization, affirmations, or even journaling to reinforce your new beliefs. Your reality is a reflection of your mindset. Reprogram your thoughts, and your life will follow suit. You have the power to create the life you desire—begin with your mind, and reflect often on your progress to keep the momentum going.

October 11: Biohacking For Emotional Resilience

Our lives are not perfect. They are full of unexpected challenges and events, and emotional resilience is what allows you to face them with confidence and clarity. Imagine approaching stress, fear, or frustration with a sense of calm—not as obstacles but as signals guiding you toward balance. This is where biohacking becomes invaluable. By using natural tools like breathwork, meditation, and sleep optimization, you can fine-tune your mental and emotional resilience, staying grounded and productive—even in the most difficult times—without losing touch with your joy.

Hacking Tip To build resilience, try incorporating breathwork at least once a week and practicing daily meditation. Meditation helps you step back from thoughts and emotions, allowing you to process them without impulsive reactions. This practice rewires your brain, strengthening your ability to handle stress. And remember—sleep optimization is a vital component for achieving mental clarity and resilience.

Coaching Prompt Reflect on a recent challenge. How might these tools have helped you respond with greater resilience?

October 12: Mental Clarity Through Balanced Routines

Let's be real—you know those days where everything feels like a chaotic blur, right? Those are the days when you just can't seem to focus, keep your concentration, and when decisions or thinking feel heavy and almost impossible. Well, here's the thing: mental clarity isn't something that magically shows up when you need it. It's something you create through balanced routines.

Think of your mind as a finely-tuned instrument. If you're constantly running on stress, overloading yourself with information, and forgetting to take a breather, that instrument is going to sound a bit off-key. But when you integrate physical activity, mental focus, and emotional care into your daily routine, you tune yourself back into harmony.

Try a morning walk, yoga, or even dancing around your kitchen to start your day. Movement gets the brain juices flowing, releasing those feel-good chemicals that make everything seem clearer.

Then there's mental focus. Dedicate time each day for deep, uninterrupted work. This is where you really engage that brainpower. But here's the kicker: balance it with moments of relaxation. I'm talking about genuine breaks, where you step away, breathe, and let your mind recharge. Meditation? Game-changer. It's like hitting the reset button on your brain.

And don't forget emotional care. Self-care isn't just bubble baths and spa days (though those are nice).

Hacking Tip: Build a routine that flows. Start with movement, focus deeply for a set time, take breaks, and allow moments for self-care. When you balance your physical, mental, and emotional well-being, it's like giving yourself the ultimate mental clarity hack. You'll be sharper, more productive, and—let's face it—just a lot more fun to be around.

October 13: Enhancing Neuroplasticity With Meditation

Contrary to old beliefs, our brains have a remarkable ability to reshape themselves by forming new neural connections. One of the most powerful tools to boost neuroplasticity is regular meditation. Meditation doesn't just help you relax—it literally changes the structure and function of your brain.

Let's break it down and see how you can benefit from it. When you meditate, particularly with mindfulness techniques, you're training your brain to be more present. This practice strengthens the prefrontal cortex, the area responsible for decision-making, attention, and self-control. At the same time, it shrinks the amygdala, the part of the brain that processes fear and stress. That's why meditation helps you stay calm under pressure and improves emotional regulation.

Studies show that regular meditation can increase the density of gray matter in the hippocampus, the region associated with learning and memory. That's right—by sitting quietly and focusing on your breath, you're not only reducing stress but also physically enhancing your brain's ability to remember and process information.

Another fascinating effect of meditation is its impact on the brain's default mode network (DMN), the part responsible for mind-wandering and self-referential thoughts. Meditation quiets the DMN, which is why it helps you stay focused and reduces the endless mental chatter that clouds your thinking.

Neuroscience Fact: Regular meditation has been shown to increase the production of brain-derived neurotrophic factor (BDNF), a protein that supports the growth of new neurons and synapses. BDNF is like fertilizer for your brain, helping it stay adaptable and resilient to stress. When you meditate consistently, you're giving your brain the tools to stay sharp, learn new things, and handle challenges with more grace and clarity.

Biohacking Tip: Meditation is like a workout for your brain, training it to stay strong, adaptable, and ready to take on life's challenges. By enhancing neuroplasticity through meditation, you're not just rewiring your brain for the short term—you're setting the stage for lifelong cognitive health and emotional well-being. It's a biohack with profound, lasting effects.

Mauro dos Santos
October 14: Practicing Self-Compassion

Practicing self-compassion is vital, especially during failures and setbacks. Being kind to yourself in tough times not only fosters resilience but also promotes personal growth. When you treat yourself with compassion, you create a nurturing environment where you can learn from mistakes instead of wallowing in self-criticism.

Negative self-talk can be incredibly damaging, leading to feelings of inadequacy and discouragement. By replacing those harsh inner critiques with understanding and support, you cultivate a positive mindset that empowers you to move forward.

Hacking Tip: The next time you face a challenge, pause and ask yourself how you would respond to a friend in a similar situation. Allow yourself the same kindness and encouragement you would offer them.

Remember, self-compassion isn't about making excuses; it's about acknowledging your humanity and allowing room for growth.

October 15: Your Body Is A Temple

An interesting fact is that in modern cars, we have around 50 sensors monitoring every detail, from oil levels to engine temperature. The moment a sensor indicates low oil, we rush to the mechanic. When the engine temperature rises, we don't rest until it's back to normal. If an unfamiliar warning light appears, our attention is immediately drawn to it, and we prioritize finding the best fuel and maintenance to keep our vehicle running smoothly. We do all this to preserve our cars, which are replaceable objects.

Yet, despite this vigilance over our vehicles, computers, and smartphones, we often neglect the one "machine" that's irreplaceable—our own body. This lack of self-care is evident in our choices, where convenience and taste often outweigh the value of quality nutrition and lifestyle habits that nurture our well-being. In 2013, the American Medical Association (AMA) formally recognized obesity as a disease. According to their standard, over 73% of the American population now suffers from this disease. It's a visible condition, yet it often appears as though people are unaware or unconcerned. On top of that, people carrying extra weight often also have, or are at risk of developing, high blood pressure, high cholesterol, and diabetes. In fact, studies show that about 85% to 90% of individuals with type 2 diabetes are above the normal weight range.

One influential study linking physical activity with mental health is the 2018 study published in *The Lancet Psychiatry* titled "Association between physical exercise and mental health in 1.2 million individuals in the USA." The study found that physically active individuals reported significantly fewer days of poor mental health compared to those who were sedentary.

Key findings from this study include:

- People who exercised regularly experienced nearly 40% fewer "bad mental health days" than sedentary individuals.

Mauro dos Santos

- Exercising for 30 to 60 minutes, three to five times a week, was associated with the best mental health outcomes.

The study underscores the relationship between physical activity and mental well-being, suggesting that regular exercise plays a crucial role in maintaining mental health.

The Bible reminds us, "Your body is a temple" (1 Corinthians 6:19-20), calling for reverence toward our bodies as the dwelling of the spirit. This sacred concept encourages us to nurture, respect, and honor our bodies by giving them the best fuel—foods rich in nutrients, clean water, sufficient rest, and regular movement. Just as we wouldn't put low-quality fuel into a luxury car, why should we treat our bodies, which are priceless, with any less care?

Biohacking Tip: Use sensors to monitor your body, start viewing it as a temple, and make decisions that align with a deeper respect for yourself. Prioritize food choices that nourish rather than deplete, exercise routines that strengthen rather than exhaust, and self-care habits that fortify rather than wear down. In doing so, you honor not only your physical health but also your mental, emotional, and spiritual well-being, creating a holistic approach to self-care that allows you to thrive in every sense.

371

October 16: Strengthening Neuroplasticity With Learning

Do you enjoy learning? When was the last time you challenged your brain with something new—like picking up a language, trying an instrument, or diving into a new sport? These activities do more than just teach you new skills—they reshape your brain. That's neuroplasticity in action, the brain's ability to form new neural connections.

According to Dr. Joe Dispenza, every time you push yourself to learn something unfamiliar, your brain builds 10,000 new pathways, making it sharper and more adaptable. It's like giving your brain a workout—just like you strengthen your muscles through exercise, you strengthen your brain by learning.

Science Fact: Learning new skills boosts cognitive reserve, protecting your brain from age-related decline and keeping you mentally agile, while also boosting your intelligence.

Hacking Tip: Try something new regularly—whether it's a hobby or a small daily challenge. Consistent learning keeps you sharp, adaptable, and mentally resilient.

October 17: Step Back

Have you noticed how easy it is to spot solutions for someone else who's in a conflict? You can be a certified armchair therapist when it comes to other people's dilemmas. But when it's your turn to deal with a sticky situation, suddenly you're as confused as a cat at a dog show! That's why stepping back can be a game changer.

Taking a step back allows you to view your life from a different angle, like changing your perspective on a painting by moving to the other side of the room. Instead of getting lost in the details of your daily grind, this moment of pause can help you assess the bigger picture. Are you truly happy with where you are? Are your choices aligned with your values? Or are you just going through the motions, like a robot on autopilot?

When you create space for reflection, you're giving yourself a chance to think critically. This is especially important during stressful times when life can feel overwhelming. Instead of feeling like you're swimming upstream, stepping back helps you catch your breath and figure out your next move—preferably without the flailing!

Tip: Schedule regular "step back" moments for yourself—whether it's sipping your morning coffee in peace, going for a stroll, or jotting down your thoughts in a journal. Ask yourself the important questions: What's working? What isn't? What changes should I make?

By stepping back, you gain valuable insights and can navigate your life with a clearer mind. So, take a breather, laugh at the chaos, and remember: sometimes all you need is a little distance to see the way forward!

October 18: Biohacking For Energy Optimization

In order to feel energized throughout the day, it's not just about caffeine or taking a nap—there's a science behind optimizing your energy levels that can keep you sharp and fueled for whatever life throws at you. With a few simple biohacking tricks, you can take control of your energy and sustain it without the crashes or mental fog that come with quick fixes.

First and foremost, diet is your foundation. Think of it like high-octane fuel for your engine. Whole foods—rich in fiber, protein, and healthy fats—provide steady, long-lasting energy, unlike the spikes and crashes you get from processed junk.

MCT Oil: The Ultimate Biohacking Fuel. One of the most powerful additions to your diet for energy optimization is **MCT oil**. Derived from coconut oil, MCT (medium-chain triglycerides) is a type of fat that your body quickly converts into fuel. Unlike regular fats, MCTs are absorbed faster, bypassing the typical digestion process and heading straight to the liver, where they are turned into **ketones**—a super-efficient fuel source for both your brain and body.

MCT oil is particularly effective if you're looking for sustained energy throughout the day. It doesn't just provide quick energy—it also supports **mental clarity** by fueling your brain, keeping you sharp and focused. I love combining it in my **Super Coffee**, as described on April 9.

Biohacking Tip: Start your morning with **Super Coffee (April 10)**—a blend of coffee, MCT oil, and grass-fed butter. This combo not only kickstarts your day but also gives you a steady release of energy that lasts for hours without the typical caffeine crash.

By incorporating biohacks like optimizing your diet and staying hydrated, you're setting yourself up for enhanced physical endurance and mental sharpness. It's about feeling energized all day, without the dips, allowing you to perform at your peak, whatever the task at hand.

October 19: Physical Strength For Longevity

Let's talk about something simple but life-changing: strength training. If you think lifting weights or doing bodyweight exercises is just about building muscle, think again. Strength training is one of the most powerful tools for extending your healthspan and ensuring long-term vitality.

When you engage in strength training, you're not just sculpting your body. Strength training helps balance hormones like testosterone and growth hormone, both of which play a critical role in how your body ages and recovers. Muscle contractions also stimulate the production of Brain-Derived Neurotrophic Factor (BDNF), which promotes neurogenesis in the hippocampus—a region of the brain associated with memory and learning. On top of that, strength training increases the production of neurotransmitters like dopamine, serotonin, and acetylcholine.

And it doesn't stop there. Regular weightlifting or bodyweight exercises improve metabolic health. This means better blood sugar control, reduced inflammation, and a more efficient fat-burning system. In short, strength training keeps your body running like a well-oiled machine for years to come.

Hacking Tip: You don't need a gym membership to start. Try the calisthenic exercises mentioned on February 19, or go for simple bodyweight moves like push-ups, squats, or planks—they can be just as effective.

By investing in your physical strength now, you're ensuring your body stays strong, your bones remain healthy, and your metabolism stays sharp—all crucial for living a long, full life.

October 20: Embracing Solitude For Self-Reflection

Spending time alone is like hitting the reset button for your mind. It fosters self-awareness and gives you the clarity needed for personal growth. In our busy world, finding moments of solitude can feel like a luxury, but it's essential for checking in with yourself.

When you embrace solitude, you create the space to reflect on your thoughts, actions, and goals without the noise of outside influences. It's an opportunity to reconnect with what really matters to you and to evaluate where you are on your journey.

This quiet time doesn't have to be long—whether it's sitting quietly with a cup of coffee, going for a walk, or journaling for a few minutes. The key is being intentional about tuning into your inner voice. Self-reflection helps you understand your emotions, identify patterns in your behavior, and recognize areas for improvement. It's in these moments of stillness that real growth happens.

Hacking Tip: Make solitude a regular part of your routine, even if it's just for a few minutes a day. Use that time to reflect on your actions, evaluate your goals, or simply clear your mind. Embracing solitude doesn't mean being lonely; it's about recharging and gaining insight into your personal journey.

October 21: Optimizing Brain Health with Omega-3s

Omega-3 fatty acids are like brain food, and *you* can easily get them from fish oil or algae supplements. These fats reduce inflammation in *your* brain, improve *your* mood, and boost neuroplasticity, which is *your* brain's ability to form new neural connections. Studies show that regular intake of Omega-3s helps *you* stay mentally sharp, enhances memory, and keeps *your* brain agile as *you* age.

Science Fact: Omega-3s, particularly DHA, are key structural components of *your* brain cells, helping *you* maintain cognitive function and mental clarity.

Hacking Tip: Add Omega-3 supplements or Omega-3-rich foods like fatty fish to *your* diet to support long-term brain health and keep *you* sharp as the years go by.

October 22: Harnessing Breathwork For Mental Clarity

Breathwork isn't just about taking deep breaths—it's a powerful way to boost brainpower and manage emotions. Techniques like Soma Breath increase oxygen flow to the brain, sharpening mental clarity, reducing stress, and supporting cognitive function. During my certification, I even experienced a natural, almost psychedelic effect—no substances needed.

Science Fact: Oxygen fuels brain activity, producing neurotransmitters that enhance mood, focus, and mental clarity. Studies show that increased oxygen levels through breathwork help regulate emotions and sharpen cognitive skills.

Hacking Tip: Make breathwork a daily ritual. Start with 5 minutes each morning or evening—whether it's slow, controlled breaths for calm or an invigorating practice like Wim Hof or Soma Breath for energy and focus. Feel the mental fog lift as oxygen powers your mind and body, leaving you ready to handle any stress with calm and control.

Mauro dos Santos

October 23: Enhancing Focus Through Ketosis

When you follow a ketogenic diet, you're not just losing weight—you're boosting your brain and body's performance. By focusing on high fat and low carbohydrates, you promote ketosis, a state where your body burns fat for energy instead of glucose. This metabolic shift can enhance mental clarity, improve focus, and boost physical endurance, making it a powerful biohack for optimizing both performance and longevity.

Science Fact: In ketosis, your brain runs on ketones, which are more efficient than glucose. Studies show that ketones provide more sustained energy for your brain, leading to improved focus, cognitive function, and reduced oxidative stress, supporting cellular health and longevity.

Biohacking Tip: Try a 16:8 intermittent fasting schedule or incorporate more ketogenic foods like avocados, nuts, and olive oil to enter ketosis. Pay attention to how your energy, focus, and endurance evolve as your body adapts—this metabolic shift might just be the edge you're looking for.

October 24: Enhancing Physical Health Through Movement

Let's face it—many of us spend way too much time sitting, whether it's at a desk, in front of a screen, or during a commute. But here's the good news: improving your physical health doesn't require hours in the gym. Simply adding a few 5-minute movement breaks throughout your day can make a huge difference.

Movement doesn't just boost your body; it recharges your brain, too. Quick breaks to stand up, stretch, or walk around can clear the mental fog, reduce fatigue, and help you stay focused. Think of it as plugging into a quick recharge station for both body and mind. Regular movement helps circulation, keeps muscles from stiffening, and releases feel-good endorphins to elevate your mood. Even if it's just getting up from your chair, doing a few shoulder rolls, or walking around the room, every bit of movement counts. The key is to make it a habit—short, frequent breaks can add up to long-term health benefits.

Tip: Set a timer to remind yourself to take a 5-minute movement break every hour. Reward yourself each day for sticking with it! You'll notice a difference not only in how your body feels but also in your mental clarity.

By embracing these small but consistent movement breaks, you're setting yourself up for better physical health and mental well-being. Sometimes, it's the little things that make the biggest difference!

October 25: Enhancing Longevity With Anti-Inflammatory Foods

Chronic inflammation is one of the silent culprits behind accelerated aging and a reduced healthspan. The good news? You can combat it with what you put on your plate. By incorporating anti-inflammatory foods, you're not only reducing inflammation but also promoting cellular repair, boosting physical health, and improving mental clarity.

Here's a quick list of anti-inflammatory foods to add to your diet:

- Turmeric
- Ginger
- Berries
- Leafy greens
- Fatty fish (like salmon)
- Walnuts
- Olive oil

Biohacking Tip: Start adding these powerful foods into your meals to help reduce inflammation, support longevity, and keep both your body and mind functioning at their best.

October 26: Strengthening Memory With Brain Games

Keeping your brain sharp is just as important as keeping your body fit, and brain games are a powerful tool to help you do just that. By challenging your mind with puzzles, memory exercises, or apps like Lumosity, you stimulate neuroplasticity—your brain's ability to form new connections. This doesn't just enhance cognitive function; it strengthens memory, sharpens focus, and keeps your brain agile as you age.

The brain thrives on challenge. When you push it to solve problems, recall information, or focus intensely, you're essentially giving it a workout. Just like lifting weights for your body, engaging in brain games helps keep your mind strong and resilient, reducing the risk of cognitive decline.

Hacking Tip: Try dedicating just a few minutes a day to brain games like puzzles, crosswords, or memory exercises. Over time, you'll notice sharper recall, better concentration, and a more agile mind ready to tackle whatever comes your way.

October 27: Developing Empathy

Empathy is a powerful quality that enhances our relationships with others. The Stoics taught that practicing empathy cultivates compassion and fosters mutual growth. Through empathy, we build common ground with those around us. Empathy allows us to step into another person's shoes. It doesn't mean we need to agree with everyone's views, but it does mean we actively listen and make an effort to understand where they're coming from. With this understanding, we can respond in a way that is meaningful and supportive.

Developing empathy changes the quality of our relationships, allowing us to create deeper connections based on trust and understanding. When others feel that someone is genuinely present with them, they're more likely to respond with openness and kindness in return. This deeper understanding can lead to stronger, healthier relationships in both personal and professional settings.

By reaching for empathy in our conversations, we ensure our responses are productive rather than defensive. In challenging situations where a tactful response is needed, empathy helps us handle emotions with grace.

Hacking Tip: Work on your listening skills to ignite empathy. Pay full attention when someone shares their thoughts and feelings. Ask open-ended questions like, "How did that make you feel?" or "What would be helpful right now?" Reflect back what you understand to show that you genuinely hear their perspective. Empathy not only helps you grow as a person but also reveals your true character to those around you. Remember, empathy is a tool that can enhance your relationship skills and help create a gentler, more understanding society!

October 28: Optimizing Longevity Through Hormonal Balance

You might not think about your hormones every day, but they have a huge impact on how you age, how you feel, and how much energy you have. The good news is that *you* can take control of your hormonal balance, and it's easier than you think. With the right lifestyle choices, you can optimize key hormones like testosterone, estrogen, and cortisol, and feel the benefits in both the short and long term.

So, how can *you* do it?

Start with Sleep When *you* don't get enough sleep, your body's hormonal balance gets thrown out of whack. Cortisol, the stress hormone, spikes, which leaves you feeling anxious and tired. At the same time, sleep deprivation can lower testosterone and estrogen, affecting *your* energy, mood, and even your metabolism. Aim for 7-9 hours of quality sleep a night, and you'll notice the difference in how you feel each day.

Adaptogens Are Your Friend Adaptogens like ashwagandha and rhodiola are natural compounds that help *your* body adapt to stress. These herbs have been shown to regulate cortisol levels, ensuring that *you* don't experience the negative effects of chronic stress. Lower cortisol means better mood, more energy, and improved focus. You can incorporate adaptogens through supplements or herbal teas—simple additions with powerful effects.

Strength Training for Hormone Boost When *you* engage in regular strength training, *you're* not just building muscle. Strength training helps balance *your* hormones by boosting testosterone and growth hormone levels. These hormones are essential for maintaining muscle mass, energy levels, and overall vitality as *you* age. Just two or three sessions a week can give *you* a significant hormonal advantage, leading to increased longevity and well-being.

Mauro dos Santos

Science Fact: Research shows that regular strength training can increase testosterone by up to 40%, while studies on adaptogens have demonstrated their effectiveness in lowering cortisol and improving stress response.

Biohacking Tip: Start by optimizing your sleep and adding adaptogens into your daily routine. Then, layer in strength training a few times a week. *You'll* start to notice better mood, increased energy, and a body that feels younger and more resilient.

By taking control of *your* hormonal balance, you're giving yourself the tools to optimize *your* longevity. Small, manageable changes can help *you* stay vibrant, energetic, and youthful for years to come!

October 29: Improving Neuroplasticity With Novelty

When was the last time *you* tried something new? Learning a language, picking up a new sport, or simply stepping out of *your* comfort zone does more for *you* than just add excitement—it rewires *your* brain. This process, called neuroplasticity, helps *your* brain form new neural connections, keeping it agile and sharp as *you* age.

Novel experiences force *your* brain to adapt and grow, which boosts cognitive function and mental flexibility. Whether it's as simple as taking a different route to work or as challenging as mastering a musical instrument, *you* can strengthen *your* brain just by embracing newness.

Science Fact: Studies show that novel activities stimulate the production of Brain-Derived Neurotrophic Factor (BDNF), which supports learning and memory.

Biohacking Tip: Challenge *yourself* to do something new every week. Whether it's a hobby, skill, or experience, *you'll* keep *your* brain sharp and open to growth.

Mauro dos Santos

October 30: Biohacking Emotional Balance With Gratitude Practices

Gratitude isn't just about being polite to others—it's a powerful tool to rewire your brain for positivity and emotional balance. You can even shout gratitude from the rooftops, thanking God or the universe for the simple gift of being alive. This practice does wonders for your mind, body, and brain. By regularly focusing on what you're thankful for—like the beauty of nature, the kindness of loved ones, or even your morning coffee—you're training your mind to shift away from stress and negativity. This shift improves emotional well-being and boosts neuroplasticity, helping your brain adapt and grow for long-term resilience.

By taking just a few minutes each day to reflect on what you appreciate, you're creating lasting mental clarity and calm. Gratitude can literally change how your brain functions, keeping you centered even when life gets tough.

Science Fact: Studies show that practicing gratitude increases activity in the prefrontal cortex, the brain's decision-making and emotional regulation center, and reduces cortisol, the stress hormone, to help you feel calmer and less anxious.

Biohacking Tip: Start a daily gratitude practice by saying aloud or writing down three to five things you're thankful for. Take it deeper by reflecting on why each item matters to you. Over time, you'll experience more emotional stability, less stress, and improved mental clarity.

October 31: Strengthening Focus With Meditation

Insight:
Meditation isn't just about finding peace in the moment—it's a scientifically-backed powerhouse for improving focus, emotional balance, and mental resilience. With over 1,400 scientific studies to back it up, meditation has been proven to enhance mental clarity, extend your ability to focus, and increase neuroplasticity, keeping your brain sharp and adaptable as you age.

Studies show that regular meditation improves sustained attention, allowing *you* to focus on tasks for longer periods without getting easily distracted. Not only that, but it also lowers cortisol levels—the stress hormone—leading to better emotional regulation and an overall sense of calm. So, instead of being overwhelmed by life's daily stressors, *you* can handle them with greater ease, keeping emotional balance and maintaining mental clarity. Meditation has also been linked to improved emotional well-being, boosting positive emotions while reducing symptoms of anxiety and depression.

But the benefits don't stop there. Meditation promotes neuroplasticity, the brain's remarkable ability to rewire itself. This means *you're* not just calming your mind for the moment but actually improving *your* brain's capacity for learning, memory, and cognitive flexibility in the long term. With a regular meditation practice, *you'll* notice sharper mental performance and better emotional stability as you go about *your* day.

Biohacking Tip: Incorporating even a short meditation session into *your* daily routine can do wonders for strengthening *your* focus and emotional balance. As *you* continue meditating, *you'll* enjoy improved memory, greater cognitive performance, and a healthier, more resilient brain for the long haul.

November

Introduction:

November is a powerful month of transformation and adventure, guided by the deep emotional energy of Scorpio and the adventurous, expansive spirit of Sagittarius. This is a time to push your boundaries—both in your inner world and in the outer world—embracing personal growth through emotional resilience, physical challenges, and spiritual exploration.

Scorpio's influence invites you to go deep within yourself, facing your fears and embracing the process of transformation. This is the time to confront the emotions and habits that are holding you back, using biohacks like breathwork, meditation, and cold exposure to strengthen your emotional resilience. Growth requires discomfort, and this month encourages you to lean into that discomfort, knowing it leads to greater strength and clarity.

Sagittarius' energy pushes you to explore new frontiers. Whether it's trying a new fitness routine, embarking on an adventure, or challenging yourself in your daily life, this is the time to step out of your comfort zone and take risks. Adventure doesn't have to mean travel—it's about trying new things, learning, and expanding your horizons. The more you explore, the more you grow.

Finally, November is about self-mastery. Scorpio's transformative energy encourages you to commit to your personal evolution, to become the best version of yourself. Whether through mental resilience, emotional healing, or spiritual exploration, this month asks you to take control of your growth journey and embrace the power that comes from inner strength.

November 1: Enhancing Mental Resilience With Stoic Practices

Mental resilience isn't something you're born with—it's something you build, and Stoic practices offer a powerful way to strengthen it. When I started reading about Stoicism, I realized how much it teaches you to focus on what you can control, accept challenges as opportunities for growth, and practice detachment from outcomes. These principles help you navigate life's ups and downs with grace, maintaining emotional balance even in stressful situations. One of the core tenets of Stoicism is recognizing that, while you can't control external events, you can control how you respond to them. By focusing only on what's within your control, you free yourself from the anxiety of things that are out of your hands—like other people's actions or unpredictable circumstances. This shift in focus strengthens your mental resilience, helping you maintain a sense of peace and stability, no matter what life throws your way.

Another key Stoic practice is accepting challenges and seeing them as essential for personal growth. When you approach difficulties with the mindset that they are opportunities to strengthen yourself, you become more adaptable and resilient. Instead of fearing adversity, you face it head-on, knowing that each challenge is a stepping stone toward greater emotional and mental fortitude.

Stoicism also encourages practicing detachment from outcomes. This doesn't mean you don't care about results—it means you understand that the outcome is often beyond your control, so you focus on doing your best in the moment.

Hacking Tip: Start applying Stoic practices in small ways. Gradually incorporate the teachings you find in this book, and when faced with a stressful situation, pause and ask yourself, "What part of this can I control?" Focus on that and let go of the rest. Over time, you'll build mental resilience, strengthening your ability to stay grounded and emotionally balanced through life's challenges.

November 2: Biohacking For Full-Body Recovery

Recovery is often overlooked but is just as important as your workouts or daily grind. By prioritizing recovery, you're not only setting yourself up for long-term health but also ensuring your body performs at its best. Biohacking techniques can speed up this process, helping you bounce back faster and stronger.

Incorporating practices like foam rolling helps loosen and improves circulation, which accelerates healing. Infrared saunas are a powerful way to reduce inflammation and detoxify your body, all while promoting relaxation. And don't forget magnesium—it's key for muscle recovery and quality sleep, which is where real healing happens.

Biohacking Tip: Start incorporating these recovery hacks into your routine. A few minutes of foam rolling or a regular magnesium supplement can make a noticeable difference. Prioritize recovery, and your body will thank you with better performance and longevity.

Remember, not every day has to be a push-hard day.

Mauro dos Santos

November 3: Embracing Personal Transformation

Have you ever noticed how some amazing people seem to stop growing, and the traits that once made them stand out become dulled by complacency? Failing to embrace new challenges can lead to a gradual erosion of what once set them apart. Growth and transformation aren't one-time events; they're an ongoing process of shedding layers and evolving into the best version of yourself. True personal transformation begins when you're ready to let go of outdated habits, open yourself to new learning, and move past limiting beliefs and behaviors that no longer serve who you're becoming. It's about creating space for a more aligned version of yourself to emerge.

How will your life look 3 or 5 years from now if you grow just 1% every day? Remember, in life, there's no stagnation—you're either growing or declining.

Hacking Tip: Each day, say to yourself, "Today, I will be better than yesterday." Or repeat, "Every day, in every way, I'm getting better and better." Start by identifying one habit or belief you're ready to let go of and replace it with something that aligns with your future self. Consistently working on these small shifts will create profound, lasting transformation over time.

November 4: Exploring New Frontiers In Health

Adventure isn't just about scaling mountains or traveling to exotic places; it's also about pushing the boundaries of what your body and mind are capable of. Exploring new frontiers in health means taking a curious, proactive approach to your well-being.

Since each one of us is different, biohacking is a way of discovering and personalizing this journey—testing and tweaking various methods to find out what works best for your unique biology. For instance, tracking your nutrients allows you to fuel your body with exactly what it needs to function at its best and provides a personal approach in this field where one diet doesn't fit all.

Exploring these biohacks gives you the tools to not only improve your health but also increase your energy, focus, and vitality. It's about staying curious, trying new things, and continually refining your approach to wellness.

Biohacking Tip: Start small—try different approaches a couple of days a week or track your patterns to identify areas for improvement. Over time, you'll discover what truly works for your body, helping you live longer, healthier, and with a sense of adventure in optimizing your own health.

November 5: Foot Roll On A Tennis Ball

Most of us already know that rolling your foot on a tennis ball or lacrosse ball releases tension, improves circulation, activates reflexology points, and promotes neuroplasticity. But science goes beyond that. By performing this simple act for 10 minutes on each foot, you stimulate the fascia, tapping into what's known as *fascial tensegrity*, where localized input influences global structural alignment and releases tension up to your neck.

This practice also stimulates the plantar cortex—the region in the brain associated with foot sensation and proprioception (our sense of body position). This activation has been shown to improve the brain's body map, which fine-tunes balance, spatial awareness, and coordination. When rolling the foot, you're indirectly engaging the vague nerve while also activating peripheral nerves that connect to the central nervous system.

What fascinates me is that you're not only activating physical mechanisms but also promoting biochemical shifts. Stimulating nerve endings in the foot applies subtle pressure that can release endorphins and serotonin through what's known as *mechanotransduction*. Biohackers and yogis alike value this practice for its ability to help regulate emotions naturally, as increased body intelligence can make you more intuitive and balanced under stress. Additionally, it naturally increases pain tolerance while aiding recovery from physical stress, intense workouts, and fatigue.

Biohacking Tip: For an extra boost, try incorporating essential oils, such as peppermint or eucalyptus, on your foot before rolling. These oils not only enhance circulation but also promote a calming effect, combining physical release with aromatherapy to amplify relaxation and recovery.

November 6: Biohacking For Peak Performance

Achieving peak physical and mental performance isn't just for elite athletes or top-level executives—it's something you can unlock through the power of biohacking. By optimizing your diet, incorporating nootropics, and adding strategic movement throughout your day, you can experience enhanced energy, focus, and endurance.

Start with your diet. Fueling your body with whole, nutrient-dense foods gives you the steady energy you need to stay sharp. Add nootropics to the mix—these cognitive enhancers help boost brain function and improve focus, memory, and creativity. And don't forget movement. Strategic bursts of exercise, even just a few minutes a day, help get your blood flowing, increasing both your physical endurance and mental clarity.

Biohacking Tip: Begin by making small tweaks to your routine. Optimize your diet, experiment with nootropics, and find ways to integrate movement into your day. Soon, you'll notice that your energy levels and performance start to rise, allowing you to operate at your peak.

November 7: Why Running Falls Short for Optimal Fat Loss

I can't count the number of overweight people I see by the beach in the first weeks of January, struggling and hurting themselves by running on hard surfaces. If this sounds like you, **stop**. Running will not make you lose weight—at least not in the way you might expect. Instead, it may cause injuries or joint damage that can be irreparable. And trust me, I'm one of the biggest running enthusiasts out there. But I never recommend it, especially if you're overweight.

So, why isn't running ideal for fat loss?

1. **High Impact with Limited Muscle Engagement**: Running, especially on hard surfaces, is a high-impact activity that primarily engages the lower body. However, it doesn't stimulate as many muscle groups as other forms of exercise, like strength training or metabolic conditioning, which limits its effectiveness for building lean muscle.
2. **Potential for Muscle Loss**: Excessive cardio, if not combined with strength training or adequate protein intake, can actually promote muscle loss. This leads to a slower resting metabolism over time, meaning you burn fewer calories throughout the day, which can work against your weight loss goals.
3. **Limited Afterburn Effect (EPOC)**: Running, particularly at a steady pace, does not generate a strong afterburn effect (excess post-exercise oxygen consumption, or EPOC). The afterburn effect is when your body continues to burn calories after the workout as it recovers. High-intensity exercises tend to create a much higher EPOC, which keeps your metabolism elevated for hours.
4. **Stress, Cortisol, and Abdominal Fat**: A study by Epel, McEwen, and Seeman (2000), *"Stress and body fat distribution: A review and theoretical integration"* published in *Psychosomatic Medicine*, reviews the mechanisms

397

linking chronic stress to abdominal fat. It concluded that prolonged cardio can elevate cortisol levels, particularly if you're already under stress or not getting enough recovery. Elevated cortisol can lead to fat storage, especially in the abdominal area, making it harder to lose weight effectively. **Yes, in some cases, running may actually make you accumulate belly fat.**

Biohacking Tip: Want to Exercise for Effective Weight Loss?

Engage in **HIIT (High-Intensity Interval Training)**. HIIT generates a high afterburn effect, boosting metabolism for up to 24 hours post-workout, making it far more efficient for calorie burn and fat loss than steady-state cardio. Incorporate **strength training with compound movements** to build lean muscle and improve metabolism.

If you haven't exercised in over five years, consider investing in a **personal trainer**. A competent trainer will save you time, frustration, and even money by setting you on the right path, keeping you accountable, and helping you build a sustainable habit.

Mauro dos Santos

November 8: Think About What You Are Thinking

Self-mastery is your ability to control your thoughts, emotions, and behaviors to achieve personal goals and maintain inner harmony. It involves becoming aware of your inner world, understanding your strengths and weaknesses, and taking conscious steps to align your life with your values and aspirations. It's a journey of personal growth that requires discipline, self-reflection, and a commitment to continuous improvement. Self-mastery isn't an end destination but a continuous process of growth and self-awareness, helping you shift patterns to become the best version of yourself.

Moving toward self-mastery begins with mindfulness—tuning into your thoughts and emotions without judgment. By observing your mental patterns, you can understand the unconscious habits influencing your actions. The next step is setting clear, intentional goals. Intentions serve as your compass, guiding your actions and decisions toward growth rather than stagnation.

Hacking Tip: Start by noticing what you're thinking and tracking your daily habits. Practice mindfulness each morning, set intentions for the day, and follow through with disciplined action. Small, consistent efforts will gradually lead you toward self-mastery.

November 9: Talk To Your Body And Say Good Things

For a long time, science largely ignored the 'gut feeling,' body energy, and the wisdom of ancient teachings about the mind-body connection. But today, we understand far more about how your thoughts and words influence your health. What you say to your body matters—it can promote healing or contribute to illness.

Studies now show that the mind and body are closely interconnected. People who speak negatively about themselves tend to experience more health issues. This isn't just metaphorical—there's actual science behind it. Self-criticism, like saying 'I'm so tired' or 'I hate how I look,' triggers stress responses, signaling to your body that something is wrong. Over time, these patterns can lead to chronic stress, inflammation, and a weakened immune system.

On the flip side, speaking positively about your body—saying 'You are beautiful' or 'I love you'—sends an entirely different message. Positive self-talk helps create an internal environment where healing and balance thrive. Studies reveal that words of affirmation can lower stress hormones like cortisol, boost immune function, and even support a healthier gut microbiome, which plays a crucial role in mood and overall health.

Gut Feeling: The Science Behind It. You may have heard that the gut is like your 'second brain.' With its vast network of neurons connected to your central nervous system, certain types of gut bacteria actually produce neurotransmitters like serotonin and dopamine, directly affecting mood, focus, and mental clarity. A balanced microbiome supports emotional resilience and cognitive sharpness, adding another layer to mental well-being.

When you speak kindly to your body, you're not just influencing your mind; you're sending signals to your gut as well. Positive affirmations, by reducing stress, create a healthier environment for beneficial bacteria. Chronic stress, however, disrupts digestion and can reduce the diversity of helpful microbes. By managing stress through affirmations like 'I love my body' or 'Thank you for supporting me,' you help maintain a balanced microbiome, fostering vitality and mental clarity.

Biohacking Tip: Try incorporating daily affirmations that align with your health goals, letting your mind and body work together for holistic well-being.

The Power of Words and Energy. Ancient cultures valued positive self-talk and self-love, and now modern science validates this wisdom. Whether through spoken words, affirmations, or mindful awareness, what you say impacts your body's energy. Positive words carry high vibrational energy that supports natural healing, while negative words carry lower vibrations, contributing to disharmony.

Hacking Tip: Start your day by speaking kindly to your body. As you look in the mirror, say, 'I love you,' or 'You're strong, healthy, and beautiful.' Practice consistently, and observe the shift in how you feel both physically and emotionally. You'll be nurturing your health from within, creating a positive environment for healing and growth.

By speaking love and kindness to your body, you're not just boosting mental well-being—you're actively cultivating health, longevity, and balance. Your body listens, so be sure to send messages of care, appreciation, and love.

November 10: Challenge Your Existence

Your beliefs shape your reality. What you know influences what you believe, and that, in turn, affects how you perceive the world. Your perception drives your emotions, which ultimately defines your state of being. But when was the last time you questioned where those beliefs and perceptions came from?

By challenging your beliefs, you open the door to new understanding. According to Dr. Joe Dispenza, this new understanding is the foundation of wisdom, which leads to personal evolution. When you challenge the thoughts that define your reality, you create space for transformation and growth, evolving into a higher version of yourself.

Hacking Tip: Start questioning your beliefs and perceptions. What's shaping how you see and experience the world? Break free from limiting beliefs and aim for the next level of evolution in your life.

November 11: Emotional Healing Through Personal Evolution

Emotional healing is a key part of personal evolution, and as you evolve, you naturally begin to process and release past emotional wounds. The journey of growth involves shedding the layers of hurt, pain, and limiting beliefs that no longer serve you. As you challenge your perceptions, beliefs, and understanding of the world, you gain the clarity to move forward with greater emotional balance.

When you start to evolve, you gain wisdom that allows you to revisit past experiences with a new perspective. Instead of seeing challenges or emotional pain as roadblocks, you start to view them as stepping stones for growth. Each layer of emotional healing brings you closer to a more balanced and resilient self, creating space for greater joy, peace, and personal freedom.

Hacking Tip: Reflect on past emotional wounds that may still be affecting you. Ask yourself how these experiences can be reframed to support your personal growth. If you're ready to take this healing journey to a deeper level, consider a Reiki massage, where a skilled practitioner can help identify emotional blocks and traumas stored in your body, releasing muscular tension and restoring the natural flow of energy. As you evolve, allow healing to become part of the process, bringing emotional clarity and balance into your life.

November 12: Praise Someone Today

"What progress have I made? I am beginning to be my own friend. That is progress indeed." **(*Letters to Lucilius* 6.2)**

Seneca reminds us that by recognizing and praising the virtues in others, we can refine our own character. When you praise someone, you don't just uplift them—you elevate your own spirit as well. Genuine praise strengthens relationships, builds confidence, and creates a positive ripple effect.

But avoid vague compliments like "You're beautiful" or "You're intelligent." Find something unique and special to acknowledge. Point out their kindness, their resilience, or the effort they've put into a task. This kind of thoughtful praise is far more meaningful and will truly lift the other person's spirit.

Hacking Tip: Today, take a moment to praise someone. Be specific and sincere, highlighting a quality or effort that often goes unnoticed. You'll not only make their day, but you'll also grow in virtue and self-awareness.

Mauro dos Santos

November 13: Be That Person

When we meet someone new, we often hope to find qualities we like or admire. But what if, instead of expecting others to impress us, you focused on being the person others admire and appreciate—not to impress but simply to become a better version of yourself?

Marcus Aurelius, in *Meditations*, emphasizes leading by example and focusing on our own growth and moral improvement. He says, *"Waste no more time debating what makes a good person. Be one."* (Meditations 10.16). This powerful reminder encourages us to stop expecting others to live up to certain ideals and instead take responsibility for embodying those ideals ourselves.

Hacking Tip: Today, embody the qualities you wish to see in others. Be the kindness, the patience, the positivity you often seek. By focusing on your own character, you inspire others without needing to say a word.

November 14: Advice From Your Godly Self

One afternoon, I was relaxing in Laguna Beach when I noticed a crowd gathered around a chess game. As a chess enthusiast, I couldn't resist stopping to watch. I stood behind one of the players, my mind racing with all the possible moves that the other player could make to gain an advantage—even to win the game. He was struggling to escape a check, but to me, the solutions seemed simple. After a while, he invited me to play a round. Confident, I sat down, but the moment I took my place, those once-clear solutions didn't feel so simple anymore. The difference? When I was just observing, I had the freedom of an outside perspective, without the pressure to perform. Once I was the player, the weight of each move—and the responsibility for the outcome—shifted my view entirely.

Have you ever noticed how easy it seems to solve other people's problems? When a friend comes to you for advice, their solution often appears clear. But, like in the chess game, this clarity comes from seeing the situation from a different angle—an outside perspective without the emotional weight of responsibility. It's much simpler to see a way forward when you're not the one in the hot seat.

Now imagine if, during your own challenges, you could access that same calm, elevated perspective—your godly, higher self—giving you the clarity and insight you'd have for a friend. This is the essence of this "hack": learning to tap into that outside viewpoint to guide yourself with wisdom and compassion.

Hacking Tip: When you're facing a difficult situation, activate your godly side. Start by sitting in silence. Visualize yourself rising above, as if you're floating up and outside your house. Imagine looking down, seeing your neighborhood, your home, and then focusing on that person—yourself—sitting in the living room or lying in bed, wherever you might be.

Mauro dos Santos

Now, from this high vantage point, observe yourself with kindness and insight. You know this person well; you know their strengths, their potential, and the conflicts they face. With this higher perspective, ask yourself: What solution do I see? What advice would my godly self give to this person who is struggling? How can they approach this situation with clarity and calm?

By practicing this, you are accessing the "quantum field," a place of limitless possibilities and perspectives. From this elevated view, you may find that your conflict isn't as overwhelming as it seemed, or that the solution is far simpler than you thought.

November 15: Physical Health Through Adventure

When you engage in an adventure like hiking through new terrain, picking up a new sport, or trying a new physical challenge, you're not just rewarding your body with strength and power—you're also increasing your resilience and mental toughness while building more self-confidence.

Engaging in outdoor activities or more adventurous workouts doesn't just benefit your body—it sharpens your mind, enhances your emotional well-being, creates more mindfulness of the present, reduces stress, and reconnects you with nature, bringing you more joy. Every climb, run, or new skill learned taps into your mental resilience, creating a more balanced and energized version of yourself.

Think about it: adventure stimulates new neural connections and keeps you mentally agile. It shakes up your routine, forcing your brain to adapt, which boosts cognitive function and keeps you emotionally vibrant. The best part? It doesn't have to be a grand trip across the world. You can find adventure in everyday moments—a new recipe, a different way to exercise, or learning something you've always wanted to try.

By embracing these small adventures, you'll notice a shift in how you handle stress and uncertainty. You'll feel more alive, more present, and mentally clear.

Hacking Tip: This week, try something different—whether it's a long hike, a bike ride, or even a new sport. Push your limits and see how physical adventure transforms not only your body but also your mindset. The key is to keep your mind stimulated and your sense of adventure alive. You're not just expanding your world—you're growing mentally, emotionally, and spiritually.

November 16: Have Your Own Mission Statement

What are you living for? What's your purpose in life? Creating a personal mission statement is one of the best ways to define your purpose, the values you live by, and what you want to achieve each day. A mission statement provides clarity on your core beliefs and guides how you aim to live, highlighting what's truly most important to you.

Just as every successful business crafts a mission statement to gain clarity, focus, and purpose, the same approach in personal life can be transformational. Your mission statement becomes a compass—directing your choices, fortifying your values, and sustaining motivation and focus. This simple step may be what you need to wake up with enthusiasm and direction every morning, feeling aligned with your goals and values.

Hacking Tip: Create your mission statement and use it as a daily guide. Write it down, reflect on it, and revisit it over time as you grow. Allow it to inspire you to live intentionally and with purpose, every single day.

November 17: Success Can Be A Vague Failure

While we live in a world where people feel rewarded by money, the ambition for riches and wealth can be a double-edged sword. Growth and success are essential in any man's life; however, when you see success only through the accumulation of money and possessions, you may be setting yourself up for failure and life's disappointment.

Stoicism advised against the relentless pursuit of material success, as it can distract from the pursuit of wisdom and inner peace. As Seneca wrote, "It is not the man who has too little, but the man who craves more, that is poor."

The Stoics warned against ambition that centers around fame, wealth, or status, as these external rewards are fleeting and can lead to moral compromise. Pursuing such goals without consideration for virtue can lead to frustration, dissatisfaction, or unethical behavior.

Marcus Aurelius also wrote, "Do not dream of the future or worry about it, but be content with what is in your hand now."

Hacking Tip: Does this mean we should never think about money or success? No. But do not make money your final goal for freedom and happiness to avoid being disappointed. *To ensure that your ambitions align with your core values, set aside time for regular self-reflection. This simple practice can help you stay grounded and motivated in a way that transcends material rewards.*

November 18: Do Not Take It Personally

Have you ever noticed that politicians, despite being constantly bombarded with insults, accusations, and criticism, often remain composed, sometimes even smiling through it all? While we may not be politicians, there's something we can learn from their resilience in the face of personal attacks.

In many ways, we should adopt a similar mindset when it comes to hearing someone else's opinion—especially when it's negative or contrary to our own. People are entitled to their opinions, and when those opinions clash with ours, or even come across as an insult, it's important to remember one key thing: it's not about you. When someone expresses a harsh thought or criticism, they're simply projecting their perspective—how they see the world in that moment. Their words reflect their own emotions, biases, or experiences, not necessarily the truth about who you are.

When you learn not to take insults personally, you free yourself from the emotional weight of other people's opinions. You become like the politician who can stand in the storm of words, unaffected, grounded in your own truth. You understand that what others say or do is a reflection of them, not you.

Hacking Tip: The next time you feel criticized or insulted, take a breath and remind yourself: "This is their opinion, not my truth." Respond with calm and poise, knowing that their words say more about them than they do about you.

November 19: Drink Water

If there's one crucial habit many neglect, it's proper hydration. Dehydration comes with a huge health price—one that we often don't realize until it's too late. You don't have to feel thirsty to know it's time to drink water. In fact, by the time you feel thirst, your body has likely already lost about 1-2% of its water content, putting you in the early stages of dehydration.

We've all heard the classic "8 cups of water a day" rule, but this one-size-fits-all guideline doesn't work for everyone. The amount of water you need depends on several factors: your weight, activity level, climate, and overall lifestyle. A more accurate approach to water intake considers your body weight. The Institute of Medicine suggests drinking between 0.5 to 1 ounce of water per pound of body weight per day.

But here's a catch—men generally need 45-50% more water than women because they have more muscle mass, burn more energy, and typically run at a higher temperature. Here's a simple breakdown, but not a rule:

- A **160-pound woman** should aim for around **9 cups** of water per day.
- A **160-pound man** should aim for around **10 to 12 cups** of water per day.
- A **280-pound woman** should target **14+ cups** daily.
- A **280-pound man** should drink **17.5+ cups** per day.

Biohacking Tip: The next time you feel hungry, try drinking a glass of water first. Often, we confuse thirst with hunger, and staying hydrated can prevent unnecessary snacking while keeping you in balance. Water is your body's fuel—use it wisely!

November 20: Listen And Understand Before Responding

Have you ever watched two people argue over the same thing, yet they seem miles apart in understanding? It's common, especially when discussing sensitive topics like philosophy or politics. But why does this happen so often? It's simple—we're often more focused on preparing our response than on truly understanding the other person's perspective.

In our eagerness to be heard, we forget the power of listening. True wisdom lies in listening with the intent to understand, not just to reply. When you pause and ask thoughtful questions, you're not only gaining clarity but also positioning yourself as someone calm, wise, and in control. In sales, we learn that the one who asks the most questions leads the conversation. The same holds true in life—those who seek to understand before speaking often gain deeper insights and control the direction of the dialogue.

Hacking Tip: Next time you're in a discussion, focus on listening more than speaking. Ask questions with the genuine intent to understand the other person's view. You'll not only avoid misunderstandings but also foster better connections and more productive conversations. Be teh wise person in the room.

November 21: Be Truly Thankful

As December approaches and Thanksgiving is here, now is the perfect moment to do a life evaluation and find one thousand reasons to be thankful. It's easy to be grateful for those who bring joy into your life, but true freedom lies in being able to thank those who have acted as your personal trainers, challenging your emotions and pushing your growth. These mentors—whether they were tough, friendships that faded, or critics who doubted you.

Marcus Aurelius, in *Meditations* 4.10, reminds us: *"Everything that happens, happens as it should, and if you observe carefully, you will find this to be so."* His Stoic wisdom points to the idea that each person, especially those who may have hurt or disappointed us, plays a role in our journey. Their actions—whether intentional or accidental—were part of a grander plan, helping you develop resilience, empathy, or insight. Forgiving them is not just an act of grace but an acknowledgment of their place in your personal evolution. Here lies true wisdom: in shifting your focus from resentment to recognition that every experience, good or bad, has its rightful place in your story.

Hacking Tip: Take a moment to make peace with yourself and those around you. List three challenging experiences from your past, noting what each taught you. Follow this with a simple statement of gratitude, thanking each experience or person involved. By forgiving freely and expressing gratitude, you open up space for growth and carry forward the lessons that make you stronger.

November 22: Physical Fitness As A Tool For Personal Evolution

Did you know that physical fitness is much more than just building muscle or staying in shape? It's a powerful tool for personal evolution. When you challenge your body through exercise, you're also training your mind to develop qualities like discipline, mental toughness, and resilience. Every time you push through a tough workout or achieve a new personal best, you're not just strengthening your muscles—you're sharpening your focus, building determination, and reinforcing the mindset that you can overcome obstacles.

Fitness becomes a practice of resilience, showing you that you can handle discomfort, overcome barriers, and continue evolving into the best version of yourself.

Hacking Tip: Start viewing your workouts as a mental and physical training ground. Push through when it's hard, and remind yourself that every physical challenge conquered strengthens not just your body but also your mind.

November 23: Mental Agility And Flexibility In Communication

Mental agility is like yoga for your brain—keeping you flexible, adaptable, and prepared to handle complex situations with ease. In leadership, mental agility is a high-value skill that lets you pivot, reassess, and remain open to learning from each experience. When your mind is flexible, you move through challenges, picking up insights and adapting your approach.

We've all encountered conversations where someone clings to a rigid viewpoint, making us feel as if we're running into a brick wall. Mental flexibility, however, allows you to shift perspectives, adjust your communication style, and actively listen rather than just waiting for your turn to talk. From a spiritual standpoint, it's also about letting go of the need to be "right," which frees you to connect authentically and compassionately.

Hacking Tip: Elevate mental agility by practicing active listening: put down the phone, look people in the eye, and really hear them out. Challenge your brain by reading outside your comfort zone or exploring opposing viewpoints. The more you stretch your mind, the more adaptable it becomes—a critical skill for effective communication and leadership.

Quick Hack: In your next conversation, pause before you respond. Resist the urge to immediately reply; instead, consider a perspective you hadn't initially thought of. This pause improves communication and helps you become a more thoughtful and engaging conversationalist.

Takeaway: Stay curious, stay flexible, and remain open to learning something new. Avoid trying to argue or convince those unwilling to listen; true growth lies in communicating with compassion, respect, and a willingness to see things from different angles.

November 24: Crisis Is A Moment Of Opportunity

When You're Facing a Crisis, Discover the Opportunity Within
When a crisis hits, it's easy to become consumed by chaos, fear, and uncertainty. Yet within every crisis lies an opportunity—an invitation to grow, learn, and transform. Crises push you out of your comfort zone, challenging your limits and revealing solutions that might never have surfaced in calmer times.

Instead of viewing crisis as purely negative, reframe it as a catalyst for personal evolution. The Stoics believed that adversity unveils our true character, acting as a refining force. In these moments, you have the chance to sharpen your resilience, adapt to change, and tap into an inner strength you didn't know existed. The pressure of a crisis prompts strategic thinking and bold decisions, turning fear into fuel for growth and pushing you to embody courage and adaptability.

Hacking Tip: The Stoics viewed hardship not as a curse but as a test of character and a way to cultivate resilience. Marcus Aurelius said, *"A blazing fire makes flame and brightness out of everything that is thrown into it."* Embrace crises as fuel for personal growth, seeking out the lesson each challenge offers. As Seneca noted, *"Difficulties strengthen the mind, as labor strengthens the body."* Reflect on your current hardships and consider how they're shaping you for the better.

Takeaway: Crises, when faced with courage and resilience, reveal your capacity to adapt, thrive, and transform. Embrace each one as an essential part of your journey toward personal strength, high performance, and wisdom.

November 25: Enhancing Decision-Making Skills For Success

Thoughtful decision-making is key to achieving positive outcomes and avoiding regret. Strengthening your decision-making skills combines critical thinking, emotional agility, and reflection—turning you into a decision-making pro!

When faced with choices, it's easy to feel overwhelmed. Should you pursue that new job opportunity or finally take that pottery class? Improving decision-making skills allows you to confidently weigh your options rather than guessing or reacting impulsively.

Strategic Thinking Decision-making starts with clarity about your long-term goals and values. Critical thinking helps you evaluate the pros and cons, but it's equally important to ask, *"Does this choice align with my goals?"* or, *"Will this decision contribute to my overall happiness and fulfillment?"* By making choices that align with your vision, you're paving the way for sustained success.

Reflection for Consistency and Growth Each decision provides an opportunity to reflect, learn, and refine your approach. Consider how previous choices have impacted you and how you might approach similar decisions differently next time. Over time, this process of reflection builds your confidence and consistency, making decision-making less stressful and more empowering.

Hacking Tip Remember, great decision-making is built from smaller, intentional choices. Embrace each decision as an opportunity for growth, and don't be afraid to laugh at mistakes—every experience adds to your expertise. With time, you'll approach decisions with clarity, focus, and the confidence that comes from a well-honed skill!

This refined approach not only enhances immediate decisions but also supports your broader journey toward personal and professional excellence.

November 26: The Journey Toward Self-Mastery

Are you a master of yourself? Self-mastery isn't achieved overnight—it's a lifelong journey of consistent effort, self-discipline, and deep introspection. It requires self-knowledge, understanding your thoughts, habits, and behaviors, and more importantly, learning to control them instead of letting them control you.

Epictetus taught that while you can't control external events, you can control how you respond to them. Imagine the power in that— no matter what chaos life throws your way, you have the ability to maintain inner calm and resilience by mastering your thoughts and reactions. That's where self-mastery begins.

Seneca took this idea further, saying, "No man is free who is a slave to his flesh." In other words, if you're constantly giving in to your desires, emotions, or impulses, you're not truly free. Self-discipline is the key to unlocking this freedom. It's about staying focused on your long-term goals instead of being derailed by short-term temptations or distractions.

But how do you cultivate self-mastery? It starts with mindfulness. Tune into your thoughts, emotions, and habits without judgment. Once you're aware of your patterns, set clear intentions for how you want to live and respond. Then, practice discipline. It's not about being perfect—it's about making a conscious effort each day to align your actions with your values.

Hacking Tip: Every day, take a few moments to reflect on your actions. Did you stay in control of your responses, or were you swept away by emotions or impulses? The more you practice, the closer you'll come to mastering yourself. And with that mastery comes true freedom—freedom from external circumstances and from the internal chaos that disrupts your peace.

November 27: The Power Of Binaural Beats

Binaural beats are a fascinating auditory illusion where two slightly different tones are played in each ear, creating a third perceived tone in your brain. This effect offers several potential benefits for your mental and emotional health:

When you listen to binaural beats in the theta (4-7 Hz) or delta (1-4 Hz) range, your brain naturally shifts into a deeply relaxed state. These frequencies activate your parasympathetic nervous system, responsible for calming you down and reducing stress. Studies show that binaural beats can lower cortisol levels, helping you manage stress more effectively.

If you've ever struggled to concentrate, binaural beats in the beta range (13-30 Hz) can be highly beneficial. These frequencies are linked to heightened alertness and cognitive function. By using binaural beats during demanding tasks, you'll notice sharper focus and an extended attention span.

These frequencies may also help you fall asleep faster and stay in deeper sleep cycles, improving overall sleep quality. Additionally, they can boost creativity. Whether you're a writer, artist, or simply looking for fresh ideas, binaural beats can help you enter a "flow state" where problem-solving and creative thinking thrive.

Hacking Tip: If you're looking for an easy way to boost focus, reduce stress, or enhance creativity, start incorporating binaural beats into your daily routine. Whether you're at work, meditating, or preparing for sleep, this biohack could significantly elevate your mental wellness and cognitive performance.

Mauro dos Santos

November 28: The Power Of Holistic Transformation For Lasting Growth

Transformation isn't just about changing one part of yourself; it's about creating a shift that impacts every area of your life.

When you embrace holistic transformation, you're no longer improving in isolation. Rather than focusing solely on fitness and neglecting mental health, or advancing in your career while overlooking relationships, holistic growth means you create balance in all areas. Emotionally, you become stronger and more resilient; socially, you build deeper, more meaningful connections; spiritually, you align with a greater sense of purpose. This balanced transformation fosters sustained growth and resilience, as each area of your life works in harmony to support the others.

The Benefits of Balanced Growth Holistic transformation not only ensures that each part of your life flourishes, but it also builds a foundation of adaptability. When every area is nourished, you're better equipped to handle change and challenges, creating a more resilient, well-rounded self.

Hacking Tip: Pick one area that needs attention, and reflect on how it connects to your overall growth. Every small improvement you make can create a ripple effect, strengthening and balancing other areas of your life. This interconnected approach forms a solid foundation for sustainable transformation and personal evolution.

November 29: Biohacking Your Environment For Optimal Performance And Growth

Your environment has a profound influence on both mental clarity and physical well-being. Biohacking your surroundings not only fosters health but sets the stage for personal growth and professional success. By reducing toxins, aligning lighting with your circadian rhythms, and minimizing distractions, you create a space that strengthens your focus and supports your goals.

Start with simple adjustments. Declutter to create an organized, stress-free zone that enhances mental clarity. Minimize harmful chemicals in your home or workspace by using natural cleaning products, and consider adding air-purifying plants for cleaner air and an improved atmosphere. Lighting is equally important—opt for soft, natural lighting during the day, and reduce blue light exposure at night to align with your body's natural rhythms, promoting better sleep and improved mood. Reducing digital noise and designating a focused work zone minimizes distractions and keeps you on task.

Strategic Hacking Tip Curate your environment to empower success. Each small, intentional adjustment aligns your space with your personal goals, helping you stay energized, focused, and in a mindset that supports personal evolution. By creating a healthy, well-organized environment, you cultivate a space conducive to sustained growth and resilience, allowing you to perform at your best both mentally and physically.

November 30: Enjoy The Present Instead Of Romanticizing The Past

It's easy to look back at the past and view it through rose-colored glasses, romanticizing what was while overlooking the beauty of the present. But the truth is, life is happening now, in this moment, and it's too valuable to let slip by while you're lost in nostalgia. By remaining present, you're not only cultivating a growth-oriented mindset but also positioning yourself to recognize opportunities for connection, growth, and advancement that exist right now. Romanticizing the past often distracts you from the opportunities right in front of you. The present is where growth, joy, and connection truly take place. While reflecting on the past can offer lessons, living in it robs you of the chance to create something new and fulfilling right now. Living in the now builds emotional resilience, empowering you to adapt to life's challenges and appreciate each moment's unique value.

Hacking Tip: Whenever you catch yourself drifting into nostalgia, ground yourself by focusing on something in the present—your breath, a conversation, or an experience. Mindfulness keeps you grounded, especially in moments of pressure, helping to maintain focus on what's truly meaningful in the here and now. Embrace the richness of the moment and build your future from the now, not from memories. Grounding yourself in the present.

December

Introduction

Introduction:

December is a month of adventure, reflection, and planning for the future, guided by the expansive energy of Sagittarius and the disciplined, grounded influence of Capricorn. It's a time to close out the year with strength, clarity, and a clear vision for what's to come.

With Sagittarius leading the way, December encourages you to expand your horizons. This is the perfect time to push yourself mentally, emotionally, and physically. Whether it's trying new biohacks to boost your endurance, exploring new ideas, or learning something new, this is a month to embrace adventure. Growth happens when you challenge yourself, and December invites you to keep exploring beyond your comfort zone.

At the same time, Capricorn's grounded energy asks you to take a step back and reflect on the year. What have you accomplished? Where have you grown? What lessons have you learned? Reflection is key to understanding where you've been and where you're headed. Use this time to assess your progress and plan your next steps. Capricorn's influence encourages you to set clear, actionable goals for the new year, so you enter it with purpose and direction.

December is about balance—between adventure and reflection, between pushing forward and pausing to assess. It's a month to close the year with strength, learn from the past, and set yourself up for a successful future.

December 1: The Power of Aromatherapy

Aromatherapy is a powerful way to improve your mental, physical, and even energetic well-being. Essential oils like lavender, eucalyptus, and peppermint contain compounds that interact with neurotransmitters, promoting effects like reduced stress, elevated mood, and enhanced cognitive function. By engaging your sense of smell, you can create a calming environment, lift your spirits, or energize your mind in ways that become more effective over time.

Aromatherapy works by stimulating the olfactory system, which directly connects to the limbic system—the part of your brain that controls emotions, memory, and behavior. Essential oils can also resonate with specific energy centers or chakras. Lavender supports emotional healing by balancing the heart chakra, while eucalyptus aids communication and respiratory health by aligning with the throat chakra. This means that different scents evoke relaxation, clarity, or emotional balance on both a physical and subtle level.

Hacking Tip: Incorporate essential oils into your daily routines to build intentional shifts in your mental and emotional states. Diffuse lavender before sleep to train your body to relax, use peppermint for a mental energy boost, or apply eucalyptus to soothe both respiratory issues and your energy flow. With regular use, aromatherapy can biohack your mood, harmonize your energy, and create an environment that supports holistic clarity and well-being.

December 2: Challenge Your Existence

Existentialist thinkers like Jean-Paul Sartre, Albert Camus, and Friedrich Nietzsche wrestled with the concept of human existence in a world that may seem indifferent or even absurd. They focused on personal responsibility, the search for meaning, and the courage to face life's uncertainties.

Challenge your existence by asking yourself: Am I truly living according to my values? Am I reaching my highest potential? This kind of self-inquiry is the foundation for growth and transformation. It pushes you beyond the comfort of routine and superficial success, driving you to explore your purpose and what genuinely motivates you.

Jean-Paul Sartre famously said, "Man is condemned to be free." In existentialism, this freedom implies that, while we have the power to choose how we live, we also bear the responsibility of creating our own meaning. Living authentically means aligning your life with your true self and values, even in the face of societal pressures. Heidegger warned that many people fall into the trap of living inauthentically by following the "they" (society) instead of taking ownership of their existence.

Viktor Frankl's *Man's Search for Meaning* echoes this concept beautifully. Through his own suffering, Frankl discovered that even in the harshest conditions, one can find purpose. He argues that the quest for meaning, rather than power or pleasure, is what truly sustains us, adding depth to the idea of living authentically and purposefully.

Hacking Tip: Every time you challenge your beliefs, habits, or comfort zones, you open yourself up to new possibilities. Growth comes from the willingness to evolve, face discomfort, and pursue what makes you feel truly alive. It's about rejecting mediocrity and embracing the unknown. The journey to a more meaningful life begins with the courage to question everything and transform.

December 3: Authenticity: A Path To Higher Vibration

Authenticity has the profound power to elevate your energy— sometimes even more than love. When you align with your true self—embracing your values, beliefs, and feelings—you create harmony between your inner truth and outer actions.

According to the Hawkins Scale of Consciousness (introduced by Dr. David R. Hawkins), love vibrates at a frequency of 500, where enlightenment, considered the highest vibration, falls between 700-1000. While authenticity isn't explicitly measured on this scale, it is closely linked to states like truth and self-actualization, which rank higher.

Authenticity offers a different kind of energy, one rooted in self-awareness and truth. When you're authentic, you're not seeking validation from others but living in harmony with your soul's purpose. This powerful, transformative energy can uplift your life and inspire those around you.

From a psychological perspective, research suggests that authenticity is associated with greater emotional regulation, self-esteem, and overall mental health. By freeing yourself from societal constraints and false identities, you create emotional clarity and mental peace. This groundedness in truth may surpass love in its ability to raise your vibration because it's about fully living in alignment with who you are at your core.

Hacking Tip: Practice authenticity daily by making small, intentional choices that align with your true self. Whether through setting boundaries, expressing genuine thoughts, or staying true to your values, each action will gradually elevate your energy and deepen your connection to self.

December 4: Find A New Way

Have you ever thought about finding a new way to solve a problem, make a decision, or even live your day? Sometimes, we get so caught up in routine and habit that we forget there's always another path—a fresh perspective that could change everything.

Neuroscience has shown that the brain is incredibly adaptable and capable of creating new pathways through neuroplasticity. This means that when we intentionally adopt new ways of thinking or problem-solving, our brain forms new neural connections. The brain's ability to rewire itself allows us to break free from habitual patterns of thought, which is essential for innovation.

Quantum mechanics teaches us that particles can exist in multiple states simultaneously, which mirrors the idea that multiple solutions can coexist until we "choose" one. This challenges traditional, linear decision-making and opens the door to more holistic, multi-dimensional problem-solving approaches.

Hacking Tip: By combining neuroscience, quantum science, and spiritual insights, you can:

- Rewire your brain through new habits (neuroplasticity)
- Expand your perception beyond limited frameworks (quantum thinking)
- Tap into intuition for guidance (spiritual insight)

Stay present, flexible, and open to possibilities, and you'll enhance your capacity for creative and effective problem-solving.

December 5: Reviewing Your Progress For The Year

Have you taken the time to truly reflect on your journey this year? We often get so caught up in what's next that we forget to pause and acknowledge how far we've come. Reflection isn't just about looking back—it's a tool to rewire your brain and shape your future. Neuroscience shows that reflection activates neuroplasticity, reinforcing new neural pathways. When you review successes and lessons learned, you engage your brain's reward systems, boosting motivation and priming yourself for future growth. Reflecting on challenges strengthens the prefrontal cortex, helping you make better decisions moving forward.

From a quantum science perspective, reviewing the past is an act of creation. By focusing on what worked and what didn't, you collapse potential realities and align yourself with the future you want to create. Reflection becomes an opportunity to consciously choose from multiple possibilities. Psychologically, reflecting on your progress activates neural pathways linked to self-awareness and emotional regulation. It also builds confidence by reinforcing a sense of accomplishment, fueling your motivation to keep evolving.

Hacking Tip:

- **Rewire Your Brain:** Reflection strengthens neural pathways, enhancing growth and adaptability.
- **Shape Your Reality:** By reflecting intentionally, you collapse multiple potential futures into the one you desire.
- **Achieve Coherence:** Weekly or monthly reflection sessions can create clarity and a sense of purpose, empowering you to build a life aligned with your goals.

In summary, reviewing your year isn't just about assessing progress; it's a chance to redefine your future, using the tools of neuroscience and quantum thinking.

December 6: Boost Your Longevity With NAD+

NAD+ (Nicotinamide Adenine Dinucleotide) is a coenzyme found in every living cell, playing a crucial role in energy production and cellular repair. As we age, our NAD+ levels naturally decline, leading to a decrease in energy, impaired DNA repair, and accelerated aging. By boosting NAD+ levels, you can potentially enhance longevity, improve metabolic function, and maintain youthful energy.

Research suggests that increasing NAD+ levels supports mitochondrial health, which is key to slowing the aging process and improving overall vitality. Additionally, NAD+ helps activate sirtuins, proteins that regulate cellular health and promote longevity.

Hacking Tip: Support your NAD+ levels through a combination of biohacks like intermittent fasting, regular exercise, and supplements such as nicotinamide riboside (NR) or nicotinamide mononucleotide (NMN). These strategies can help maintain your energy and vitality as you age, giving your cells the boost they need to function optimally.

December 7: Embracing The Unknown For Self-Growth

Growth happens when you step outside your comfort zone and embrace the unknown. Whether it's taking risks, trying new things, or making bold decisions, uncertainty is where real personal evolution occurs. By stepping into unfamiliar territory, you open yourself up to new possibilities and opportunities that you might never have imagined. It's in these moments of uncertainty that you discover new strengths, gain wisdom, and experience growth that pushes you toward becoming the best version of yourself.

Hacking Tip: The next time you feel hesitant to try something new, remind yourself that the unknown is where growth lives. Start with small steps outside your comfort zone, gradually building your tolerance for uncertainty. Visualize positive outcomes, take the leap, and trust that each step in the unknown accelerates your evolution.

December 8: Reviewing Your Successes And Failures

Success and failure are not opposites; they're partners in your growth. Every success reflects alignment with your potential, and every failure signals where new possibilities lie. When you review your year, you're not just looking back—you're collapsing time, accessing the quantum field where all possibilities exist, and bringing the lessons of the past into your future.

"Success comes to both the wise and the foolish, but only the wise know how to make good use of it." Seneca, in his works like *Letters to Lucilius* and *On the Shortness of Life*, often discusses the nature of success, wisdom, and how we should respond to life's fortunes and misfortunes. He emphasizes that external success is fleeting, but true wisdom comes from how we use both success and failure to grow in virtue. Seneca's teachings align well with modern self-improvement, where we find that true success is measured by personal growth rather than fleeting achievements.

Quantum physics teaches us that observation shapes reality. Just as focused observation in quantum physics collapses multiple possibilities into one, reflecting on your year anchors potential into reality, shaping your future by concentrating on what matters. As you reflect on your successes, you integrate them into your identity. Equally important, when you observe your failures without judgment, you transform them into opportunities. This neutral approach to observation channels these experiences into constructive energy, where the energy of failure becomes a catalyst for change, allowing you to rewire your approach and align more closely with your true path.

Hacking Tip: Instead of simply looking back, observe your year through the lens of potential. Where did you succeed? Where did you stumble? Both offer energy for transformation. Approach each with curiosity rather than judgment. Your failures, just like your successes, can shift your reality, setting the stage for a more aligned future.

December 9: Your Emotions Hold Your Pain: Nocebo Effect

The concept of emotional pain manifesting as physical pain, often referred to as the "nocebo effect," is essentially the opposite of the placebo effect. While the placebo effect involves positive outcomes based on the belief in a treatment's efficacy, the nocebo effect occurs when your brain takes a condition, for example, a painful movement after a trauma or accident, and creates a memory. After the treatment, the symptoms are no longer there, but the memory that your brain created still exists, and every time you make that particular movement, your brain remembers that it's painful. The nocebo effect or emotional pain, particularly from traumatic events, can become deeply embedded in the body, manifesting as chronic pain or illness.

It can be even worse or more difficult if it's associated with an emotional trauma. Research shows that individuals who have experienced trauma are more likely to develop chronic pain conditions.

Dr. Bessel van der Kolk, a renowned psychiatrist and trauma expert, discusses this phenomenon in his groundbreaking book *The Body Keeps the Score*. He explains that trauma isn't merely psychological; it has deep physical roots. The body holds onto traumatic experiences, resulting in various forms of physical pain, from muscle tension and migraines to gastrointestinal issues and even autoimmune disorders. Often, this "holding" of pain occurs subconsciously, so individuals may be unaware of the connection between their physical symptoms and unresolved emotional trauma.

The Science Behind the Nocebo Effect

Research into the nocebo effect has shown that negative emotions and expectations significantly impact physical health. Studies conducted by **Dr. Luana Colloca at the University of Maryland** reveal that patients who expect pain or negative side effects from treatment are more likely to report these symptoms. The expectation of pain can actually amplify the body's experience of it, illustrating how powerfully our minds influence our physical health.

This response is driven by brain regions involved in pain perception, such as the **anterior cingulate cortex** and **insular cortex**. These regions are highly active when negative expectations and emotions are present, leading to an intensification of the physical experience of pain. Emotional pain can manifest in or worsen physical conditions through the power of belief and negative expectation.

How to Heal: The Mind-Body Connection

Healing from emotional pain that has manifested as physical symptoms requires an approach that addresses both the mind and body. Here are several therapeutic practices and mind-body techniques to facilitate healing:

- **Trauma-focused therapies**: Approaches like **EMDR (Eye Movement Desensitization and Reprocessing)**, **somatic experiencing**, and trauma-focused psychotherapy allow individuals to process and release trauma stored in the body. Studies have shown that EMDR, in particular, reduces symptoms of PTSD and chronic pain by stimulating the brain's natural healing processes, leading to improvements in both emotional and physical well-being.
- **Mind-body practices**: Techniques such as **yoga**, **meditation**, and **breathwork** have been shown to reduce the physical impact of stress and trauma. Yoga has been found to lower cortisol levels and help the nervous system return to a more balanced state, while meditation enhances the brain's capacity for emotional regulation and resilience. These practices encourage relaxation, helping the body release stored emotional pain.
- **Somatic Experiencing**: Developed by Dr. Peter Levine, somatic experiencing focuses on releasing trauma held in

the body by increasing awareness of physical sensations. This method has been shown to reduce both physical and emotional symptoms and facilitate holistic healing.

- **Reiki massage** has proven to be highly effective for treating chronic and emotional pain. By combining muscle tension release through massage with the healing energy of Reiki, this approach supports clients in creating new beliefs while releasing both physical and emotional pain together.

Biohacking Tip

Incorporate mind-body practices to foster healing and resilience. **Practice mindfulness** to increase awareness of sensations in your body, allowing you to identify and release tension that may be linked to unresolved emotional trauma. Integrate **calming exercises like breathwork or progressive muscle relaxation** to help regulate your nervous system and reduce chronic pain related to hyperactivation. Additionally, **seek for a reiki master or reiki massage professional** to help you work through and release trauma stored in the body.

December 10: Planning Your Financial Goals For The Future

The end of the year is a great time to reassess your financial habits, especially as holiday spending can quickly add up. Financial security is a crucial pillar of long-term stability and success. As you think about your future, it's worth reflecting on how you've been managing your finances and setting clear, actionable goals to promote growth and security.

Whether your focus is on saving more, investing smarter, or paying off debt, intentional financial planning will set the foundation for long-term success. This is not just about cutting back, but about creating a financial strategy that supports your future aspirations. By taking control now, you're building a life where your financial decisions work in your favor rather than against you.

Hacking Tip: Start small. Set a specific savings goal, automate a percentage of your income for investments, or create a debt payoff plan. The consistency of these small steps can lead to significant financial growth over time, helping you navigate life with more confidence and stability.

December 11: Change Your Friends Or Change Your Friends

If you're holding this book, it's a clear sign you're on a journey of personal growth, aiming to become the best version of yourself. Congratulations on your decision! Trust me, by applying the principles within these pages, you will elevate your life to a whole new level. However, as you look around, if your friends aren't supporting your growth or aren't willing to grow alongside you, it might be time to make a change. Share your learnings, share this book, and encourage them to grow with you. Remember, growth is unique to everyone, so self-compassion is essential.

Some of your friends may choose to stay where they are, and that's okay. There's no judgment or criticism in their choice. Since you're walking a new path, however, it's important to connect with people who are on a similar journey. Changing your social focus doesn't mean cutting ties; it means deciding who to invest time in and recognizing where each relationship fits best within your journey. Surround yourself with people who lift you up and share your ambitions.

Hacking Tip: Some people are meant to be close friends who share your goals and values, while others may be acquaintances you meet occasionally. Respect both, but invest your time with those who inspire and elevate you.

December 12: Enjoy Without Guilt

Remember the 80/20 rule? In biohacking, it means eating mindfully 80% of the time while allowing yourself to relax the other 20%. This doesn't mean you should fill your body with junk food; rather, during that 20%, you can enjoy a meal or drink with friends, fully present, and without guilt. Mindful indulgence is key to maintaining this balance.

The holidays are the perfect time to practice this awareness, self-control, and inner resilience. With parties, business events, and more food invitations than usual, finding this balance becomes even more valuable. Enjoy the social connections without overthinking every bite—embrace the freedom to indulge mindfully, knowing you're supporting your health long-term.

Hacking Tip: Life is meant to be enjoyed, and while responsibility is key, balance is just as essential. Allow yourself to indulge mindfully and guilt-free, savoring each moment and every bite. This approach builds resilience, reinforcing a positive relationship with food and connection during the holiday season.

December 13: In A War There's No Winner

Sometimes, what seems crystal clear and logical to you is utterly baffling to someone else. What begins as a simple explanation can quickly spiral into an argument, and trust me, I've been there many times. But here's the truth: I can't recall a single argument that ever gave me a truly positive result. Sure, you might "win" the argument, proving yourself smarter or more knowledgeable, but it often comes at the cost of something far greater—peace of mind, a friendship, or even your reputation for wisdom and respect.

Engaging in a heated debate doesn't just affect the relationship; it affects you physically and mentally. Arguing elevates cortisol levels, triggering stress responses that cloud your clarity and make it harder to engage empathetically. On the other side, the person you're debating may feel humiliated or attacked, even if that wasn't your intent. In the end, "winning" often leaves both parties feeling drained rather than uplifted.

Hacking Tip: It's often more valuable to lose an argument than to lose a friend. Ask yourself, "What do I really gain by proving I'm right?" More often than not, agreeing with the other person—or simply letting the debate go—brings more peace and fulfillment than "winning" ever could. Choosing understanding over conflict is a conscious, empowered choice that reflects your growth and self-control.

Mauro dos Santos

December 14: Release Trauma And Self-Limitation To Become A Better Person

"I am like this, and nobody can change me." This is one of the most common phrases you'll hear from someone who seems angry at the world, resigned to their current state. But if you dig deeper, you'll often find that they aren't naturally this way—they've built a protective shell around their pain, shaped by past traumas, to guard themselves. We are, in many ways, the result of our personal histories, and those histories are often marked by pain and trauma. These experiences leave scars that shape our behaviors, thoughts, and the way we interact with the world. However, when we take the time to confront the true source of our pain, we open the door to release it, along with the self-limitations it has imposed on us.

By addressing and healing these old wounds, you allow yourself to shed the layers of defense mechanisms that no longer serve you. In doing so, you free yourself to become the person you were meant to be—one not defined by past hurts, but by your ability to grow beyond them. This process is both liberating and transformative, helping you step into a version of yourself that's rooted in strength, healing, and possibility.

As Dr. Joe Dispenza explains in *Breaking the Habit of Being Yourself*, by reconditioning our thoughts and beliefs, we can change how our bodies and minds interact with past traumas. Dispenza teaches that we can "lose our old mind" and create a new one, effectively reshaping how we respond to our past. This shift allows us to replace old thought patterns with empowering beliefs, leading to profound personal change.

Hacking Tip: Take time to reflect on your pain, not with the intent to dwell on it, but to release it. Seek out ways to heal—whether through therapy, journaling, or mindfulness practices. By doing so, you'll dismantle the walls that hold you back, freeing yourself to evolve into a better, more authentic version of yourself.

December 15: Time To Do A Self-evaluation

How was your year? Did you grow? What changes have unfolded in your life? Which habits have you embraced, and what have you removed that no longer serves you? These questions are not just reflective—they're essential steps in your personal growth journey.

Seneca advocated for a daily practice of self-evaluation. He suggested reviewing your actions, thoughts, and behaviors each day as a way to improve character and maintain accountability. In *Letters to Lucilius*, he writes, "When the light has been removed and my wife has fallen silent, aware of this habit of mine, I examine my entire day and go back over what I've done and said. I hide nothing from myself, I pass nothing by." This practice of honest reflection allows you to see where you aligned with your virtues and where you fell short, giving you the chance to correct your path. Similarly, Epictetus encouraged people to define the person they wanted to become and align their actions accordingly. "First tell yourself what kind of person you want to be, then do what you have to do."

Reflecting on these teachings, Dr. Joe Dispenza's work also supports the importance of self-evaluation as a way to reprogram our thoughts. In *Breaking the Habit of Being Yourself*, he explains that our daily reflections shape the neural pathways in our brains, influencing how we act and respond in the future. By consistently aligning our thoughts and actions with our values, we're effectively "rewiring" ourselves to become the person we aspire to be. As the year draws to a close, now is the perfect time to assess whether your actions reflect your goals and values.

Hacking Tip: Set aside time for a year-end reflection. Review what you accomplished, where you fell short, and how you can improve. Use this process to establish clear intentions for the new year, ensuring that your actions align with the person you aspire to become.

December 16: New Year Dreams

As we reach the second half of December, it's the perfect time to start thinking about what you want to accomplish in the coming year. Don't wait for the last day of December or the start of January to begin creating a new life for yourself. Start now. What are the things you truly desire? Beyond resolutions, your dreams are the visions that guide your growth and fulfillment. They provide direction, purpose, and the motivation to keep moving forward.

Marcus Aurelius once said, *"The soul becomes dyed with the color of its thoughts."* So, dream big and envision a life filled with the things that inspire and uplift you. Whether it's a career shift, personal transformation, or new adventures, this is the moment to turn those dreams into actionable plans.

Hacking Tip: Write down your top three dreams for the coming year. Break them into achievable steps and revisit them regularly to stay on track. And most importantly, act immediately—why wait?

The new year offers a clean slate—a chance to align your goals with the deeper aspirations of your heart.

December 17: Embrace Your Company Mission

Think about where you spend most of your week—the workplace. It's more than just a place where you complete tasks; it's where you invest your time, energy, and skills. When you align yourself with the company's mission, you're not just doing a job—you're becoming part of something bigger. This sense of shared purpose not only elevates the company but also strengthens your role within it, creating a more fulfilling and impactful work experience.

Success thrives on cooperation. By working together, sharing ideas, and supporting your colleagues, you create a winning environment. Being a team player doesn't just benefit the company—it benefits you. When the team wins, everyone wins. This opens the door for more opportunities, growth, and advancement for all. As a business coach would emphasize, contributing to a shared goal makes you indispensable in your role, enhancing both job satisfaction and professional growth.

Tony Robbins, a renowned motivational speaker, often talks about the importance of focusing on your purpose and the power of shared goals. When you connect with the company's mission, you tap into a drive that fuels motivation and commitment, helping you rise above challenges and push for excellence. This alignment fosters a sense of ownership and responsibility, making you not only a valuable employee but also a leader in your own right.

Hacking Tip: Show up with a mindset of cooperation and support. Ask yourself, "How can I contribute to our collective success today?" By embracing the mission and actively seeking ways to uplift the team, you're not only helping the company grow—you're paving the way for your own success. The journey of collective success is where individual advancement finds its roots.

December 18: Practice Patience

Patience is a powerful tool that helps you navigate life's delays and setbacks without falling into frustration. The Stoics recognized that cultivating patience allows you to approach challenges calmly and thoughtfully, leading to better decision-making instead of reacting impulsively. In today's fast-paced world, patience becomes an asset that not only aids in personal growth but also supports professional effectiveness, enhancing resilience in high-stress environments. When you practice patience, you create space to evaluate situations more clearly. Instead of rushing to judgment or action, you can consider your options and respond in a way that aligns with your goals and values. As a business coach would suggest, patience strengthens leadership, allowing you to remain composed under pressure and make strategic decisions. This balanced approach, seen in effective leaders, promotes trust and respect among teams and colleagues, building a foundation for lasting success.

Reflecting on patience, high-performance experts emphasize that the ability to delay gratification or withstand discomfort can lead to significant breakthroughs. Patience encourages a growth mindset—one where setbacks are seen as learning experiences rather than obstacles. This mindset, essential for sustained progress, enables you to focus on long-term goals, rather than immediate rewards, driving meaningful and lasting change.

Hacking Tip: To cultivate patience, start by taking a deep breath when you feel frustration rising. Remind yourself that some things are beyond your control, and focus on what you can influence. Practice waiting a little longer in everyday situations—whether it's in line at the store or during a meeting. Each moment spent in patience is an opportunity to strengthen your ability to remain calm and collected. Embrace patience, and you'll find it easier to navigate life's ups and downs with resilience and clarity, building a stronger foundation for personal and professional growth.

December 19: Talk When You Have Something To Say

There's great wisdom in knowing when to speak and when to remain silent. A wise person speaks with purpose, choosing their words carefully to convey meaning, while a fool talks just to fill the silence. Proverbs 17:28 reminds us, "Even fools are thought wise if they keep silent, and discerning if they hold their tongues." This is a powerful reminder that silence often speaks louder than unnecessary words.

In a world filled with constant chatter, it's easy to feel pressure to always contribute. Social dynamics often tempt us to speak simply to show presence or affirmation, yet true wisdom lies in waiting until you have something genuinely valuable to offer. Neuroscientifically, silence allows us to regulate emotions more effectively, preserving mental clarity and minimizing stress. When you hold back until your words are purposeful, your contributions resonate more deeply, gaining both respect and attention. This approach is often essential in professional settings, where speaking with intentionality can elevate team cohesion, reduce conflicts, and foster a culture of respect.

The art of speaking less and listening more also aligns with philosophical teachings on self-discipline and introspection, as it shows you value the conversation and those around you. When we follow this path of discernment, our silence reflects wisdom and helps create a more thoughtful world.

Hacking Tip: Next time you're in a conversation, pause and ask yourself, "Is what I'm about to say necessary and valuable?" Speaking with intention gives your words meaning and encourages others to do the same. Embrace purposeful silence, and let your words reflect the wisdom within.

December 20: Reflecting On Your Relationships

How was your year? Did you grow? What changes have unfolded in your life? Which habits have you embraced, and what have you removed that no longer serves you? These questions are not just reflective—they're essential steps in your personal growth journey.

Seneca advocated for a daily practice of self-evaluation. He suggested reviewing your actions, thoughts, and behaviors each day as a way to improve character and maintain accountability. In *Letters to Lucilius*, he writes, *"When the light has been removed and my wife has fallen silent, aware of this habit of mine, I examine my entire day and go back over what I've done and said. I hide nothing from myself, I pass nothing by."* This practice of honest reflection allows you to see where you aligned with your virtues and where you fell short, giving you the chance to correct your path.

Self-evaluation also holds an insightful place in neuroscience and social behavior. In *Social*, Matthew Lieberman highlights how reflection and self-assessment engage brain regions responsible for understanding our place within social contexts. This enhances our mental flexibility, essential for adapting to challenges. Moreover, Amir Levine and Rachel Heller, in *Attached*, explain that understanding attachment styles and relational patterns can elevate self-awareness, allowing you to make better choices and strengthen key relationships.

As the year draws to a close, now is the perfect time to assess whether your actions reflect your goals and values. By doing this self-evaluation, you not only acknowledge your progress but also refine who you want to become in the year ahead.

Hacking Tip: Set aside time for a year-end reflection. Review what you accomplished, where you fell short, and how you can improve. Use this process to establish clear intentions for the new year, ensuring that your actions align with the person you aspire to become.

December 21: If You Are Selfish At Your Workplace, You Need Help

One of the biggest challenges in many organizations today is a lack of cooperation, often driven by underlying insecurities and self-centered behaviors. With experience working alongside corporate teams, I've seen firsthand how damaging these attitudes can be—not only to individual progress but to the overall success of the company.

When employees withhold information or hesitate to collaborate, it's frequently rooted in insecurity. The fear of losing relevance or being outshone can make people overly protective of their contributions. But in a thriving organization, success is the result of collective effort, not isolated achievements. A workplace shouldn't feel like a battleground where resources are guarded; rather, it should be a dynamic ecosystem where shared knowledge and teamwork fuel innovation, efficiency, and growth.

Self-centered actions in the workplace—like hoarding information, declining to mentor, or resisting team initiatives—often appear in subtle ways. While some may believe that withholding knowledge protects their personal value, this approach actually limits their own growth and can create isolation from the team. True professional success arises from creating value for others and embracing the collaborative spirit.

Insecure employees may believe they're safeguarding their roles, but this mindset often holds them back. In contrast, those who willingly share, mentor, and support their colleagues often find themselves recognized for leadership qualities and trusted for higher roles.

Coaching Insight: If you ever feel reluctant to cooperate, pause and consider why. Are feelings of inadequacy or competition holding you back? Reflecting on these areas can be transformative because the most successful professionals are those who uplift others and contribute to a shared purpose. In the long run, your own success is closely linked to how well you collaborate, communicate, and contribute to the team.

By addressing insecurities and embracing a mindset of cooperation, you're not only supporting your company's success—you're building a foundation for your own growth as a valuable, indispensable team player.

December 22: The Power Of Sound Healing

Sound healing, particularly through the use of tuning forks, is an ancient practice that is regaining recognition for its profound impact on our physical, emotional, and energetic well-being. Tuning forks are designed to resonate at specific frequencies that can align with different parts of the body, energy centers (or chakras), and even your mental state.

When a tuning fork is struck, it creates a vibration that interacts with your body at a cellular level. These sound waves work to restore energetic balance, promoting vibrational healing that can penetrate deep into your tissues. It's like giving your cells a gentle, energetic "massage," allowing them to recalibrate and heal. The fork's frequency creates harmony in the body, encouraging a state of deep relaxation and stress reduction. Each tuning fork is specifically tuned to a certain frequency, which can correspond to various aspects of the body or mind. For example, certain frequencies are believed to stimulate circulation, reduce muscle tension, and even relieve physical pain. Tuning fork therapy is often used in conjunction with energy healing practices to target the body's chakras, helping to unblock stagnant energy and promote overall well-being.

Science of Sound Healing: Sound frequencies can alter brainwave states, promoting relaxation and emotional clarity. Research shows that sound therapy can shift the brain into alpha or theta states, which are linked to deep meditation, creativity, and healing. Additionally, sound waves stimulate the nervous system, promoting circulation and aiding in the body's natural healing processes.

Hacking Tip: If you're new to sound healing, start by experimenting with tuning forks that resonate with your energy centers. Whether you use them for chakra alignment, stress relief, or pain management, the vibrational frequencies can bring balance to both your mind and body.

December 23: Sound Healing And Disease: What It Offers

Sound healing has long been recognized for its ability to alleviate stress, balance energy, and promote overall well-being. While it's not a cure for diseases, certain practitioners suggest that specific sound frequencies can help restore the body's natural vibrational state, offering potential support for healing and recovery.

Potential Benefits in Disease Management:

1. **Stress Reduction**: Sound healing can help calm the nervous system, reduce stress, and indirectly support the immune system. By promoting deep relaxation, it creates a space where the body can focus on healing.
2. **Pain Relief**: Some evidence suggests that sound therapy may help manage pain by enhancing relaxation and improving circulation. When the body is in a relaxed state, it may experience less tension, which can alleviate physical discomfort.
3. **Emotional Support**: Chronic conditions often lead to emotional strain, including anxiety and depression. Sound healing is known to ease these emotional burdens, providing a sense of calm and mental relief, which is crucial for overall well-being.

Limitations and Complementary Use: While sound healing offers significant emotional and stress-reducing benefits, scientific evidence supporting it as a standalone treatment for diseases is limited. Sound therapy should be considered a complementary practice, supporting conventional medical treatments rather than replacing them.

Hacking tip: Sound healing offers valuable relaxation, emotional relief, and stress reduction, which can contribute to enhanced well-being. However, it should always be used in conjunction with traditional medical care for a holistic approach to health management.

December 24: Silence For An Exceptional Mind

Silence is an underrated tool, especially when it comes to mastering your business mind. In a world filled with constant noise and distractions, embracing silence can provide clarity, sharpen focus, and empower better decision-making.

1. **Develop a Clear Vision**: In silence, you can disconnect from the external chaos and tune in to your deeper thoughts. It gives you the mental space to refine your vision for your business and set clear goals without distraction.
2. **Master Decision-Making**: Silence helps you avoid reactive decisions and fosters thoughtful, deliberate choices. By quieting the noise around you, you're able to weigh options more effectively and focus on long-term outcomes.
3. **Calm the Mind in Stressful Situations**: When you practice silence regularly, it becomes a natural way to calm your mind during high-pressure situations. This inner calm enhances your ability to think clearly, even in the face of challenges.
4. **Enhance Self-Awareness and Emotional Intelligence**: Silence allows you to reflect on your emotions, building greater self-awareness. It's in these quiet moments that you can assess your strengths and areas for growth, leading to greater emotional intelligence.
5. **Enhance Listening Skills**: By practicing silence, you also sharpen your ability to listen. Active listening is a key leadership skill that helps you understand others better and respond more thoughtfully.

Hacking Tip: Incorporate moments of silence into your daily routine—whether through meditation, reflection, or simply stepping away from the noise. You'll notice a shift in how you approach challenges, make decisions, and lead with clarity. Silence sharpens the mind, allowing you to be more effective in your business and personal life.

December 25: Celebrate Christmas, Or Join Us In Celebrating Life

Christmas is a time of joy, connection, and reflection for many, a moment to celebrate love, gratitude, and togetherness with family and friends. Yet even if you don't observe Christmas, today can be a special opportunity to celebrate life itself. Whether you embrace the spirit of the holiday or simply take a moment to pause and appreciate your journey, this day offers a moment to reflect on life's beauty. It's a time to express gratitude for the experiences that have shaped you, the people who support you, and the moments—of growth, joy, and even challenge—that have brought you to this point. Consider how these connections and experiences contribute to the richness of life.

Hacking **Tip:**
Reach out to loved ones, appreciate the present, and celebrate the gift of life. Whether or not you celebrate Christmas, let today be a reminder to embrace love, kindness, and gratitude in everything you do. Take a moment to reflect on where you've been, celebrate small wins, and envision growth for the year ahead.

Happy holidays to all, and here's to celebrating the richness of life together!

This approach maintains the text's essence while deepening its resonance across different life experiences and enhancing its impact as both a call to gratitude and a foundation for intentional living

December 26: Creating Harmony In Your Daily Life

Your harmony in life doesn't just happen by accident—you create it by aligning your actions with your values. When what you do each day reflects what truly matters to you, there's a sense of flow, balance, purpose, and joy. Imagine waking up knowing that everything on your to-do list moves you closer to your dreams and long-term goals, while also supporting your overall well-being.

What's your purpose—your personal growth, family, health, or career aspirations? Once you know what drives you, it becomes easier to align your daily tasks with those values. Instead of feeling pulled in a million directions, your actions start to serve a greater purpose, making even small tasks feel meaningful.

This alignment doesn't just boost productivity—it fosters emotional well-being too. When you spend most of your time living in harmony with your values, stress is reduced, and you feel more fulfilled. It's like everything in your life is working together, rather than against you.

Hacking Tip: Make a living by never working one day in your life. When your actions reflect your values, life becomes more than just a checklist of tasks—it becomes a journey filled with purpose, fulfillment, joy, and balance. That's true harmony.

December 27: Reflecting On Your Emotional Growth

Emotional growth is an essential aspect of your overall development, often overlooked but just as vital as physical or mental progress. Take a moment to reflect on how your emotional intelligence has evolved over the past year. How have you handled stress? How have your relationships with others improved? Have you become better at managing and understanding your own emotions?

This kind of self-reflection is key to cultivating stronger emotional health in the future. The more aware you are of your emotional patterns, the better equipped you'll be to navigate challenges with grace and empathy.

Hacking Tip: Regularly assess your emotional responses and interactions. By understanding how you've grown emotionally, you can set clear intentions to continue building resilience, empathy, and emotional intelligence in the year ahead.

December 28: Mental Resilience For The Upcoming Year

As you approach the new year, building mental resilience will be crucial for navigating the inevitable challenges ahead. Fortunately, you can start preparing now. Mental resilience isn't just about enduring tough times—it's about equipping your mind to stay steady, focused, and calm when obstacles arise, enhancing both adaptability and creativity.

Biohack your brain with practices like mindfulness, stress-reduction techniques, and focus exercises. Meditation, breathwork, or even journaling can help regulate your nervous system and reduce stress. Regular mental training strengthens your brain's ability to remain adaptable and centered, regardless of what comes your way.

Hacking Tip: Begin incorporating short mindfulness sessions or brain-boosting exercises into your daily routine, and set specific resilience goals, like meditating for 10 minutes each day. Take a moment to reflect on how you handled past challenges, recognizing your growth. A calm and resilient mind is your greatest tool for handling the uncertainty and challenges of the new year—building a future where you thrive, no matter the circumstances.

December 29: Reflecting On Your Personal Evolution

Personal evolution is a slow, transformative process, but taking time to reflect reveals how far you've truly come. Look back on the past year and consider your growth—mentally, emotionally, physically, and spiritually. Each step, big or small, has shaped who you are today.

This kind of self-awareness gives you the clarity to understand what's working, what's not, and how you want to continue evolving in the future. It's through this reflection that you prepare yourself for even more meaningful growth in the years to come.

Hacking Tip: Set aside time to journal or meditate on your personal evolution. Recognize the shifts you've made and consider how you'll continue to build on them in the upcoming year.

December 30: Reviewing Your Accomplishments And Setting New Goals

Before you dive into setting new goals for the upcoming year, take a moment to reflect on what you've already accomplished. Celebrate your wins, no matter how big or small, and acknowledge the effort, persistence, and dedication that went into achieving them. Recognizing your progress fuels the momentum for even greater things ahead.

Now, as you set your new goals, let your biggest ambition be this: to create happiness and fulfillment that lasts a lifetime. Whether it's through personal growth, career achievements, or nurturing relationships, aim for goals that bring you genuine joy and long-term well-being.

Hacking Tip: Use your past accomplishments as a springboard. Set goals that not only challenge you but also align with your happiness and personal fulfillment. Keep happiness as your ultimate milestone.

December 31: Expanding Your Horizons For the Future

As you enter a new year, embrace the spirit of adventure and open yourself up to new possibilities. Expanding your horizons means stepping out of your comfort zone, trying new things, and seeking experiences that push your personal boundaries. Growth and evolution happen when you dare to explore beyond what you already know.

Whether it's learning new skills, traveling to unfamiliar places, or meeting new people, every step you take into the unknown enriches your journey and broadens your perspective.

Hacking Tip: Set an intention to challenge yourself in the coming year. Seek out opportunities that inspire curiosity and excitement, and let your sense of adventure guide you toward personal and professional growth.

Note From The Author

This is not the end—rather, it may be the beginning of your journey of growth and transformation. My hope is that you join me in this pursuit, so together we can spread these lessons and create a meaningful impact on the lives we touch.

Remember, the insights here are not meant to be final answers. Use them as a guideline, experimenting to find what resonates with you, your needs, or this moment in your life. Absorb what feels right, and keep the rest as a reference—maybe for a future need or to help someone else on their path.

Every page is a product of countless hours of reflection, analysis, and the selection of the teachings that have had the most powerful impact. For those of you who have chosen this book, my goal is that some of these lessons connect with you and bring value to your life.

Throughout the year, I'll continue to share additional resources, insights, and lessons related to this book, all freely available to you. And if there's anything you'd like to see expanded or explored further, please reach out directly at <u>mauro@coachmauro.com</u>.

Mauro dos Santos

My Instagram

@MAURO.HEALTHCOACH

About The Author

Mauro dos Santos
**International Speaker |
Health Specialist |
Biohacker
Personal Trainer | Massage
Therapist | Reiki Master**

From Adversity to Transformation

My name is Mauro dos Santos, and my journey is a testament to the resilience of the human spirit and the body's incredible capacity to heal. From facing life-threatening health challenges at a young age to emerging as an international speaker and health expert, my path has been all about transforming adversity into a mission to help others reach their fullest potential.

When I was 11 years old, I was diagnosed with chronic, intense nosebleeds that landed me in the hospital every few months. With each visit, my condition seemed hopeless to the doctors, who couldn't identify the cause. On several occasions, I slipped into a coma, only to wake up feeling weak and drained. Lacking resources to fully investigate my condition, the doctors sent me home with severe restrictions: no lifting, running, sports, or even sun exposure.

One day, I came across a magazine article about someone who had overcome a severe illness through karate. I was intrigued by the idea that physical discipline could bring about such change. Shortly after, a friend invited me to join a local karate group. Though my family was concerned about my health and safety, I was determined to try, so I joined—keeping it a secret, especially from my mother. Despite being the smallest and skinniest in the group, I faced each challenge with all the determination I had.

Around this time, I began to devour every book and magazine I could find on karate and martial arts. I learned to push through my limitations and gained a resilience that would carry me through my life. When I started high school, I noticed the physical education instructor, Professor Natanael, inviting talented soccer players to join the city's new track and field team. Gathering my courage, I asked if I could join too. They needed a long-distance runner, and I volunteered, committing to cross-country and the 5K.

This was the beginning of my sports career and a new chapter in my journey of self-discovery. I dedicated myself to understanding high performance from every angle—massage, nutrition, recovery. By the time I was 14, I was already teaching new members in my karate group. I trained for track each morning, trained or taught karate in the evenings, and attended night school, all while working a full-time job to help support my family.

Over the years, I have spent more than 35 years in the health and fitness field, guiding hundreds of clients to transformative results. My expertise spans fitness, nutrition, yoga, Pilates, and core strength training, allowing me to design wellness programs tailored to each person's unique needs and goals. My love for learning and passion for health took me deeper into understanding the science behind the body and mind, and I began studying human performance, philosophy, spirituality, and self-growth.

Then, in 2011, life brought another defining challenge. A severe back injury left me unable to walk, and doctors recommended surgery. But in the midst of pain, uncertainty, and feeling lost, I was guided to explore quantum science and neuroscience, seeking to understand what was truly happening in my life. I leaned on everything I knew—massage, energy work, yoga, and Pilates—and chose a path of self-rehabilitation. Through unwavering belief in the body's ability to heal and a deep commitment to self-discipline, I regained my mobility and emerged stronger, more certain than ever of the body's power to heal when the mind and spirit are fully engaged.

Today, as an international speaker, health specialist, and biohacker, I combine a lifetime of learning with personal experience to help others break through chronic pain, trauma, and limiting beliefs. Through the years, I've developed a deep knowledge of human sciences, philosophy, spirituality, and self-growth. My approach to wellness is holistic, incorporating personalized fitness programs, therapeutic massage, and Reiki-infused healing to empower clients to overcome physical, mental, and emotional barriers. My mission is to support people in transforming not only their bodies but their entire approach to health and well-being.

At one point in my life, I made a personal commitment to create a positive impact on every person I meet. This commitment drives my work and fuels my desire to reach a broader audience. It is my hope to reach one million people worldwide through my teachings, books, and programs, sharing the lessons I've gathered with anyone who seeks change.

This book is a concise collection of the most effective, straightforward ways to improve health and promote longevity, drawn from years of personal experience, study, and dedication. By following the teachings here and embracing self-discipline, you will discover the joy of taking care of your body and the profound fulfillment that comes with it.

Join me, and let's unlock the extraordinary potential within you. Together, we can transform challenges into opportunities, building a life filled with vitality, purpose, and balance.

Appendix

My top 51 reading recommendations.

I've always loved reading and learning, and it's rare that I don't have a book recommendation ready for someone who shares the same drive to grow and explore new ideas. Over the years, I've come across books that left a mark on me—insights and perspectives that have, in one way or another, guided me to where I am today.

Because you're reading this, I thought it would be the perfect time to share a list of 51 books that I consider "must-reads." Each one is a treasure of its own, with a unique perspective on the topics that matter most, from self-improvement to science, philosophy, and beyond. To make it easier, I've included the category for each book and a quick idea of what it covers.

I hope you find something here that inspires you or gives you that new spark of insight. Enjoy the journey!

1. **Alder, D. (2017).** *The New Health Rules: Simple Changes to Achieve Whole-Body Wellness.* Ten Speed Press.
   Category: Health & Wellness
   Why read this book? Provides practical guidance for integrating healthy, sustainable habits into everyday life, making wellness accessible for all.
2. **Asprey, D. (2014).** *The Bulletproof Diet: Lose up to a Pound a Day, Reclaim Energy and Focus, Upgrade Your Life.* Rodale Books.
   Category: Biohacking
   Why read this book? A biohacker's guide to optimizing energy and focus, offering insights into the impact of nutrition on cognitive performance.
3. **Brach, T. (2003).** *Radical Acceptance: Embracing Your Life with the Heart of a Buddha.* Bantam.
   Category: Mindfulness & Spirituality
   Why read this book? A compassionate approach to self-

acceptance, Brach's work is a guide to overcoming self-judgment and cultivating inner peace.

4. **Brown, B. (2010).** *The Gifts of Imperfection: Let Go of Who You Think You're Supposed to Be and Embrace Who You Are.* Hazelden Publishing.
   Category: Self-Improvement
   Why read this book? Encourages embracing vulnerability as a path to personal freedom, authenticity, and deeper relationships.

5. **Brown, B. (2012).** *Daring Greatly: How the Courage to Be Vulnerable Transforms the Way We Live, Love, Parent, and Lead.* Gotham Books.
   Category: Personal Development
   Why read this book? Inspires readers to take risks and live authentically, challenging societal norms around vulnerability.

6. **Carol Dweck, C. (2006).** *Mindset: The New Psychology of Success.* Random House.
   Category: Psychology
   Why read this book? A foundational guide to understanding and adopting a "growth mindset" to overcome challenges and achieve personal growth.

7. **Chopra, D. (1994).** *The Seven Spiritual Laws of Success: A Practical Guide to the Fulfillment of Your Dreams.* New World Library.
   Category: Spirituality
   Why read this book? Outlines principles for aligning with one's purpose, providing a spiritual approach to achieving success and fulfillment.

8. **Clear, J. (2018).** *Atomic Habits: An Easy & Proven Way to Build Good Habits & Break Bad Ones.* Penguin.
   Category: Self-Improvement
   Why read this book? Offers actionable strategies for forming positive habits, making lasting changes attainable.

9. **Cohen, S. (2007).** *Social Relationships and Health.* American Psychologist.
   Category: Psychology & Health
   Why read this book? Examines the impact of social connections on health, revealing how strong relationships foster well-being.

10. **Cozolino, L. (2010).** *The Neuroscience of Psychotherapy: Healing the Social Brain.* W.W. Norton & Company.
    Category: Neuroscience
    Why read this book? Explores the brain's capacity for healing through relationships and therapy, combining science with therapeutic insight.

11. **Covey, S. R. (1989).** *The 7 Habits of Highly Effective People: Powerful Lessons in Personal Change.* Simon & Schuster.
    Category: Personal Development
    Why read this book? Covey's seven principles provide a framework for effective personal and professional relationships.

12. **Covey, S. R. (2004).** *The 8th Habit: From Effectiveness to Greatness.* Free Press.
    Category: Leadership
    Why read this book? Encourages finding one's voice and inspiring others, adding depth to Covey's original seven habits.

13. **Davidson, R. J., & Goleman, D. (2017).** *Altered Traits: Science Reveals How Meditation Changes Your Mind, Brain, and Body.* Avery.
    Category: Neuroscience & Mindfulness
    Why read this book? A scientific look at how meditation changes the brain, adding rigor to the practice of mindfulness.

14. **Duhigg, C. (2012).** *The Power of Habit: Why We Do What We Do in Life and Business.* Random House.
    Category: Psychology
    Why read this book? Explores the science of habits, providing strategies for change in both personal and business contexts.

15. **Duckworth, A. (2016).** *Grit: The Power of Passion and Perseverance.* Scribner.
    Category: Personal Development
    Why read this book? Emphasizes grit as a key to achieving long-term goals, combining passion with resilience.

16. **Dyer, W. W. (2004).** *The Power of Intention: Learning to Co-create Your World Your Way.* Hay House.
    Category: Spirituality & Self-Empowerment

Why read this book? Focuses on intention as a force for shaping one's reality, blending personal empowerment with spiritual guidance.

17. **dos Santos, M. (2023).** *Healing from Within.* Amazon.
    Category: Holistic Health
    Why read this book? Bridges scientific and spiritual practices for healing, encouraging a holistic approach to mind-body health.

18. **Friedman, J. (2017).** *The 5 Elements of Effective Thinking.* Princeton University Press.
    Category: Critical Thinking
    Why read this book? A practical guide to improving thinking skills, focusing on problem-solving and creativity.

19. **Friedman, M. D. (2016).** *The Longevity Book: The Science of Aging, the Biology of Strength, and the Privilege of Time.* Atria Books.
    Category: Health & Longevity
    Why read this book? Explores the science of aging, providing insights on how to extend health and vitality.

20. **Gibbons, J. (2015).** *The Art of Possibility: Transforming Professional and Personal Life.* Harvard Business Review Press.
    Category: Personal Growth
    Why read this book? Expands perspectives to maximize potential, blending personal and professional growth principles.

21. **Goldsmith, M. (2010).** *What Got You Here Won't Get You There.* Hyperion.
    Category: Leadership
    Why read this book? Offers strategies for overcoming personal limitations that may block future success.

22. **Goleman, D. (1995).** *Emotional Intelligence.* Bantam.
    Category: Emotional Intelligence
    Why read this book? Introduces EQ as essential for success, covering self-awareness, empathy, and emotional regulation.

23. **Goleman, D. (2011).** *The Brain and Emotional Intelligence: New Insights.* More Than Sound.
    Category: Neuroscience & EQ

Why read this book? Builds on *Emotional Intelligence* with insights into the brain's role in emotional skills.

24. **Gribbin, J. (2007).** *In Search of Schrödinger's Cat: Quantum Physics and Reality.* Random House.
    Category: Quantum Science
    Why read this book? A reader-friendly journey through quantum physics, revealing the mysteries of reality.

25. **Halvorson, H. G. (2013).** *Succeed: How We Can Reach Our Goals.* The American Psychological Association.
    Category: Psychology
    Why read this book? Offers a research-based approach to setting and achieving goals, blending psychology with practical advice.

26. **Hansen, J. (2019).** *Be the Hero: The Six Keys to a Life of Purpose and Success.* Per Capita Publishing.
    Category: Self-Empowerment
    Why read this book? Provides actionable steps to create a purpose-driven life, emphasizing control and personal growth.

27. **Hansen, R. (2018).** *The Power of Intentional Leadership: The Key to Success and Growth.* High Performance Leadership Press.
    Category: Leadership
    Why read this book? Examines leadership through intentionality, offering strategies for successful growth.

28. **Harari, Y. N. (2011).** *Sapiens: A Brief History of Humankind.* Harper.
    Category: Anthropology
    Why read this book? A sweeping history of human evolution and civilization, exploring cultural and societal shifts.

29. **Hawking, S. (2018).** *Brief Answers to the Big Questions.* Bantam.
    Category: Science & Philosophy
    Why read this book? Hawking addresses profound scientific questions with clarity, offering insights into the future of humanity.

30. **Hawkins, D. R. (2010).** *Power vs. Force: The Hidden Determinants of Human Behavior.* Hay House.
    Category: Psychology

Why read this book? Examines the energy dynamics behind human behavior, blending science with consciousness studies.

31. **Kabat-Zinn, J. (1990).** *Wherever You Go, There You Are: Mindfulness Meditation in Everyday Life.* Hachette Books.
Category: Mindfulness & Meditation
Why read this book? A foundational guide to mindfulness, teaching readers how to bring awareness to daily life through meditation.

32. **Kaku, M. (2011).** *Physics of the Impossible: A Scientific Exploration of the World of Phasers, Force Fields, Teleportation, and Time Travel.* Doubleday.
Category: Science & Futurism
Why read this book? Explores futuristic scientific concepts, challenging readers to imagine what may be possible through advances in physics.

33. **Kahneman, D. (2011).** *Thinking, Fast and Slow.* Farrar, Straus and Giroux.
Category: Psychology & Decision-Making
Why read this book? A deep dive into the dual processes that drive our thinking, helping readers understand and improve decision-making.

34. **Mullins, J., & Komisar, R. (2009).** *Getting to Plan B: Breaking Through to a Better Business Model.* Harvard Business Press.
Category: Entrepreneurship & Innovation
Why read this book? Offers a practical framework for refining business models, ideal for entrepreneurs adapting to new challenges.

35. **Neff, K. D. (2011).** *Self-Compassion: The Proven Power of Being Kind to Yourself.* William Morrow.
Category: Psychology & Self-Improvement
Why read this book? Advocates for self-compassion as a means to build resilience and emotional strength, shifting away from self-criticism.

36. **Penrose, R. (2005).** *The Road to Reality: A Complete Guide to the Laws of the Universe.* Vintage.
Category: Physics & Science
Why read this book? An ambitious, comprehensive look at

the principles governing our universe, challenging readers to deepen their understanding of reality.

37. **Robbins, A. (1992).** *Awaken the Giant Within: How to Take Immediate Control of Your Mental, Emotional, Physical, and Financial Destiny!* Free Press.
   Category: Self-Improvement & Motivation
   Why read this book? Offers powerful strategies for personal mastery, guiding readers to take control of their lives and reach their full potential.

38. **Roe, A. (2015).** *Biohacker's Handbook: How to Take Control of Your Body.* Fox Chapel Publishing.
   Category: Biohacking
   Why read this book? A hands-on guide to biohacking practices for optimizing health, focus, and energy, ideal for health enthusiasts.

39. **Sartre, J. P. (1946).** *Existentialism Is a Humanism.* Yale University Press.
   Category: Philosophy
   Why read this book? An introduction to existentialist philosophy, discussing themes of freedom, responsibility, and self-creation.

40. **Sinclair, D. A. (2019).** *Lifespan: Why We Age—and Why We Don't Have To.* Atria Books.
   Category: Health & Longevity
   Why read this book? Offers insights from cutting-edge research on aging, providing a glimpse into the science of extending healthspan.

41. **Sinek, S. (2009).** *Start with Why: How Great Leaders Inspire Everyone to Take Action.* Portfolio.
   Category: Leadership
   Why read this book? Highlights the importance of purpose in leadership, showing how a clear "why" fosters loyalty and drives impact.

42. **Tolle, E. (2004).** *The Power of Now: A Guide to Spiritual Enlightenment.* New World Library.
   Category: Spirituality & Mindfulness
   Why read this book? Teaches readers the power of presence and mindfulness, essential for reducing stress and finding inner peace.

43. **Tolle, E. (2005).** *A New Earth: Awakening to Your Life's Purpose.* Penguin Group.
    Category: Spirituality & Self-Development
    Why read this book? Guides readers in transcending ego-driven behavior to find deeper purpose and connection with life.

44. **Turner, T. (2019).** *The Art of Business Coaching: A Practical Guide to Helping Your Clients Achieve Success.* Business Expert Press.
    Category: Coaching & Business Development
    Why read this book? Provides essential tools for effective coaching, making it a valuable resource for those guiding clients toward success.

45. **Tim Ferriss.** *Tools of Titans: The Tactics, Routines, and Habits of Billionaires, Icons, and World-Class Performers.*
    Category: Self-Improvement & Productivity
    Why read this book? Shares insights from top performers in various fields, offering strategies for productivity, health, and success.

46. **Whitmore, J. (2009).** *Coaching for Performance: GROWing Human Potential and Purpose.* Nicholas Brealey Publishing.
    Category: Coaching & Leadership
    Why read this book? Introduces the GROW model for coaching, an essential guide for leaders and coaches seeking to unlock potential.

47. **Freeman, M. (2019).** *The Science and Art of Healing.* Synthesis Press.
    Category: Holistic Health
    Why read this book? Blends science and holistic approaches, exploring healing practices that integrate mind and body for wellness.

48. **Friedman, M. D. (2016).** *The Longevity Book: The Science of Aging, the Biology of Strength, and the Privilege of Time.* Atria Books.
    Category: Health & Longevity
    Why read this book? Examines the science behind aging, offering readers insights on staying vital and healthy throughout life.

49. **Hawkins, D. R. (2010).** *Power vs. Force: The Hidden Determinants of Human Behavior.* Hay House.
    Category: Psychology & Consciousness
    Why read this book? Explores the subtle energies that drive behavior, connecting consciousness to human potential and empowerment.

50. **Hansen, J. (2019).** *Be the Hero: The Six Keys to a Life of Purpose and Success.* Per Capita Publishing.
    Category: Purpose & Motivation
    Why read this book? Outlines practical steps for creating a meaningful life, empowering readers to lead with purpose and resilience.

51. **Yogananda, P. (1946).** *Autobiography of a Yogi.* Self-Realization Fellowship.
    Category: Spirituality
    Why read this book? Yogananda shares his spiritual journey, insights, and encounters with various gurus, offering an introduction to Eastern philosophy and meditation. This memoir has inspired readers worldwide with its teachings on self-realization and inner peace.

Glossary

- **Achterberg, J., et al.** (1994). "Psychosomatic Studies on Healing: Sound and Music Therapy." *Alternative Therapies, 1*(2), 55-60. This study explores the therapeutic effects of sound and music on health and emotional well-being.
- **Ackerman, D.** (1990). *A Natural History of the Senses.* Vintage. Ackerman provides an exploration of the senses and their impact on human experience and awareness.
- **Alder, D. (2017).** *The New Health Rules: Simple Changes to Achieve Whole-Body Wellness.* Ten Speed Press. Provides practical guidance for integrating healthy, sustainable habits into everyday life, making wellness accessible for all.
- **Adler, M.J.** (1983). *How to Speak, How to Listen.* Scribner. Adler discusses effective communication strategies, emphasizing the importance of both speaking and listening skills.
- **Ader, R., & Cohen, N.** (1975). "Behaviorally Conditioned Immunosuppression." *Psychosomatic Medicine, 37*(4), 333-340. This paper examines how psychological factors can influence immune function.
- **Aggarwal, B. B., & Sung, B.** (2009). "Pharmacological basis for the role of curcumin in chronic diseases: An age-old spice with modern targets." *Trends in Pharmacological Sciences, 30*(2), 85–94. The authors discuss curcumin's potential health benefits and its application in treating chronic diseases.
- **Albers, S.** (2012). *Eating Mindfully: How to End Mindless Eating and Enjoy a Balanced Relationship with Food.* New Harbinger Publications. Albers provides strategies for cultivating mindfulness around eating to enhance enjoyment and health.
- **Allen, D.** (2001). *Getting Things Done: The Art of Stress-Free Productivity.* Penguin Books. Allen outlines a time management system designed to improve productivity and reduce stress.
- **Aman, Y., Qiu, Y., Tao, J., et al.** (2018). "The NAD+ World: New Discoveries in NAD+ Metabolism and Roles in Aging and Disease." *Cell Metabolism, 27*(3), 529-547. This article

discusses new findings regarding NAD+ metabolism and its implications for aging and health.

- **Anderson, B., & Anderson, J.** (2010). *Stretching.* Shelter Publications. This book provides insights into the benefits of stretching for flexibility, injury prevention, and overall health.
- **Arany, P. R., et al.** (2013). Low-Level Laser Therapy (LLLT) for Wound Healing: Mechanism and Application. *Advances in Wound Care.* This paper examines how low-level laser therapy can enhance wound healing processes.
- **Arden, J.B., & Linford, L.** (2009). *Rewire Your Brain: Think Your Way to a Better Life.* Wiley. The authors discuss neuroplasticity and how changing thought patterns can lead to personal growth and improved well-being.
- **Ariely, D.** (2010). *The Upside of Irrationality: The Unexpected Benefits of Defying Logic.* Harper. Ariely explores the hidden benefits of irrational behaviors and their impact on decision-making.
- **Aristotle.** (1999). *Nicomachean Ethics* (M. Ostwald, Trans.). Prentice Hall. Aristotle discusses the nature of ethical behavior and the path to achieving virtue and happiness.
- **Asprey, D.** (2014). *The Bulletproof Diet: Lose up to a Pound a Day, Reclaim Energy and Focus, Upgrade Your Life.* Rodale Books. Asprey presents a dietary approach aimed at improving mental clarity and physical health.
- **Asprey, D.** (2017). *Head Strong.* Harper Wave. This book focuses on enhancing brain function and mental performance through diet and lifestyle changes.
- **Asprey, D.** (2018). *Game Changers: What Leaders, Innovators, and Mavericks Do to Win at Life.* Harper Wave. Asprey explores strategies employed by successful individuals to achieve greatness.
- **Atkinson, D.** (2016). "Effect of Binaural Beats on Brain Activity." *The Journal of Alternative and Complementary Medicine, 22*(6), 430-436. This study investigates how binaural beats can influence brain activity and mood.
- **Aurelius, M.** (180 A.D.). *Meditations.* Translated by Gregory Hays, Modern Library. Aurelius offers personal reflections on Stoic philosophy and the nature of self-discipline.

- **Aurelius, M.** (2002). *Meditations.* Penguin Classics. This edition provides insights into the thoughts and teachings of the Roman emperor on personal growth and virtue.
- **Aurelius, M.** (circa 161–180 AD). *Meditations.* Translation by Gregory Hays, 2002. Modern Library. Aurelius reflects on the importance of rationality and virtue in daily life.
- **Bailey, C.** (2016). *The Productivity Project: Accomplishing More by Managing Your Time, Attention, and Energy.* Crown Business. Bailey explores strategies for effectively managing time and energy to enhance productivity.
- **Bandura, A.** (1997). *Self-Efficacy: The Exercise of Control.* W.H. Freeman and Company. Bandura discusses the role of self-efficacy in motivating individuals to pursue goals and overcome challenges.
- **Baron-Cohen, S.** (2011). *The Science of Evil: On Empathy and the Origins of Cruelty.* Basic Books. Baron-Cohen investigates the roots of empathy and cruelty, examining how brain function affects moral behavior.
- **Batmanghelidj, F.** (2008). *Your Body's Many Cries for Water.* Global Health Solutions. Batmanghelidj emphasizes the importance of hydration for maintaining health and preventing chronic diseases.
- **Baumeister, R. F., & Tierney, J.** (2011). *Willpower: Rediscovering the Greatest Human Strength.* Penguin Books. The authors examine the science behind willpower, offering insights into self-control and decision-making.
- **Becker, E.** (1973). *The Denial of Death.* Free Press. Becker explores how humans cope with the fear of death and its implications for psychology and culture.
- **Berger, W.** (2014). *A More Beautiful Question: The Power of Inquiry to Spark Breakthrough Ideas.* Bloomsbury. Berger highlights the significance of asking profound questions to foster innovation and creativity.
- **Bialystok, E.** (2011). "Reshaping the Mind: The Benefits of Bilingualism." *Canadian Journal of Experimental Psychology, 65(4),* 229–235. Bialystok discusses the cognitive advantages of bilingualism and its effects on mental flexibility.

- **Blagosklonny, M. V.** (2013). "MTOR-driven aging: Speeding up mammalian aging by resource utilization and waste disposal." *Cell Cycle, 12(24),* 3735–3741. Blagosklonny examines the mechanisms of aging related to cellular processes and nutrient sensing.
- **Blake, S.** (2007). *Resveratrol: A Miraculous Antioxidant for Anti-Aging.* Blake Publications. Blake explores the anti-aging properties of resveratrol and its potential health benefits.
- **Blanton, B.** (1996). *Radical Honesty: How to Transform Your Life by Telling the Truth.* Sparrowhawk Publications. Blanton advocates for complete honesty as a means to transform relationships and personal well-being.
- **Blumenthal, J. A., et al.** (1999). "Effects of Exercise Training on Older Patients with Major Depression." *Archives of Internal Medicine, 159(19),* 2349-2356. This study investigates the impact of exercise on alleviating depression in older adults.
- **Bohm, D.** (1980). *Wholeness and the Implicate Order.* Routledge. Bohm discusses the interconnectedness of all things, proposing a new framework for understanding reality.
- **Bostock, D.** (2018). *Nootropics: Unlocking Your True Potential with Smart Drugs and Mind Enhancing Supplements.* Createspace Independent Publishing. Bostock examines various nootropics and their potential to enhance cognitive function.
- **Boyle, M.** (2016). *New Functional Training for Sports.* Human Kinetics. Boyle presents innovative training techniques aimed at improving athletic performance and functional movement.
- **Bradberry, T., & Greaves, J.** (2009). *Emotional Intelligence 2.0.* TalentSmart. The authors provide insights into emotional intelligence and strategies for improving interpersonal skills.
- **Brach, T.** (2003). *Radical Acceptance: Embracing Your Life with the Heart of a Buddha.* Bantam. Brach emphasizes the importance of acceptance and mindfulness in achieving emotional healing and resilience.
- **Breus, M. J.** (2016). *The Power of When: Discover Your Chronotype—and the Best Time to Eat Lunch, Ask for a Raise, Have Sex, Write a Novel, Take Your Meds, and More.* Little,

Brown and Company. Breus explores how understanding one's chronotype can optimize productivity and health.

- **Broad, W. J.** (2012). *The Science of Yoga: The Risks and the Rewards.* Simon & Schuster. Broad evaluates the benefits and potential risks associated with yoga practice.
- **Brown, B.** (2010). *The Gifts of Imperfection: Let Go of Who You Think You're Supposed to Be and Embrace Who You Are.* Hazelden Publishing. Brown encourages readers to embrace vulnerability and authenticity for personal growth.
- **Brown, B.** (2015). *Rising Strong: How the Ability to Reset Transforms the Way We Live, Love, Parent, and Lead.* Spiegel & Grau. Brown discusses the power of resilience and the importance of rising after failures.
- **Brown, B.** (2018). *Dare to Lead: Brave Work. Tough Conversations. Whole Hearts.* Random House. Brown offers insights into effective leadership, emphasizing courage, vulnerability, and trust.
- **Brown, B. (2012).** *Daring Greatly: How the Courage to Be Vulnerable Transforms the Way We Live, Love, Parent, and Lead.* Gotham Books. Inspires readers to take risks and live authentically, challenging societal norms around vulnerability.
- **Brown, P. C., Roediger III, H. L., & McDaniel, M. A.** (2014). *Make It Stick: The Science of Successful Learning.* Belknap Press. The authors explore effective learning strategies grounded in cognitive psychology.
- **Bucci, L. R.** (1993). *Nutrients as Ergogenic Aids for Sports and Exercise.* CRC Press. Bucci discusses various nutrients that can enhance athletic performance and recovery.
- **Buettner, D.** (2008). *The Blue Zones: Lessons for Living Longer From the People Who've Lived the Longest.* National Geographic. Buettner explores the lifestyles of centenarians around the world to identify common habits that promote longevity.
- **Buckle, J.** (2015). *Clinical Aromatherapy: Essential Oils in Healthcare.* Churchill Livingstone. Buckle examines the therapeutic benefits of essential oils and their applications in clinical settings.

- **Burns, D. D.** (1980). *Feeling Good: The New Mood Therapy.* William Morrow & Co. Burns presents cognitive therapy techniques to improve mood and mental health.
- **Burkeman, O.** (2021). *Four Thousand Weeks: Time Management for Mortals.* Farrar, Straus and Giroux. Burkeman reflects on the limitations of time management and the importance of meaningful living.
- **Bailey, C.** (2016). *The Productivity Project: Accomplishing More by Managing Your Time, Attention, and Energy.* Crown Business. Bailey explores techniques for enhancing productivity through effective time and energy management.
- **Bandura, A.** (1997). *Self-Efficacy: The Exercise of Control.* W.H. Freeman and Company. Bandura presents the concept of self-efficacy and its influence on motivation and behavior change.
- **Baron-Cohen, S.** (2011). *The Science of Evil: On Empathy and the Origins of Cruelty.* Basic Books. Baron-Cohen examines the psychological underpinnings of cruelty and the role of empathy in human behavior.
- **Batmanghelidj, F.** (2008). *Your Body's Many Cries for Water.* Global Health Solutions. Batmanghelidj discusses the critical role of water in health and its impact on various bodily functions.
- **Baumeister, R. F., & Tierney, J.** (2011). *Willpower: Rediscovering the Greatest Human Strength.* Penguin Books. This book explores the science of willpower and how it can be strengthened for better self-control.
- **Becker, E.** (1973). *The Denial of Death.* Free Press. Becker analyzes humanity's fear of death and how it shapes our behavior and culture.
- **Berger, W.** (2014). *A More Beautiful Question: The Power of Inquiry to Spark Breakthrough Ideas.* Bloomsbury. Berger emphasizes the importance of asking the right questions to drive innovation and creativity.
- **Bialystok, E.** (2011). "Reshaping the Mind: The Benefits of Bilingualism." *Canadian Journal of Experimental Psychology, 65*(4), 229–235. Bialystok discusses how bilingualism enhances cognitive flexibility and mental acuity.

- **Blagosklonny, M. V.** (2013). "MTOR-driven aging: Speeding up mammalian aging by resource utilization and waste disposal." *Cell Cycle, 12*(24), 3735–3741. This study examines the role of mTOR signaling in aging processes.
- **Blake, S.** (2007). *Resveratrol: A Miraculous Antioxidant for Anti-Aging.* Blake Publications. Blake explores the health benefits of resveratrol, particularly its anti-aging properties.
- **Blanton, B.** (1996). *Radical Honesty: How to Transform Your Life by Telling the Truth.* Sparrowhawk Publications. Blanton advocates for honesty in communication as a means of personal transformation.
- **Blumenthal, J. A., et al.** (1999). "Effects of Exercise Training on Older Patients with Major Depression." *Archives of Internal Medicine, 159*(19), 2349-2356. This study highlights the positive effects of exercise on mental health, particularly in older adults with depression.
- **Bohm, D.** (1980). *Wholeness and the Implicate Order.* Routledge. Bohm presents a new perspective on reality, emphasizing the interconnectedness of all things.
- **Bostock, D.** (2018). *Nootropics: Unlocking Your True Potential with Smart Drugs and Mind Enhancing Supplements.* Createspace Independent Publishing. Bostock reviews various nootropics and their potential cognitive benefits.
- **Boyle, M.** (2016). *New Functional Training for Sports.* Human Kinetics. Boyle discusses innovative training methods for enhancing athletic performance.
- **Bradberry, T., & Greaves, J.** (2009). *Emotional Intelligence 2.0.* TalentSmart. This book provides practical strategies for improving emotional intelligence and interpersonal skills.
- **Brach, T.** (2003). *Radical Acceptance: Embracing Your Life with the Heart of a Buddha.* Bantam. Brach explores the concept of radical acceptance as a means of achieving emotional healing and well-being.
- **Breus, M. J.** (2016). *The Power of When: Discover Your Chronotype—and the Best Time to Eat Lunch, Ask for a Raise, Have Sex, Write a Novel, Take Your Meds, and More.* Little, Brown and Company. Breus examines how understanding one's chronotype can optimize daily routines for better health.

- **Broad, W. J.** (2012). *The Science of Yoga: The Risks and the Rewards.* Simon & Schuster. Broad investigates the scientific evidence behind yoga's benefits and risks.
- **Brown, B.** (2010). *The Gifts of Imperfection: Let Go of Who You Think You're Supposed to Be and Embrace Who You Are.* Hazelden Publishing. Brown discusses the importance of embracing imperfections to foster authenticity and belonging.
- **Brown, B.** (2015). *Rising Strong: How the Ability to Reset Transforms the Way We Live, Love, Parent, and Lead.* Spiegel & Grau. Brown explores the power of vulnerability in overcoming setbacks and building resilience.
- **Brown, B.** (2018). *Dare to Lead: Brave Work. Tough Conversations. Whole Hearts.* Random House. Brown offers insights on courageous leadership and the importance of empathy in the workplace.
- **Brown, P. C., Roediger III, H. L., & McDaniel, M. A.** (2014). *Make It Stick: The Science of Successful Learning.* Belknap Press. This book outlines effective learning strategies based on cognitive science.
- **Bucci, L. R.** (1993). *Nutrients as Ergogenic Aids for Sports and Exercise.* CRC Press. Bucci discusses the role of various nutrients in enhancing athletic performance.
- **Buettner, D.** (2008). *The Blue Zones: Lessons for Living Longer From the People Who've Lived the Longest.* National Geographic. Buettner identifies common lifestyle habits among the world's longest-lived populations.
- **Buckle, J.** (2015). *Clinical Aromatherapy: Essential Oils in Healthcare.* Churchill Livingstone. Buckle examines the therapeutic uses of essential oils in clinical settings.
- **Burns, D. D.** (1980). *Feeling Good: The New Mood Therapy.* William Morrow & Co. Burns presents cognitive therapy techniques for overcoming depression and improving mental health.
- **Burkeman, O.** (2021). *Four Thousand Weeks: Time Management for Mortals.* Farrar, Straus and Giroux. Burkeman discusses how to make the most of limited time by prioritizing what truly matters.

- **Carol Dweck, C. (2006).** *Mindset: The New Psychology of Success.* Random House.
- **Chopra, D. (1994).** *The Seven Spiritual Laws of Success: A Practical Guide to the Fulfillment of Your Dreams.* New World Library.
- **Clear, J. (2018).** *Atomic Habits: An Easy & Proven Way to Build Good Habits & Break Bad Ones.* Penguin.
- **Cohen, S. (2007).** *Social Relationships and Health.* American Psychologist. Examines the impact of social connections on health, revealing how strong relationships foster well-being.
- **Cunnane, S. C.,** & **Crawford, M. A.** (2003). "Survival of the fattest: Fat babies were the key to evolution of the large human brain." *Comparative Biochemistry and Physiology Part A: Molecular & Integrative Physiology,* 136(1), 17-26.
- **Cotman, C. W.,** & **Berchtold, N. C.** (2002). "Exercise: A behavioral intervention to enhance brain health and plasticity." *Trends in Neurosciences,* 25(6), 295–301. A study on how physical exercise promotes brain plasticity, highlighting the impact of BDNF in brain growth and memory.
- **Coyle, D.** (2009). *The Talent Code: Greatness Isn't Born. It's Grown. Here's How.* Bantam. Coyle discusses how perseverance and practice create pathways to mastering skills and overcoming challenges.
- **Cozolino, L. (2010).** *The Neuroscience of Psychotherapy: Healing the Social Brain.* W.W.
- Explores the brain's capacity for healing through relationships and therapy, combining science with therapeutic insight.
- **Covey, S. R. (1989).** *The 7 Habits of Highly Effective People: Powerful Lessons in Personal Change.* Simon & Schuster. Covey's seven principles provide a framework for effective personal and professional relationships.
- **Covey, S. R. (2004).** *The 8th Habit: From Effectiveness to Greatness.* Free Press. Encourages finding one's voice and inspiring others, adding depth to Covey's original seven habits.
- **Csikszentmihalyi, M.** (1996). *Creativity: Flow and the Psychology of Discovery and Invention.* Harper Perennial. Csikszentmihalyi discusses how engaging in creative activities fosters mental flexibility, joy, and resilience.

- **Davidson, R. J.**, & **Goleman, D.** (2017). *Altered Traits: Science Reveals How Meditation Changes Your Mind, Brain, and Body*. Avery. Davidson and Goleman examine how meditation enhances focus, emotional balance, and neuroplasticity.

- **Davidson, R. J.**, & **McEwen, B. S.** (2012). "Social Influences on Neuroplasticity: Stress and Interventions to Promote Well-Being." *Nature Neuroscience*, 15(5), 689-695. This study explains how engaging in unfamiliar activities, such as using the non-dominant hand, enhances neuroplasticity and resilience.

- **Davis, D. L.** (2010). *Disconnect: The Truth about Cell Phone Radiation, What the Industry Has Done to Hide It, and How to Protect Your Family*. Dutton. A thorough exploration of the potential health risks of cell phone radiation, highlighting steps for minimizing exposure.

- **Dean, C.**, & **Shealy, N.** (2017). *The Magnesium Miracle (Second Edition)*. Ballantine Books. An in-depth guide on magnesium's role in supporting muscle recovery, mental health, and cardiovascular function.

- **Deci, E. L.**, & **Ryan, R. M.** (2000). *Self-Determination Theory and the Facilitation of Intrinsic Motivation, Social Development, and Well-Being. American Psychologist*, 55(1), 68–78. This foundational study examines how intrinsic motivation drives growth and achievement.

- **Dispenza, J.** (2013). *Breaking the Habit of Being Yourself: How to Lose Your Mind and Create a New One*. Hay House. Focuses on the neuroscience of spirituality, showing how thoughts shape personal reality and spiritual well-being.

- **Dispenza, J.** (2017). *Becoming Supernatural: How Common People Are Doing the Uncommon*. Hay House. Dispenza discusses the science and spirituality of personal transformation.

- **Dispenza, J.** (2019). *Becoming Supernatural: How Common People Are Doing the Uncommon*. Hay House. Explores visualization techniques for accessing higher states of mind and achieving extraordinary personal transformation.

- **Doidge, N.** (2007). *The Brain That Changes Itself: Stories of Personal Triumph from the Frontiers of Brain Science.* Penguin. Doidge explores neuroplasticity and how adopting new habits can rewire the brain.
- **Dos Santos, M. (2023).** *Healing from Within.* Amazon. Bridges scientific and spiritual practices for healing, encouraging a holistic approach to mind-body health.
- **Duckworth, A.** (2016). *Grit: The Power of Passion and Perseverance.* Scribner. Examines the role of perseverance in long-term success, exploring how small, consistent efforts create meaningful results.
- **Duckworth, A. L.**, et al. (2007). "Grit and perseverance." *Journal of Personality and Social Psychology.* This study examines the role of grit in achieving success.
- **Duhigg, C.** (2012). *The Power of Habit: Why We Do What We Do in Life and Business.* Random House. Analyzes the science of habit formation and how recognizing achievements can reinforce motivation.
- **Dweck, C. S.** (2006). *Mindset: The New Psychology of Success.* Ballantine Books. Discusses the importance of a growth mindset and how breaking free from limiting beliefs can foster personal and professional success.
- **Dyer, W. W. (2004).** *The Power of Intention: Learning to Co-create Your World Your Way.* Hay House. Focuses on intention as a force for shaping one's reality, blending personal empowerment with spiritual guidance.
- **Ecclesiastes 8:15.** *The Bible.* Biblical insights into enjoying life's moments, reflecting the value of gratitude and appreciation as essential elements of relaxation.
- **Elrod, H.** (2012). *The Miracle Morning: The Not-So-Obvious Secret Guaranteed to Transform Your Life (Before 8AM).* Hal Elrod. Advocates for an early morning routine as a foundation for personal growth, focus, and productivity.
- **Emerson, R. W.** (1844). *The Essays of Ralph Waldo Emerson.* Emerson's views on learning from others highlight the importance of humility and openness in communication as tools for self-growth.

- **Emmons, R. A.** (2007). *Thanks!: How the New Science of Gratitude Can Make You Happier*. Houghton Mifflin Harcourt. Emmons explores the transformative power of gratitude, including for small, sensory experiences, and how it improves emotional well-being and resilience.

- **Emmons, R.A.**, & **McCullough, M.E.** (2003). *Counting Blessings Versus Burdens. Journal of Personality and Social Psychology*. Emmons and McCullough discuss the effects of gratitude on psychological well-being.

- **Enright, R. D.** (2001). *Forgiveness Is a Choice: A Step-by-Step Process for Resolving Anger and Restoring Hope*. American Psychological Association. Enright offers a comprehensive approach to self-forgiveness and healing from emotional pain through forgiveness.

- **Epel, McEwen, and Seeman** (2000), *"Stress and body fat distribution: A review and theoretical integration"* published in *Psychosomatic Medicine*, reviews the mechanisms linking chronic stress to abdominal fat.

- **Epictetus** (circa 55-135 AD). *The Enchiridion*. Various editions. A Stoic guide to managing emotions and actions, emphasizing rational responses and inner control over external events.

- **Epictetus** (1995). *The Handbook (Enchiridion)*. Hackett Publishing. Epictetus emphasizes the importance of focusing on what's within our control for a fulfilling life.

- **Fasano, A.**, & **Catassi, C.** (2001). "Current approaches to diagnosis and treatment of celiac disease: An evolving spectrum." *Gastroenterology*, 120(3), 636–651. Scientific insights on gluten sensitivity and the impact of gluten on gut health, detailing the importance of a gluten-free diet for those affected.

- **Ferriss T.** *Tools of Titans: The Tactics, Routines, and Habits of Billionaires, Icons, and World-Class Performers*. Shares insights from top performers in various fields, offering strategies for productivity, health, and success.

- **Field, T.** (2009). *Complementary and Alternative Therapies Research*. American Psychological Association. Discusses alternative therapies, including inversion, and their effects on physical relaxation and mental clarity.

- **Fisher, R., Ury, W., & Patton, B.** (1991). *Getting to Yes: Negotiating Agreement Without Giving In*. Penguin Books. This book emphasizes conflict resolution through empathy and understanding rather than confrontation.
- **Fitzgerald, B.** (2018). *The Healing Power of Red Light Therapy*. Critical Bench Publishing. A guide to red light therapy, its cellular benefits, and its effects on skin health, muscle recovery, and energy.
- **Fleming, J.H., & Asplund, J.** (2007). *Human Sigma: Managing the Employee-Customer Encounter*. Gallup Press. This book discusses resilience in the face of uncertainty and the positive impact on growth.
- **Fletcher, G. F.**, et al. (2013). "Exercise Standards for Testing and Training: A Scientific Statement from the American Heart Association." *Circulation*, 128(8), 873–934. Outlines the impacts of cardiovascular exercise on heart health, based on extensive clinical research.
- **Fogg, B.J.** (2019). *Tiny Habits: The Small Changes That Change Everything*. Houghton Mifflin Harcourt. Fogg emphasizes the impact of small, sustainable habits on health and well-being.
- **Fontana, L., & Partridge, L.** (2015). "Promoting Health and Longevity Through Diet: From Model
- **Freeman, M. (2019).** *The Science and Art of Healing*. Synthesis Press. Blends science and holistic approaches, exploring healing practices that integrate mind and body for wellness.
- **Friedman, J. (2017).** *The 5 Elements of Effective Thinking*. Princeton University Press. A practical guide to improving thinking skills, focusing on problem-solving and creativity.
- **Friedman, M. D. (2016).** *The Longevity Book: The Science of Aging, the Biology of Strength, and the Privilege of Time*. Atria Books. Explores the science of aging, providing insights on how to extend health and vitality.

- **Gawain, S.** (2002). *Creative Visualization*. New World Library. A practical guide to using visualization to manifest goals, aligning mental focus with desired outcomes.
- **Gibbons, J. (2015).** *The Art of Possibility: Transforming Professional and Personal Life.* Harvard Business Review Press. Expands perspectives to maximize potential, blending personal and professional growth principles.
- **Goldsmith, M. (2010).** *What Got You Here Won't Get You There.* Hyperion. Offers strategies for overcoming personal limitations that may block future success.
- **Goleman, D. (2011).** *The Brain and Emotional Intelligence: New Insights.* More Than Sound. Builds on *Emotional Intelligence* with insights into the brain's role in emotional skills.
- **Goleman, D. (1995).** *Emotional Intelligence.* Bantam. Introduces EQ as essential for success, covering self-awareness, empathy, and emotional regulation.
- **Goleman, D.** (2013). *Focus: The Hidden Driver of Excellence.* HarperCollins. An analysis of focus and how it enhances performance and cognitive function.
- **Grant, A.** (2016). *Originals: How Non-Conformists Move the World.* Viking. Explores creativity and the importance of unconventional thinking for personal growth and innovation.
- **Gribbin, J. (2007).** *In Search of Schrödinger's Cat: Quantum Physics and Reality.* Random House. A reader-friendly journey through quantum physics, revealing the mysteries of reality.
- **Haidt, J.** (2006). *The Happiness Hypothesis: Finding Modern Truth in Ancient Wisdom.* Basic Books. Examines love, relationships, and emotional resilience as essential components of a disciplined, fulfilling life.
- **Halvorson, H. G. (2013).** *Succeed: How We Can Reach Our Goals.* The American Psychological Association. Offers a research-based approach to setting and achieving goals, blending psychology with practical advice.
- **Hamblin, M. R.** (2017). *Photobiomodulation in the Brain: Low-Level Laser (Light) Therapy in Neurology and Neuroscience.* Elsevier. Covers the benefits of red light therapy in neurological applications, such as recovery from brain injuries and enhancement of cognitive functions.

- **Hanh, T. N.** (2015). *Silence: The Power of Quiet in a World Full of Noise.* HarperOne. This work underscores the importance of silence for achieving inner peace and mental clarity.
- **Hansen, J. (2019).** *Be the Hero: The Six Keys to a Life of Purpose and Success.* Per Capita Publishing. Provides actionable steps to create a purpose-driven life, emphasizing control and personal growth.
- **Hansen, R. (2018).** *The Power of Intentional Leadership: The Key to Success and Growth.* High Performance Leadership Press. Examines leadership through intentionality, offering strategies for successful growth.
- **Hanson, R., & Mendius, R.** (2009). *Buddha's Brain: The Practical Neuroscience of Happiness, Love, and Wisdom.* New Harbinger. Examines brain-based techniques to foster emotional well-being and resilience.
- **Hawking, S. (2018).** *Brief Answers to the Big Questions.* Bantam. Hawking addresses profound scientific questions with clarity, offering insights into the future of humanity.
- **Hawkins, D. R. (2010).** *Power vs. Force: The Hidden Determinants of Human Behavior.* Hay House. Examines the energy dynamics behind human behavior, blending science with consciousness studies.
- **Harari, Y. N. (2011).** *Sapiens: A Brief History of Humankind.* Harper. A sweeping history of human evolution and civilization, exploring cultural and societal shifts.
- **Helmstetter, S.** (1986). *What to Say When You Talk to Yourself.* Pocket Books. Examines how self-talk influences beliefs, offering techniques to reframe negative thoughts and empower personal transformation.
- **Hof, W.** (2017). *The Wim Hof Method: Activate Your Full Human Potential.* Sounds True. A guide to cold exposure and breathing techniques, aimed at building resilience and boosting physical and mental endurance.
- **Holick, M. F.** (2004). *The UV Advantage.* iBooks. Details the importance of sunlight in vitamin D synthesis, linking it to immune health, bone density, and overall well-being.

- **Holick, M. F.** (2010). *The Vitamin D Solution: A 3-Step Strategy to Cure Our Most Common Health Problem.* Hudson Street Press. Covers the importance of sunlight for vitamin D synthesis, immune health, and mental well-being.
- **Hyman, M.** (2008). *The UltraMind Solution: Fix Your Broken Brain by Healing Your Body First.* Scribner. Explores the mind-body connection and how self-care practices, such as hygiene, impact mental and physical health.
- **Iyengar, B. K. S.** (1979). *Light on Yoga.* Schocken Books. A comprehensive guide to the physical and mental discipline of yoga, promoting resilience and flexibility.
- **James, M.** (2016). *The Little Book of Discipline: How to Achieve and Maintain Self-Discipline to Accomplish the Important Goals in Your Life.* Success Books. Offers practical advice on developing self-discipline through daily actions, making goal achievement attainable.
- **James, W.** (1890). *The Principles of Psychology.* Henry Holt and Company. A foundational text on willpower and self-discipline, emphasizing the importance of determination and consistency.
- **Judith, A.** (2004). *Wheels of Life: A User's Guide to the Chakra System.* Llewellyn Publications. A comprehensive guide on chakra balancing, connecting physical and emotional well-being.
- **Kabat-Zinn, J.** (1994). *Wherever You Go, There You Are: Mindfulness Meditation in Everyday Life.* Hyperion. A practical guide to mindfulness, emphasizing the importance of stillness for inner peace and clarity.
- **Kaku, M. (2011).** *Physics of the Impossible: A Scientific Exploration of the World of Phasers, Force Fields, Teleportation, and Time Travel.* Doubleday. Explores futuristic scientific concepts, challenging readers to imagine what may be possible through advances in physics.
- **Kahneman, D. (2011).** *Thinking, Fast and Slow.* Farrar, Straus and Giroux. A deep dive into the dual processes that drive our thinking, helping readers understand and improve decision-making.

- **Kelley, T., & Kelley, D.** (2013). *Creative Confidence: Unleashing the Creative Potential Within Us All.* Crown Business. Discusses practical ways to bring creativity into everyday life, enhancing personal growth and flexibility.
- **Kishimi, I., & Koga, F.** (2018). *The Courage to Be Disliked: How to Free Yourself, Change Your Life, and Achieve Real Happiness.* Atria Books. Encourages embracing authenticity, teaching readers to live freely without the need for external validation.
- **Krause, R., et al.** (2009). "Sunlight, Vitamin D, and Skin Cancer." *Anticancer Research.* A study examining the balance between sunlight exposure for health benefits and skin cancer risk, underscoring the importance of moderation.
- **Li, Q.** (2018). *Forest Bathing: How Trees Can Help You Find Health and Happiness.* Viking. Discusses the health benefits of connecting with nature and managing energy through environmental practices.
- **Locke, E. A., & Latham, G. P.** (2002). "Building a Practically Useful Theory of Goal Setting and Task Motivation." *American Psychologist*, 57(9), 705–717. A key study on the power of specific goals in enhancing motivation and performance.
- **Masten, A. S.** (2001). "Ordinary Magic: Resilience Processes in Development." *American Psychologist*, 56(3), 227–238. Emphasizes resilience as a fundamental skill for overcoming challenges.
- **Matthews, G.** (2016). *Success: How We Can Reach Our Goals.* Oxford University Press. Explores the psychology of goal-setting, focusing on the importance of clear, actionable goals.
- **McClellan, R., & Fisher, R.** (1999). "The Effect of Music on Immune System and Stress." *Music Therapy Perspectives*, 17(1), 21-25. This study examines the impact of sound therapy on immune health and stress reduction.
- **McDougall, S., & Parry, M.** (2016). *What Doesn't Kill Us: How Freezing Water, Extreme Altitude, and Environmental Conditioning Will Renew Our Lost Evolutionary Strength.* Rodale Books. Explores how environmental challenges like

cold immersion strengthen resilience and health, drawing on both research and McDougall's experiences.

- **McGonigal, K.** (2015). *The Upside of Stress*. Avery. McGonigal explains how stress can be harnessed as a positive force.
- **McClellan, R., & Fisher, R.** (1999). "The Effect of Music on Immune System and Stress." *Music Therapy Perspectives, 17*(1), 21-25. Examines the impact of sound therapy on immune health and stress reduction.
- **Mullins, J., & Komisar, R. (2009).** *Getting to Plan B: Breaking Through to a Better Business Model.* Harvard Business Press. Offers a practical framework for refining business models, ideal for entrepreneurs adapting to new challenges.
- **McGonigal, K.** (2015). *The Upside of Stress*. Avery. Explains how stress can be harnessed as a positive force.
- **Naparstek, B.** (2004). *Invisible Heroes: Survivors of Trauma and How They Heal*. Bantam. Offers guidance on healing trauma and breaking free from limiting beliefs.
- **Neff, K. D. (2011).** *Self-Compassion: The Proven Power of Being Kind to Yourself.* William Morrow.
- **Nelson, B. R.** (2007). *Chakra Healing and Karmic Awareness*. Healing Arts Press. Discusses how chakra balancing practices support physical and emotional well-being and unlock spiritual potential.
- **Nepo, M.** (2012). *The Book of Awakening: Having the Life You Want by Being Present to the Life You Have*. Red Wheel Weiser. Discusses the power of silence for cultivating mindfulness and clarity.
- **Nestor, J.** (2020). *Breath: The New Science of a Lost Art*. Riverhead Books. Explores the science of breathing techniques for mental clarity, stress reduction, and energy enhancement.
- **Neff, K. D.** (2011). *Self-Compassion: The Proven Power of Being Kind to Yourself*. William Morrow. Discusses self-compassion as a foundation for emotional health, encouraging supportive self-talk and nurturing self-care.
- **Newberg, A., & Waldman, M. R.** (2009). *How God Changes Your Brain: Breakthrough Findings from a Leading*

Neuroscientist. Ballantine Books. Explores meditation's effects on the brain and how stillness improves mental and emotional health.

- **Newport, C.** (2016). *Deep Work: Rules for Focused Success in a Distracted World*. Grand Central Publishing. Advocates for focused, distraction-free work, showing how deep concentration enhances productivity and success.
- **Noakes, T.** (2001). *Lore of Running*. Oxford University Press. Covers the physiological and mental benefits of endurance exercises like running for cardiovascular health.
- **Nhat Hanh, T.** (1975). *The Miracle of Mindfulness*. Beacon Press. Guides readers on how to cultivate mindfulness, emphasizing the importance of savoring daily moments for mental peace and balance.
- **Nhat Hanh, T.** (1991). *Peace Is Every Step: The Path of Mindfulness in Everyday Life*. Bantam Books. Focuses on mindfulness and emotional regulation, offering practical methods for finding peace and clarity.
- **Ober, C., Sinatra, S. T., & Zucker, M.** (2014). *Earthing: The Most Important Health Discovery Ever?* Basic Health Publications. Examines the science behind grounding and its effects on physical and mental well-being.
- **Oschman, J. L.** (2007). *Energy Medicine*. Churchill Livingstone. Investigates the role of energy healing in promoting physical and mental well-being.
- **Pareto, V.** (1906). *Cours d'économie politique*. University of Lausanne. Introduces the Pareto Principle, suggesting that focusing on the 20% of efforts that yield 80% of results can enhance productivity and success.
- **Patterson, K., et al.** (2002). *Crucial Conversations: Tools for Talking When Stakes Are High*. McGraw-Hill. Practical advice for handling difficult conversations truthfully and effectively, fostering trust and clarity in relationships.
- **Peale, N. V.** (1952). *The Power of Positive Thinking*. Prentice Hall. Discusses the transformative power of positive thinking on well-being and personal success.
- **Penrose, R. (2005).** *The Road to Reality: A Complete Guide to the Laws of the Universe.* Vintage. An ambitious,

comprehensive look at the principles governing our universe, challenging readers to deepen their understanding of reality.

- **Perlmutter, D.** (2015). *Brain Maker: The Power of Gut Microbes to Heal and Protect Your Brain for Life.* Little, Brown Spark. Discusses the connection between nutrition, brain health, and longevity.
- **Perlmutter, D., & Loberg, K.** (2015). *Brain Maker.* Little, Brown and Company. Discusses the role of gut health in brain function and mental health.
- **Peterson, C., & Seligman, M. E. P.** (2004). *Character Strengths and Virtues: A Handbook and Classification.* Oxford University Press. Foundational text on positive psychology, exploring resilience as a character strength developed through facing adversity.
- **Peterson, J. B.** (2018). *12 Rules for Life: An Antidote to Chaos.* Random House. Discusses the role of faith and belief in building resilience and purpose during challenging times.
- **Phillips, S. M., & Winett, R. A.** (2010). "Uncomplicated Resistance Training and Health-Related Outcomes: Evidence for a Public Health Mandate." *Current Sports Medicine Reports,* 9(4), 208–213. Demonstrates the role of resistance training in enhancing long-term health and resilience.
- **Pipher, M.** (1999). *Another Country: Navigating the Emotional Terrain of Our Elders.* Riverhead Books. Highlights the significance of family connections, suggesting that time management can strengthen familial relationships.
- **Pink, D. H.** (2009). *Drive: The Surprising Truth About What Motivates Us.* Riverhead Books. Investigates the science behind motivation and what truly drives human behavior.
- **Pollan, M.** (2008). *In Defense of Food: An Eater's Manifesto.* Penguin Press. Explores mindful eating and how to find balance without guilt.
- **Porges, S.** (2011). *The Polyvagal Theory: Neurophysiological Foundations of Emotions, Attachment, Communication, and Self-Regulation.* Norton & Company. Discusses how movement, rhythm, and dance can regulate emotional states and contribute to emotional resilience.

- **Pressfield, S.** (2002). *The War of Art: Break Through the Blocks and Win Your Inner Creative Battles*. Black Irish Entertainment. Emphasizes overcoming resistance and nurturing creative energy.
- **Rand, W. L.** (2004). *The Reiki Touch: Complete Home Learning System*. Sounds True. Provides an introduction to Reiki, detailing how this practice promotes healing, reduces stress, and enhances overall well-being.
- **Ratey, J. J., & Hagerman, E.** (2008). *Spark: The Revolutionary New Science of Exercise and the Brain*. Little, Brown. Explains the mental and physical health benefits of daily walking.
- **Rhind, J.P.** (2012). *Aromatherapy for Healing the Spirit: Restoring Emotional and Mental Balance with Essential Oils*. Healing Arts Press. Explores how essential oils affect the mind and body.
- **Robbins, A.** (1986). *Unlimited Power: The New Science of Personal Achievement*. Free Press. Explains how negative influences can hinder success.
- **Robbins, T.** (1991). *Awaken the Giant Within: How to Take Immediate Control of Your Mental, Emotional, Physical, and Financial Destiny!*. Free Press. Emphasizes the power of self-reflection and personal responsibility.
- **Robinson, K.** (2011). *Out of Our Minds: Learning to Be Creative*. Capstone. Encourages embracing creativity as a path to personal and professional growth.
- **Roe, A. (2015).** *Biohacker's Handbook: How to Take Control of Your Body.* Fox Chapel Publishing. A hands-on guide to biohacking practices for optimizing health, focus, and energy, ideal for health enthusiasts.
- **Rogers, C. R.** (1961). *On Becoming a Person: A Therapist's View of Psychotherapy*. Houghton Mifflin. Advocates for authenticity in communication, showing how genuine, empathetic interactions create deeper connections.
- **Rosenberg, M. B.** (2003). *Nonviolent Communication: A Language of Life*. PuddleDancer Press. Advocates for empathetic and patient communication.

- **Rubin, G.** (2015). *Better Than Before: Mastering the Habits of Our Everyday Lives*. Crown Publishing Group. Explores how healthy routines and intentional actions improve well-being.
- **Ryan, M., & Becker, J.** (2019). *The Art of Letting Go: How to Move Forward in Your Life*. CreateSpace Independent Publishing. Provides strategies for releasing anger and embracing forgiveness.
- **Ryan, R. M., & Deci, E. L.** (2000). *Self-Determination Theory and the Facilitation of Intrinsic Motivation, Social Development, and Well-Being. American Psychologist, 55*(1), 68–78. Discusses intrinsic motivation and self-determined actions.
- **Nestor, J.** (2020). *Breath: The New Science of a Lost Art*. Riverhead Books. Explores the science of breathing techniques for mental clarity, stress reduction, and energy enhancement.
- **Newberg, A., & Waldman, M. R.** (2009). *How God Changes Your Brain: Breakthrough Findings from a Leading Neuroscientist*. Ballantine Books. An exploration of meditation's effects on the brain and how stillness improves mental and emotional health.
- **Newport, C.** (2016). *Deep Work: Rules for Focused Success in a Distracted World*. Grand Central Publishing. Advocates for focused, distraction-free work, showing how deep concentration enhances productivity and success.
- **Noakes, T.** (2001). *Lore of Running*. Oxford University Press. Covers the physiological and mental benefits of endurance exercises like running for cardiovascular health.
- **Ober, C., Sinatra, S. T., & Zucker, M.** (2014). *Earthing: The Most Important Health Discovery Ever?* Basic Health Publications. Examines the science behind grounding and its effects on physical and mental well-being.
- **Patterson, K., et al.** (2002). *Crucial Conversations: Tools for Talking When Stakes Are High*. McGraw-Hill. Offers practical advice for handling difficult conversations truthfully and effectively, fostering trust and clarity in relationships.
- **Peale, N. V.** (1952). *The Power of Positive Thinking*. Prentice Hall. Discusses the transformative power of positive thinking on well-being and personal success.

- **Peterson, C., & Seligman, M. E. P.** (2004). *Character Strengths and Virtues: A Handbook and Classification.* Oxford University Press. A foundational text on positive psychology, exploring resilience as a character strength developed through facing adversity.
- **Peterson, J. B.** (2018). *12 Rules for Life: An Antidote to Chaos.* Random House. Discusses the role of faith and belief in building resilience and purpose during challenging times.
- **Phillips, S. M., & Winett, R. A.** (2010). "Uncomplicated Resistance Training and Health-Related Outcomes: Evidence for a Public Health Mandate." *Current Sports Medicine Reports,* 9(4), 208–213. A study demonstrating the role of resistance training in enhancing long-term health and resilience.
- **Porges, S.** (2011). *The Polyvagal Theory: Neurophysiological Foundations of Emotions, Attachment, Communication, and Self-Regulation.* Norton & Company. Discusses how movement, rhythm, and dance can regulate emotional states and contribute to emotional resilience.
- **Rubin, G.** (2015). *Better Than Before: Mastering the Habits of Our Everyday Lives.* Crown Publishing Group. Explores how healthy routines and intentional actions improve well-being, sleep, and overall resilience.
- **Ryan, R. M., & Deci, E. L.** (2000). "Self-Determination Theory and the Facilitation of Intrinsic Motivation, Social Development, and Well-Being." *American Psychologist.* This study discusses intrinsic motivation and how self-determined actions enhance mental clarity, well-being, and resilience.
- **Sacks, O.** (1995). *An Anthropologist on Mars: Seven Paradoxical Tales.* Knopf. Explores the intricacies of human sensory experience, emphasizing how mindful engagement with the senses enriches perception and awareness.
- **Sapolsky, R. M.** (2004). *Why Zebras Don't Get Ulcers.* Holt Paperbacks. Discusses the role of stress management and a balanced lifestyle in maintaining health, emphasizing holistic well-being.
- **Sartre, J.P.** (1946). *Existentialism Is a Humanism.* Yale University Press. Outlines existentialism and the responsibility of creating one's own meaning.

- **Schwartz, B.** (2016). *The Paradox of Choice*. Harper Perennial. Explores how excessive choice can lead to anxiety and dissatisfaction.
- **Schwartz, T.** (2010). *The Way We're Working Isn't Working: The Four Forgotten Needs That Energize Great Performance*. Free Press. Provides guidance on reflection and goal-setting to achieve better balance and growth.
- **Schoenfeld, B. J.** (2010). *Science and Development of Muscle Hypertrophy*. Human Kinetics. Explores how strength training improves muscle mass, metabolism, and bone density, essential for healthy aging.
- **Seligman, M. E. P.** (2002). *Authentic Happiness: Using the New Positive Psychology to Realize Your Potential for Lasting Fulfillment*. Free Press. Discusses how understanding one's core values and desires leads to a more fulfilling life.
- **Seneca** (circa 4 BCE–65 AD). *Letters from a Stoic*. Translation by Robin Campbell, 1969. Penguin Classics. Emphasizes reflection on both successes and failures as a means of personal development.
- **Siegel, D.J.** (2010). *Mindsight: The New Science of Personal Transformation*. Bantam. Discusses mindfulness practices for building mental resilience.
- **Sinclair, D.** (2019). *Lifespan: Why We Age—and Why We Don't Have To*. Atria Books. Explores expanding possibilities in health and longevity, encouraging curiosity and self-exploration.
- **Sinek, S.** (2009). *Start with Why: How Great Leaders Inspire Everyone to Take Action*. Portfolio. Highlights the importance of aligning goals with a clear purpose to foster sustained motivation.
- **Sinek, S.** (2017). *Leaders Eat Last: Why Some Teams Pull Together and Others Don't*. Portfolio. Emphasizes the value of putting others first for a thriving workplace culture.
- **Spencer, J. P.** (2013). "Antioxidants in coffee and health." *Journal of Nutrition*, 143(1), 88–94. Provides evidence on the antioxidant properties of coffee and its role in brain protection and overall health.

- **Starrett, K., & Cordoza, G.** (2013). *Becoming a Supple Leopard: The Ultimate Guide to Resolving Pain, Preventing Injury, and Optimizing Athletic Performance*. Victory Belt. Highlights how mobility exercises enhance joint health, prevent injuries, and improve posture, especially for sedentary lifestyles.
- **Stewart, D.** (2005). *The Chemistry of Essential Oils Made Simple: God's Love Manifest in Molecules*. Care Publications. Discusses the chemical properties of essential oils and their benefits for physical and emotional well-being.
- **Tharp, T.** (2003). *The Creative Habit: Learn It and Use It for Life*. Simon & Schuster. Offers insights on creativity and the benefits of continuous learning and new experiences.
- **Thayer, J. F., & Sternberg, E. M.** (2006). "Beyond Heart Rate Variability: Vagal Regulation of Allostatic Systems." *Annals of the New York Academy of Sciences*, 1088(1), 361-372. Explores how a calm, appreciative state before meals can enhance parasympathetic nervous function, supporting digestion and reducing stress.
- **Thich Nhat Hanh.** (2011). *The Art of Power*. HarperOne. Explores spiritual growth and mindfulness as pathways to authentic personal power.
- **Thich Nhat Hanh** (2015). *Silence: The Power of Quiet in a World Full of Noise*. HarperOne. Discusses how silence and mindfulness create space for emotional control, clarity, and self-reflection.
- **Thoreau, H.D.** (1854). *Walden*. Beacon Press. Explores self-discovery, aspirations, and the fulfillment of personal dreams in harmony with nature.
- **Tolle, E.** (1999). *The Power of Now: A Guide to Spiritual Enlightenment*. New World Library. Discusses the importance of surrounding oneself with positive influences, emphasizing that social environments shape personal growth and well-being.
- **Tolle, E.** (2004). *A New Earth: Awakening to Your Life's Purpose*. Penguin Group. Provides insights for aligning spiritual growth with life's purpose.

- **Turner, T. (2019).** *The Art of Business Coaching: A Practical Guide to Helping Your Clients Achieve Success.* Business Expert Press. Provides essential tools for effective coaching, making it a valuable resource for those guiding clients toward success.
- **Tutu, D., & Tutu, M.** (2014). *The Book of Forgiving: The Fourfold Path for Healing Ourselves and Our World.* HarperOne. Explores forgiveness as a process, providing practical steps for releasing anger and embracing peace.
- **Van der Kolk, B. A.** (2014). *The Body Keeps the Score: Brain, Mind, and Body in the Healing of Trauma.* Viking. Examines how trauma is stored in the body and offers techniques for releasing it, emphasizing holistic healing.
- **Walker, M.** (2017). *Why We Sleep: Unlocking the Power of Sleep and Dreams.* Scribner. Delves into the science of sleep, explaining how quality sleep impacts health, mood, and cognitive function.
- **Wansink, B.** (2010). *Mindless Eating: Why We Eat More Than We Think.* Bantam. Reveals how mindfulness in eating enhances enjoyment and satisfaction, aiding in fitness and nutrition goals.
- **Weil, A.** (2000). *Eating Well for Optimum Health: The Essential Guide to Food, Diet, and Nutrition.* Knopf. Discusses the health benefits of ginger, including its anti-inflammatory properties and role in improving digestion and immunity.
- **William, A.** (2015). *Life-Changing Foods.* Hay House, Inc. A guide on the healing properties of various foods, including celery juice and cilantro, with insights into their detoxifying benefits.
- **Williams, M., & Penman, D.** (2011). *Mindfulness: An Eight-Week Plan for Finding Peace in a Frantic World.* Rodale. Offers practical techniques for integrating mindfulness into everyday activities, making it accessible for reducing stress and enhancing focus.
- **Whitmore, J. (2009).** *Coaching for Performance: GROWing Human Potential and Purpose.* Nicholas Brealey Publishing. Introduces the GROW model for coaching, an essential guide for leaders and coaches seeking to unlock potential.

- **Wolf, M.** (2007). *Proust and the Squid: The Story and Science of the Reading Brain.* Harper Perennial. Explores how reading transforms the brain, expanding knowledge and fostering empathy, along with cognitive benefits over time.
- **Worwood, V. A.** (2016). *The Complete Book of Essential Oils and Aromatherapy: Over 800 Natural, Nontoxic, and Fragrant Recipes to Create Health, Beauty, and Safe Home and Work Environments.* New World Library. Provides comprehensive recipes and techniques for using essential oils to improve well-being.
- **Zeidan, F., et al.** (2010). "Mindfulness Meditation Improves Cognition." *Consciousness and Cognition.* Highlights the cognitive benefits of mindfulness meditation.
- **Zhang, X., et al.** (2019). "Anti-inflammatory and neuroprotective properties of ginger: A review." *Food Science & Nutrition*, 7(7), 3053–3070. Provides evidence on ginger's effects on reducing inflammation and protecting against neurodegenerative diseases.

Printed in Great Britain
by Amazon

56631275R10278